Study Guide to Accompa

MW00677663

Introduction to Physical Anthropology

Seventh Edition

Robert Jurmain
Harry Nelson
Lynn Kilgore
Wenda Trevathan

Prepared by

Marcus Young Owl
California State University
Long Beach, CA

Denise Cucurny
California State University
Long Beach, CA

West / Wadsworth

I(T)P® an International Thomson Publishing Company

Belmont, CA • Albany, NY • Bonn • Boston • Cincinnati • Detroit • Johannesburg
London • Los Angeles • Madrid • Melbourne • Mexico City • Minneapolis / St. Paul
New York • Paris • Singapore • Tokyo • Toronto • Washington

For more information, contact Wadsworth Publishing Company, 10 Davis Drive, Belmont, CA 94002, or electronically at http://www.thomson.com/wadsworth.html

International Thomson Publishing Europe
Berkshire House 168-173
High Holborn
London, WC1V 7AA, England

International Thomson Editores
Campos Eliseos 385, Piso 7
Col. Polanco
11560 México D.F. México

Thomas Nelson Australia
102 Dodds Street
South Melbourne 3205
Victoria, Australia

International Thomson Publishing Asia
221 Henderson Road
#05-10 Henderson Building
Singapore 0315

Nelson Canada
1120 Birchmount Road
Scarborough, Ontario
Canada M1K 5G4

International Thomson Publishing Japan
Hirakawacho Kyowa Building, 3F
2-2-1 Hirakawacho
Chiyoda-ku, Tokyo 102, Japan

International Thomson Publishing GmbH
Königswinterer Strasse 418
53227 Bonn, Germany

International Thomson Publishing Southern Africa
Building 18, Constantia Park
240 Old Pretoria Road
Halfway House, 1685 South Africa

ISBN 0-314-20872-0

Contents

PREFACE

The subject matter of physical anthropology has always been fascinating to us. However, we would be the first to admit that it is not easy to study. Students often see the word *anthropology* and think "social science." Physical anthropology's direct historical roots are from anatomy (indeed, the American Association of Physical Anthropologists was formed at the 1931 meetings of the American Anatomical Association). Thus, you need to approach the study of physical anthropology as you would any other life science like biology or anatomy and physiology. Like the textbooks in those disciplines, physical anthropology texts are information intensive.

A study guide is intended to guide you in your study so that you learn efficiently. This Study Guide is designed to help you become an interactive learner rather than a passive learner, and it will require you to write down key words as you proceed through a chapter. The act of writing down a word not only focuses you on the subject but also reinforces the ideas being dealt with.

The chapters in this Study Guide correspond to the chapters in the textbook, *Introduction to Physical Anthropology* by Jurmain, Nelson, Kilgore, and Trevathan. The Study Guide begins with a list of objectives. You should look at these objectives and then read the corresponding chapter in the text.

After reading the chapter, return to the Study Guide and go to the Fill-in Outline. The Fill-in Outline will walk you through the chapter systematically in the order that the material appears in the text chapter. Fill in the blanks as you proceed through this section. Upon completion of the Fill-in Outline, look up the answers in the back of the Study Guide chapter. Note which questions you got correct without guessing and those answers that you missed. This will give you a good indication of the areas you are weak in. Redo those sections.

The next section of the Study Guide is Key Terms. Your study of physical anthropology will introduce you to many new words. Studies have actually shown that science students learn as many new words in a course as students taking a foreign language course. Many terms are defined in the margins of your text. There is also a glossary at the end of the textbook. Many of these key terms are also repeated in this Study Guide, many rephrased so that you get a different perspective. Some of the key terms in the Study Guide were not defined in the text, but it was felt it would be of value to elucidate them in the Study Guide.

The next two sections of the Study Guide, Fill-in Questions and Multiple Choice Questions, will provide you review and reinforcement. You should view these two sections as practice tests. There is a certain amount of repetition between the two types of tests and this will help to reinforce the content of the text. The multiple choice questions will sometimes require you to apply the information you have learned to a new situation. This is entirely fair and your course instructor may expect the same of you. The answers are at the end of the Study Guide chapters. Answers for fill-in and multiple choice questions also include a page reference. If you did poorly on certain questions, reread the pages in the text that you are referred to.

Master the content. You should set a goal of learning 90% of the material before you go on to the next chapter. Review previous chapters weekly. If you do this, you should be well prepared when exam time arrives. The Study Guide can direct you in your study, but ultimately, you are responsible for learning the material. Do not wait until just before the test to study or you will be overwhelmed with the amount of material that you must assimilate.

ACKNOWLEDGMENTS

The development and composition of this Study Guide entailed more than just the work of the authors. We wish to gratefully acknowledge the patience that our families had while we secluded ourselves to produce this Study Guide. We also want to thank Denise Simon, Janine Wilson, Shannon Buckels, and Barri Breeden for their ideas, support, and understanding as we fell behind in our schedule. Finally, we want to thank Jane Docherty for the artwork that she contributed to the Study Guide.

Marcus Young Owl
Departments of Anthropology and Biological Sciences
California State university, Long Beach

Denise Cucurny
Department of Anthropology
California State University, Long Beach

CHAPTER 1

INTRODUCTION TO PHYSICAL ANTHROPOLOGY

LEARNING OBJECTIVES

After reading this chapter you should be able to:
- define the word hominid. (p. 2)
- define biocultural evolution. (pp. 4-6)
- discuss what the subject matter of anthropology is. (p. 6)
- identify the three main subfields of anthropology. (p. 6)
- identify the main research areas within physical anthropology. (pp. 9-15)
- describe the method by which scientists attempt to understand the world. (pp. 18-20)
- understand the steps involved in analyzing a situation scientifically. (pp. 18-20)
- ask questions in a critical manner. (pp. 18-20)

FILL-IN OUTLINE

Introduction
Anthropology is the scientific discipline that has the human species as its subject matter. Anthropologists study all aspects of the human species including our biology (from an evolutionary perspective).

   I. WHAT IS ANTHROPOLOGY?

      A. Anthropology is the scientific study of _____ .

      B. Anthropology is a multidisciplinary field in that it _____ the findings of many disciplines, including sociology, economics, history, psychology, and biology.

C. In the United States anthropology consists of three main subfields:

    1. _____ _____

    2. _____

    3. _____ _____

    4. Some universities include _____ _____ as a fourth area
of anthropology.

II. CULTURAL ANTHROPOLOGY

A. Cultural anthropology is the study of all aspects of _____ _____.

B. The recorded description of traditional lifestyles is called an _____ .

C. Ethnographic accounts formed the basis for _____-_____
studies which broadened the context within which cultural anthropologists studied
human behavior and enabled them to formulate theories about the fundamental
aspects of human behavior.

D. The focus of cultural anthropology has shifted over the twentieth century. Some of
the new subfields of cultural anthropology include

    1. _____ _____ which deals with issues of inner cities.

    2. _____ _____ explores the relationship between
various cultural attributes and health and disease.

    3. _____ _____ is concerned with factors that
influence the distribution of goods and resources within and between cultures.

E. Many of the subfields of anthropology have a practical application, this type of
anthropology is called _____ _____ .

III. ARCHEOLOGY

A. _____ is the discipline that studies and interprets material
remains recovered from earlier cultures.

B. Archeologists are concerned with culture, but obtain their information from

_____ and other _____ _____,

rather than from living people.

C. Archeology is very much aimed at answering specific questions.

1. _____ is conducted for the purpose of gaining information

about human behavior, not simply for the artifacts present at a site.

2. By identifying human behavior patterns on a larger scale, archeologists attempt

to recognize behaviors shared by all human groups, or _____

_____ .

IV. LINGUISTIC ANTHROPOLOGY

A. The field that studies the origin of language, as well as specific languages, is

_____ _____ .

B. Linguistic anthropologists also examine the relationship between culture and

language. These include:

1. how members of a society _____ phenomena.

2. how the use of language shapes perceptions in different _____ .

C. Language _____ is a unique human characteristic.

Research in this area may have implications for the evolution of language skills in

humans, making this area of research of interest for physical anthropologists.

V. PHYSICAL ANTHROPOLOGY

A. _____ _____ is the study of human biology

within the framework of evolution. Many physical anthropologists emphasize the

interaction between _____ and _____ .

B. Physical anthropology is divided into a number of subfields. Some of these are:

1. Paleoanthropology, which is the study of _____ _____ .

a. Paleoanthropology focuses particularly on the _____ .

    b. The ultimate goal of paleoanthropology is to identify and establish a time sequence among the early _____ .

2. Human variation is a field which looks at observable physical variation in humans.

    a. This field was prominent in the nineteenth century.

    b. Techniques used to measure human physical variation are still used today and are called _____ .

3. _____ is the field which studies gene structure and action as well as the patterns of inheritance.

    a. Genetics is crucial to the study of _____ _____ .

    b. Genetics can help anthropologists investigate the _____ _____ between living primate species.

4. _____ is the discipline that studies nonhuman primates.

    a. This is because primates are humanity's closest _____, anthropologists feel that the study of these animals can shed light on our own behavior and other aspects of our biology.

    b. The _____ number of primates species in their natural environments has placed a greater urgency on the study of these animals.

5. _____ _____ is the study of the primate fossil record.

6. The field which studies skeletal biology is _____ .

    a. The subdiscipline of osteology that studies disease and trauma in archeologically derived populations is _____ .

    b. _____ _____ is a field directly related to osteology and paleopathology. It applies the techniques of anthropology to law.

7. Many physical anthropologists specialize in _____, the study of structure.

KEY TERMS

adaptation: functional response of organisms or populations to the environment.

anthropology: the scientific discipline that studies all aspects of the human species.

anthropometry: the measurement of the human body.

archeology: the discipline of anthropology that interprets past cultures through their material remains which are recovered through excavation.

artifacts: objects that have been modified or, in some other way, used by ancient humans.

biocultural evolution: the interaction between biology and culture in human evolution.

bipedal: walking habitually on two legs as in humans and ground birds.

cultural anthropology: the area within anthropology that focuses on the study of human behavior.

culture: the behavior aspects of humans, including their technology and institutions, which is learned and transmitted between generations.

ethnography: the study of human societies.

forensic anthropology: the field that applies the techniques of anthropology to the law. This usually refers to the techniques used by osteologists and sometimes archeology.

genetics: the study of gene structure and action, and the patterns of inheritance of traits.

Hominidae: the taxonomic family that humans belong to.

hominid: a member of the family Hominidae.

linguistic anthropology: the area within anthropology that studies the origins and cultural perceptions and uses of language.

material culture: the physical remains of human cultural activity.

osteology: the study of skeletal biology. Human osteology focuses on the interpretation of the skeletal remains of past populations.

paleoanthropology: the subdiscipline within physical anthropology which studies human evolution.

paleopathology: the branch of osteology that studies the evidence of disease and injury in human skeletal remains.

primate: a member of the mammalian order Primates. Primates include lemurs, bushbabies, monkeys, apes, and humans.

primatology: the study of the mammalian order Primates. Humans are members of this order.

species: a group of interbreeding organisms that produce fertile offspring and are reproductively isolated from other such groups.

Now take the Fill-in and Multiple Choice tests. Do not guess. Following completion of the tests, correct them. The correct answers and textbook page references are at the end of this study guide chapter. Note your strong areas and your weak areas to guide you in your continuing study.

FILL-IN QUESTIONS

1. The taxonomic family to which humans belong is the family _____ .

2. A critical trait to classifying a primate fossil as a hominid is that they walk on two legs.

   Walking on two legs is referred to as walking _____ .

3. A _____ is a group of interbreeding organisms that produce fertile offspring and are reproductively isolated from other such groups.

4. _____ _____ is the study of human biology from an evolutionary perspective.

5. The strategy by which humans adapt to their natural environment is _____ .

6. _____ is a change in the genetic makeup of a population from one generation to the next.

7. The human predisposition to assimilate a particular culture and to function within it is influenced by biological factors. Culture has assumed more and more importance over the course of human evolution. This interaction between biology and culture is referred to as _____ _____.

8. The scientific discipline that focuses on the study of humankind is _____ .

9. The discipline of anthropology that studies human societies, and produces ethnographies, is _____ anthropology.

10. Archeologists study _____ _____.

11. Remains left behind, and recovered by excavation, are called _____.

12. An area within archeology that evaluates archeological sites that are threatened by development is called _____ _____ _____ .

13. An anthropologist who is interested in the origins of human language would be a(n) _____ anthropologist.

14. An anthropologist who studies human evolutionary biology is a(n) _____ anthropologist.

15. The ultimate goal of paleoanthropology is to identify and establish the relationship of the various early _____ species and to gain insights into their adaptation and behavior.

16. Physical (biological) traits that characterize the different human populations throughout the world are seen by physical anthropologists as having evolved as biological

_____ .

17. Modern physical anthropology would not exist as an evolutionary science if it were not for advances in understanding _____ principles.

18. The behavioral study of any animal species provides a wealth of data pertaining to that species' _____ .

19. Many osteologists specialize in metric studies which emphasize skeletal

_____ .

20. Skills which enable people to evaluate, compare, analyze, critique, and synthesize information are collectively called _____ _____ skills.

21. A _____ is a provisional statement about the relationships between observations.

22. Ideally, a theory should _____ how new facts may fit into an established pattern.

23. A crucial feature of scientific statements is that they are _____ ; this means that such a statement can be tested.

24. Measurements produce numbers and even observations can be assigned numbers. Numbers can be analyzed. A skill which uses numbers for analysis, such as statistics, falls into the category of _____ critical reasoning.

MULTIPLE CHOICE QUESTIONS

1. Walking on two legs, as humans and chickens do, is referred to as
   A. bipedalism.
   B. quadrupedalism.
   C. cursorial.
   D. brachiation.

2. The mammalian group that humans belong to is the order
    A. Carnivora.
    B. Rodentia.
    C. Primates.
    D. Chiroptera.

3. Culture is
    A. inherited by a simple genetic transmission.
    B. a biological trait of our species.
    C. learned.
    D. the strategy by which many mammals adapt to their environments.

4. The biological characteristics of humans enabled culture to develop and culture, in turn, influenced human biological development. This is called
    A. biocultural evolution.
    B. microevolution.
    C. quantum evolution.
    D. convergent evolution.

5. Anthropology differs from other disciplines which study humans in that anthropology
    A. studies humans exclusively.
    B. allows no biases from other disciplines to interfere in anthropological studies.
    C. never uses an evolutionary perspective.
    D. is integrative and interdisciplinary.

6. An anthropologist who is studying the subsistence strategy of the Mbuti pygmies in Zaire belongs to the anthropological subfield of
    A. archeology.
    B. cultural anthropology.
    C. linguistic anthropology.
    D. physical anthropology.

7. Anthropologists who conduct excavations in order to recover artifacts, and other aspects of material culture, are
    A. archeologists.
    B. cultural anthropologists.
    C. linguistic anthropologists.
    D. medical anthropologists.

8. The applied approach in archeology that has expanded greatly in recent years is
    A. magnetometry.
    B. climatic reconstruction.
    C. cultural resource management.
    D. dendrochronology.

9. Physical anthropology has its origins in
    A. physics.
    B. natural history.
    C. anatomical observation of human physical variation.
    D. Both B and C are correct.

10. Physical anthropologists became interested in human change over time (i.e., evolution) with the publication of
    A. Blumenbach's *On the Natural Varieties of Humankind.*
    B. Malthus' *An Essay on the Principle of Population.*
    C. Darwin's *Origin of Species.*
    D. Wood Jones' *Man's Place Among the Mammals.*

11. Anthropologists who specialize in the fossil remains and the physical evidence of early human behavior are called
    A. cultural anthropologists.
    B. linguists.
    C. paleoanthropologists.
    D. geneticists.

12. Contemporary physical anthropologists, whose main interest is in modern human variation, approach their subject matter from the perspective of
    A. racial typologies.
    B. adaptive significance.
    C. behavioral genetics.
    D. constitutional typology.

13. Physical anthropologists developed techniques for measuring the human body. Not only physical anthropologists employ these techniques. Such measurements are used at health clubs and include techniques for measuring body fat. These types of measurements are called
    A. calibration.
    B. dermatoglyphics.
    C. genetics.
    D. anthropometrics.

14. A researcher is studying the nutritional ecology of howler monkeys in Panama. Her area of expertise is
    A. primatology.
    B. paleoanthropology.
    C. osteology.
    D. genetics.

15. A family reports to the police that their dog has brought home a leg bone that appears to be human. The police also believe this bone is human. To find out vital information about the person this bone came from the police will consult a(n)
    A. forensic anthropologist.
    B. primatologist.
    C. paleoanthropologist.
    D. evolutionary geneticist.

16. A physical anthropologist who studies bones exclusively is called a(n)
    A. primatologist.
    B. paleoanthropologist.
    C. mammalogist.
    D. osteologist.

17. An important and basic discipline, for osteology, paleopathology, and paleoanthropology is
    A. ecology.
    B. anatomy.
    C. ethology.
    D. genetics.

18. A scientific hypothesis
    A. must always be a correct statement.
    B. is not a necessary part of the scientific method.
    C. is the same thing as a law.
    D. must be falsifiable.

19. If a researcher measures some biological variable and then uses the numbers obtained to arrive at conclusions we would say that this study is
    A. quantitative.
    B. qualitative.
    C. descriptive .
    D. natural history.

20. Scientific hypotheses are falsifiable. This means that they
    A. can provide proof.
    B. are testable.
    C. are subject to supernatural law.
    D. do not offer predictions.

ANSWERS TO FILL-IN OUTLINE

I. **WHAT IS ANTHROPOLOGY?**
  A. humankind
  B. integrates
  C. 1. cultural anthropology
     2. archeology
     3. physical anthropology
     4. linguistic anthropology

II. **CULTURAL ANTHROPOLOGY**
  A. human behavior
  B. ethnography
  C. cross-cultural
  D. 1. urban anthropology
     2. medical anthropology
     3. economic anthropology
     4. applied anthropology

III. **ARCHEOLOGY**
  A. archeology
  B. artifacts, material culture
  C. 1. excavation
     2. cultural universals

IV. **LINGUISTIC ANTHROPOLOGY**
  A. linguistic anthropology
  B. 1. perceive
     2. cultures
  C. acquisition

V. **PHYSICAL ANTHROPOLOGY**
  A. physical anthropology, biology, culture
  B. 1. human evolution
        a. fossil record
        b. hominids
     2. b. anthropometrics
     3. genetics
        a. evolutionary processes
        b. evolutionary distance
     4. primatology
        a. relatives
        b. declining
     5. primate paleontology
     6. osteology
        a. paleopathology
        b. forensic anthropology
     7. anatomical studies

ANSWERS & REFERENCES TO FILL-IN QUESTIONS

1. Hominidae, p. 2
2. bipedally, p. 2
3. species, p. 3
4. physical anthropology, p. 4
5. culture, p. 4
6. evolution, p. 5
7. biocultural evolution, p. 5
8. anthropology, p. 6
9. cultural, pp. 6-7
10. past cultures, p. 8
11. artifacts and/or material culture, p. 8
12. cultural resource management, p. 9
13. linguistic, p. 9
14. physical, p. 9
15. hominid, p. 10
16. adaptations, p. 11
17. genetic, p. 12
18. adaptation, p. 12
19. measurements, p. 13
20. critical thinking, p. 18
21. hypothesis, p. 18
22. predict, p. 18
23. falsifiable, p. 18
24. quantitative, p. 19

ANSWERS & REFERENCES TO MULTIPLE CHOICE QUESTIONS

1. A, p. 3
2. C, p. 4
3. C, p. 4
4. A, p. 5
5. D, p. 6
6. B, p. 6
7. A, p. 8
8. C, p. 9
9. D, p. 10
10. C, p. 10
11. C, p. 10
12. B, p. 11
13. D, p. 11
14. A, p. 12
15. A, p. 14
16. D, p. 13
17. B, p. 14
18. D, p. 18
19. A, p. 19
20. B, p. 18

CHAPTER 2

THE DEVELOPMENT OF EVOLUTIONARY THEORY

LEARNING OBJECTIVES

After reading this chapter you should be able to:
- trace the development of evolutionary thought. (pp. 22-24)
- identify the major influences on the thought of Charles Darwin. (pp. 24-28)
- describe the processes of natural selection. (pp. 32-33)
- describe a case of natural selection. (pp. 33-34)
- understand the short-comings of nineteenth-century evolutionary thought. (pp. 35-36)

FILL-IN OUTLINE

Introduction
Evolution is a theory that has been increasingly supported by a large body of evidence. Evolution is the single-most fundamental unifying force in biology. Evolution is particularly crucial to the discipline of physical anthropology because its subject matter deals with human evolution and the physiological adaptations we have made to our environment. This chapter presents the development of evolutionary thought as well as the social and political context in which it developed.

I. A BRIEF HISTORY OF EVOLUTIONARY THOUGHT

    A. The pre-scientific view

        1. The European world view throughout the middle ages was one of _____,

           the idea that the world was fixed and unchanging.

a. Part of this world view was the _____ _____ _____.

   This was a hierarchy in which life was arranged from the simplest to the most

   complex (i.e., humans).

b. It was believed that the world was "full" of species and there could not be any

   other species added, nor had any species disappeared.

c. The world was seen as the result of the "_____ _____," in

   which anatomical structures were viewed as planned to meet the purpose for

   which they were required—an argument from design.

2. The creation of the world was believed to be recent, the earth being only about

    5500 years old; this was a major obstacle to the idea of evolution, which requires

    immense time.

B. The scientific revolution

1. The discovery of the _____ _____ challenged the traditional ideas of

    Europe.

    a. The world could not be perceived as flat.

    b. Exposures to new plants and animals increased the awareness of the biological

       diversity on the planet.

2. _____ challenged the old idea that the earth was the center of

    the universe.

3. Galileo's work further pushed the notion that the universe was a place of

    motion rather than of _____.

4. By the 16th and 17th centuries, scholars began searching for natural laws rather

    than supernatural explanations. This approach viewed nature as a

    _____.

C. The path to natural selection

   1. John Ray, living in the 16th century, distinguished groups of plants and animals from other such groups.

      a. Organisms capable of reproducing and producing offspring were classified by Ray as _____ .

      b. Ray also recognized that species shared similarities with other species. He grouped similar species together in a _____.

   2. Carolus Linnaeus developed a system of classification and laid the basis for

     _____ .

      a. Linnaeus standardized the use of the genus and the species to identify each organism, a procedure called _____ _____.

      b. Linnaeus' most controversial act was to include _____ among the animals in his taxonomy.

   3. Comte de Buffon

      a. Buffon stressed the importance of change in nature.

      b. Buffon recognized that the _____ was an important agent of change.

   4. Jean Baptiste Lamarck

      a. _____ was the first scientist to produce a systematic explanation for the evolutionary process.

      b. Lamarck postulated that the environment played a crucial role in the physical change an organism would go through.

         1. As the environment changed, the organism would adjust to the environment by _____ also.

2. Lamarck believed that as an organism used structures, or did not use structures, the structures would change in response to the environment.

   a. Future _____ would inherit the modified condition.

   b. This idea of Lamarck was called _____ ___ _____ _____ . It is also called use-disuse theory.

5. Georges Cuvier was the archenemy of Lamarck.

   a. Despite founding vertebrate paleontology (as well as comparative anatomy and zoology), Cuvier believed strongly in the _____ ___ _____.

   b. Cuvier is strongly associated with the idea that animal and plant species disappeared because of local disasters.

      1. This theory was called _____.

      2. Following a set of extinctions, new life forms migrated in from unaffected neighboring areas.

6. Charles Lyell is considered the founder of modern geology.

   a. Lyell emphasized that the earth had been molded by the same geological forces observable today. This theory is called _____.

   b. In order for uniformitarianism to be explanatory, the earth would have to be immensely _____.

7. Thomas Malthus was a political economist.

   a. Malthus wrote about the relationship between food supplies and population increase. He stated that population size increases _____ while food supplies remained relatively stable.

   b. Malthus' ideas contributed to the thinking of both Darwin and Wallace, namely the idea of _____ for food and other resources.

8. Charles Darwin

   a. Many of Darwin's ideas were formed from his observations while serving as a naturalist on *HMS Beagle's* surveying voyage around the world.

   b. In the late 1830s, a number of ideas coalesced for Darwin.

      1. Darwin saw that biological variation within a species was

         _____ _____ .

      2. Darwin also recognized the importance of sexual reproduction in increasing

         _____ .

      3. Malthus' essay presented important ideas to Darwin. From Malthus, Darwin developed the ideas that

         a. in animals population, size is continuously _____ by limits of food supply.

         b. there is a constant "_____ ____ _____."

      4. Darwin essentially had completed his work by the year _____ . He would publish it fifteen years later.

9. A. R. Wallace

   a. Wallace was a naturalist who worked in South America and Southeast Asia.

   b. Wallace's observations led him to conclusions _____ to Darwin's. Namely, that

      1. species are descended from _____ _____ .

      2. the emergence of new species was influenced by the _____ .

   c. The coincidental development of evolution by natural selection by both Darwin and Wallace was resolved by the joint presentation of their papers to the Linnean Society of London.

D. The processes of natural selection

1. All species can produce offspring at a _____ rate than food supplies increase.

2. There is biological _____ within all species.

3. Over-reproduction leads to _____ for limited resources.

4. Those individuals within a species that possess favorable traits are more likely to survive than other individuals and produce _____ .

5. The _____ context determines whether a trait is favorable or not.

6. Biological traits are _____ .

    a. Individuals with traits favored by the environment contribute _____ offspring to the next generation.

    b. Over time such traits will become _____ _____ in the population.

7. Over _____ _____ ____ _____ _____ , successful variations accumulate in a population, so that later generations may be distinct from the ancestral one; thus, in time, a new species may appear.

8. Geographical _____ may also lead to the formation of new species.

    a. When populations of a species inhabit different ecological zones they begin to _____ to the different environments.

    b. Over time each population responds to the different _____ _____ and the end result, given sufficient time, may be two distinct species.

E. Natural selection operates on individuals, but it is the population that evolves.

1. The unit of natural selection is the _____ .

2. The unit of evolution is the _____ .

II. NATURAL SELECTION IN ACTION

A. Industrial melanism is one of the best documented cases of _____ _____.

    1. Two forms of peppered moth exist: a light gray mottled form and a dark form.

        a. Prior to the industrial revolution the light form predominated.

            1. When resting on lichen-covered tree trunks the mottled form was _____ from birds.

            2. In contrast, the dark moths stood out on light, lichen-covered trees.

            3. Birds served as _____ _____ which resulted in few dark moths surviving to produce offspring.

        b. By the end of the nineteenth century the dark form was the more common.

            1. As the industrial revolution progressed coal dust settled on trees.

            2. The light moths stood out on the dark tree trunks and were _____ upon by birds; this resulted in dark forms leaving more _____ to the next generation and subsequently becoming the more common variety.

    2. The example of _____ _____ emphasizes several of the mechanisms of evolutionary change through natural selection.

        a. A _____ must be inherited to have importance in natural selection.

        b. Natural selection cannot occur without _____ in inherited characteristics.

        c. Selection can work only with variation that already _____ .

            1. _____ is a relative measure that changes as the environment changes.

            2. Fitness is simply reproductive _____ .

B. _____ _____ _____ _____ refers to the number of offspring produced by an individual that survive to reproductive age.

III. CONSTRAINTS ON NINETEENTH-CENTURY EVOLUTIONARY THEORY

A. Variation

1. The _____ of variation was a major gap in 19th century evolutionary theory.

2. Darwin suggested that _____-_____ might cause variation.

B. Transmission

1. Darwin did not understand the mechanisms by which parents transmitted traits to offspring.

2. The most popular contemporary idea was _____ _____ ; the idea that offspring expressed traits intermediate between the traits of their parents.

KEY TERMS

binomial nomenclature: identifying each organism by two names, the genus and the species.
biology: the study of life.
catastrophism: a view that the earth's geology is the result of a series of cataclysmic events.
differential net reproductive success: the number of offspring that are produced, survive, and reproduce themselves.
evolution: the change in the genetic structure of a population generationally.
fitness: a measure of the relative reproductive success of individuals and, hence their genetic contribution to the next generation.
fixity of species: the idea that species do not change, i.e., they do not evolve.
genus: the taxon (category) in biological classification that consists of similar and related species.
natural selection: the mechanism of evolutionary change in which certain traits from among existing variations are favored resulting in an increase in those traits in the next generation.
reproductive success: the number of offspring that an individual produces and the genetic contribution to the next generation that this implies.
species: a group of organisms capable of interbreeding under natural conditions and producing fertile and viable offspring; the second name in a binomen.
stasis: in biology, this was the view that nature and all of its organisms were unchanging.
taxonomy: the biological discipline that names and classifies organisms.
transmutation: the word that meant change in species that predated the word evolution.
uniformitarianism: the theory that the earth's geology is the result of long-term processes, still at work today, that requires immense geological time.

Now take the Fill-in and Multiple Choice tests. Do not guess. Following completion of the tests, correct them. The correct answers and textbook page references are at the end of this study guide chapter. Note your strong areas and your weak areas to guide you in your continuing study.

FILL-IN QUESTIONS

1. The individual most responsible for the elucidation of the evolutionary process was

    _____ _____.

2. The belief that life forms cannot change is called _____ ___ _____.

3. A paradigm, dating back to Aristotle, in which a hierarchy of life forms were arranged

    from the simplest to the most complex was termed the _____ _____

    __ _____ .

4. Copernicus proposed that the sun was the center of the solar system. This idea is called

    the _____ solar system.

5. The idea of a mechanistic universe relied on natural explanations rather than

    _____ explanations.

6. The naturalist who developed the species concept was _____ _____.

7. In his work, *The Wisdom of God Manifested in the Works of Creation*, John Ray emphasized that

    nature was the deliberate outcome of a _____ _____.

8. The naturalist who developed a classification of plants and animals, the basis of the same

    system of taxonomy that we use today, was _____.

9. Linnaeus gave humans their binomen which is _____ _____.

10. A French naturalist, working in the mid-eighteenth century, who emphasized the importance

    of change in nature and the importance of the environment was _____ .

11. _____ _____ was an English physician who expressed evolutionary

    concepts in his book of poetry *Zoonomia*.

12. Lamarck went beyond the work of Buffon and Erasmus Darwin in that he attempted to

    _____ the evolutionary process.

13. Lamarck believed that if an animal was modified by the environment it could pass on the new trait to its offspring. This idea is called _____ ____

    _____ _____ .

14. _____ was a French anatomist strongly opposed to any idea of evolution. He proposed that new species appeared by occupying area vacated by extinct species that were destroyed by catastrophes.

15. _____ is considered the founder of modern geology.

16. Lyell contributed an important influence on Charles Darwin, namely that _____ processes have been uniform over a long period of time.

17. _____ influenced both Darwin and Wallace with his ideas about population increase and competition for limited food supplies.

18. The _____ _____ was a social movement that had members who supported Lamarck's evolutionary ideas. Their support actually hindered the acceptance of new revolutionary ideas like evolution.

19. A term predating evolution was _____ , which also meant the change of one species into another.

20. When Darwin set sail on the *Beagle* he believed in the _____ of species.

21. The *Beagle's* stopover on the _____ Islands was an important event in Darwin's development. He noted the similarity of the flora and fauna of these islands with that of South America and particularly gained insight from observing the finches on these islands.

22. Darwin wrote that under certain circumstances "favourable variations would tend to be preserved, and unfavourable ones to be destroyed. The result of this would be the formation of a new species." This describes _____ _____.

23. The naturalist _____ also developed a theory of evolution by natural selection at the same time as Darwin.

24. Those individuals within a species that produce more offspring, compared to other individuals, are said to have greater _____ _____.

25. The individual member of a species is the unit of _____ ; the species is the unit of _____ .

26. One of the best documented cases of natural selection acting on modern populations involves the _____ _____ in Britain.

27. Natural selection _____ occur without variation in inherited characteristics.

28. Differential net reproductive success refers to the number of offspring produced by an individual that survive to _____ .

29. A major problem for Darwin's hypothesis of natural selection acting on variation was that he could not explain where _____ came from.

30. In addition to his inability to explain the origins of variation, Darwin also did not understand the mechanism by which parents _____ traits to offspring.

MULTIPLE CHOICE QUESTIONS

1. The idea that organisms never change is called
   A. catastrophism.
   B. fixity of species.
   C. transmutation of species.
   D. evolution.

2. Which of the following is a **correct** statement?
   A. Scientific knowledge is usually gained through a series of small steps rather than giant leaps.
   B. A. R. Wallace actually developed the idea of evolution through natural selection a decade before Darwin.
   C. The predominant world view of the Middle Ages was that there was constant change in life forms with the exception of humans.
   D. The Great Chain of Being is an evolutionary scheme in which the organisms are arranged beginning with those whose ancestors first appeared in the fossil record and ending with those forms whose ancestors are the most recent.

3. The naturalist who developed the concepts of the genus and species was
   A. Charles Darwin.
   B. John Ray.
   C. Carolus Linnaeus.
   D. Jean-Baptiste Lamarck.

4. The discipline within biology that is concerned with the rules of classifying organisms on the basis of evolutionary relationships is
   A. anatomy.
   B. genetics.
   C. taxonomy.
   D. ethology.

5. Which of the following is an example of binomial nomenclature?
   A. vole
   B. chimpanzee
   C. human
   D. *Homo sapiens*

6. The system of biological classification, or taxonomy, that is used by biologists was devised by
   A. Charles Darwin.
   B. J. B. Lamarck.
   C. Georges Cuvier.
   D. Carolus Linnaeus.

7. The first person to class humans with animals was
   A. Linnaeus.
   B. Aristotle.
   C. John Ray.
   D. Archbishop James Ussher.

8. Lamarck believed that
   A. organisms do not change.
   B. only genetically determined traits are passed from parent to offspring.
   C. the environment plays a major role in evolution.
   D. only populations evolve.

9. The naturalist who believed that species could change by adapting to new environmental conditions, yet rejected the notion of one species evolving out of another, was
   A. Linnaeus.
   B. Buffon.
   C. Lamarck.
   D. Cuvier.

10. The first natural historian to codify evolutionary ideas in a comprehensive system that attempted to explain the evolutionary process was
    A. Linnaeus.
    B. Buffon.
    C. Lamarck.
    D. Erasmus Darwin.

11. The opposite of fixity of species is
    A. evolution.
    B. typology.
    C. stasis.
    D. immutability of species.

12. A body builder works hard to build large muscles. He marries a beauty queen/life guard. The body builder expects his male offspring to be born muscle-bound. His beliefs resemble those of
    A. catastrophism.
    B. uniformitarianism.
    C. the inheritance of acquired characteristics.
    D. evolution by natural selection.

13. The idea that species were fixed, but became extinct due to sudden, violent events and were replaced by neighboring new species is called
    A. evolution.
    B. phyletic gradualism.
    C. catastrophism.
    D. uniformitarianism.

14. Which scientist was most associated with the concept of catastrophism?
    A. Lamarck
    B. Cuvier
    C. Buffon
    D. Lyell

15. Uniformitarianism refers to the concept that
    A. the geological processes at work today are the same as those at work in the past.
    B. evolution is a universal fact.
    C. the basic biological processes of life are the same wherever life is found.
    D. the laws of heredity are universal.

16. Uniformitarianism implies which of the following
    A. new species are created by natural disasters.
    B. the earth is very old.
    C. the earth has a living history, short as it may be.
    D. biological species evolve.

17. Which of the following ideas of Charles Lyell contributed to Darwin's thinking?
    A. There is variation within any population of organisms.
    B. There is a "struggle for existence" between individuals.
    C. A trait must be inherited to have any importance in evolution.
    D. There is an immense geological time scale.

18. The concept of the "struggle for existence," the constant competition for food and other resources, was the idea of
    A. Charles Darwin.
    B. Charles Lyell.
    C. Thomas Malthus.
    D. A. R. Wallace.

19. Who of the following developed a theory of evolution by natural selection?
    A. Lamarck
    B. A. R. Wallace
    C. Erasmus Darwin
    D. Lyell

20. Which of the following is **not** a statement that Darwin would have made?
    A. There is biological variation within all species.
    B. The environment selects which traits are beneficial.
    C. Geographical isolation may lead to a new species.
    D. Traits acquired within an individual's lifetime are passed to the next generation.

21. Those individuals that produce more offspring, relative to other individuals in the population, are said to have greater
    A. reproductive success.
    B. selective pressure.
    C. variation.
    D. survival potential.

22. Forces in the environment which influence reproductive success are called
    A. k-selection.
    B. selective pressures.
    C. phyletic gradualism.
    D. differential reproduction.

23. Who of the following did **not** believe in the fixity of species?
    A. Lamarck
    B. Linnaeus
    C. Cuvier
    D. Buffon

24. The best documented case of natural selection acting on modern populations is
    A. starfish as keystone predators of mussels in the Pacific Northwest.
    B. mutualism involving sharks and remoras.
    C. industrial melanism involving peppered moths near Manchester, England.
    D. the symbiosis formed by cork sponges and hermit crabs.

25. What happened to the peppered moth population in England?
    A. There was a change in wing length due to the stability of the environment.
    B. There was a loss of functional wings due to a change in the environment.
    C. They became extinct because these moths could not adapt to the environment.
    D. There was a shift in body color from light to dark in this population.

26. Industrial melanism refers to
    A. a case of natural selection in Britain.
    B. Lamarck's example for the inheritance of acquired characters.
    C. Darwin's example for evolution by natural selection.
    D. Both A and C

27. Differential net reproductive success refers to
    A. an individual leaving more offspring than another.
    B. the number of offspring that survive to reproduce relative to other individuals.
    C. an evolutionary shift in a trait.
    D. the development of new traits.

28. Darwin's explanation for evolution suffered from his ability to explain
    A. the role of variation in natural selection.
    B. the origins of variation.
    C. the effects of the environment.
    D. the immense time span that would be required.

29. Darwin believed that inheritance took place by
    A. particulate inheritance.
    B. blending inheritance.
    C. spontaneous generation.
    D. the principle of independent assortment.

30. Who of the following did **not** influence Charles Darwin?
    A. Lamarck
    B. Malthus
    C. Mendel
    D. Lyell

31. Which of the following statements is **true**?
    A. Creation Science is falsifiable.
    B. A theory that is not subject to revision is not scientific.
    C. There is no dispute regarding the mechanisms and processes of evolution.
    D. Creation Science is amenable to modification based on hypothesis testing.

ANSWERS TO FILL-IN OUTLINE

I. A BRIEF HISTORY OF EVOLUTIONARY THOUGHT
- A. 1. stasis
     - a. Great Chain of Being
     - c. Grand Design
- B. 1. New World (i. e., North and South America, new worlds that the Europeans did not know existed)
  - 2. Copernicus
  - 3. fixity
  - 4. mechanism
- C. 1. a. species
     - b. genus
  - 2. taxonomy
     - a. binomial nomenclature
     - b. humans
  - 3. b. environment
  - 4. a. Lamarck
     - b. 1. changing
       - 2. a. offspring
          - b. inheritance of acquired characteristics
  - 5. a. fixity of species
     - b. 1. catastrophism
  - 6. a. uniformitarianism
     - b. ancient (or old)
  - 7. a. geometrically
     - b. competition
  - 8. b. 1. critically important
       - 2. variation
       - 3. a. checked
          - b. struggle for existence
       - 4. 1844
  - 9. b. similar
     - 1. other species
     - 2. environment
- D. 1. faster
  - 2. variation
  - 3. competition
  - 4. offspring
  - 5. environmental
  - 6. inherited
     - a. more
     - b. more common
  - 7. long periods of geological time
  - 8. isolation
     - a. adapt
     - b. selective pressures
- E. 1. individual
  - 2. population

II. Natural Selection in Action
   A. natural selection
      1. a. 1. camouflaged
           3. selective agents
        b. 2. preyed, offspring
      2. industrial melanism
        a. trait
        b. variation
        c. exists
           1. fitness
           2. success
   B. differential net reproductive success

III. Constraints on Nineteenth-Century Evolutionary Theory
   A. 1. source
      2. use-disuse, this idea was originally introduced in the section on Lamarck
   B. 2. blending inheritance

Answers & References to Fill-in Questions

1. Charles Darwin, p. 22
2. fixity of species, p. 23
3. Great Chain of Being, p. 23
4. heliocentric, p. 24
5. supernatural, p. 24
6. John Ray, p. 24
7. Grand Design, p. 25
8. Carolus Linnaeus, p. 25
9. *Homo sapiens*, p. 25
10. Buffon, p. 25
11. Erasmus Darwin, p. 25
12. explain, p. 26
13. inheritance of acquired characteristics, p. 26
14. Georges Cuvier, p. 26
15. Charles Lyell, p. 27
16. geological, p. 28
17. Thomas Malthus, p. 28
18. Reform Movement, p.29
19. transmutation, p. 29
20. fixity, p. 29
21. Galápagos, pp. 29-30
22. natural selection, p. 31
23. Wallace, p. 32
24. reproductive success, p. 33
25. selection; evolution, p. 33
26. peppered moth, p. 33
27. cannot, p. 34
28. reproduce, p. 34
29. variation, p. 35
30. transmitted, p. 35

Answers & References to Multiple Choice Questions

1. B, p. 23
2. A, p. 22
3. B, p. 24
4. C, p. 25
5. D, the other answers are the common names of these three mammals, p. 25.
6. D, p. 25
7. A, p. 25
8. C, p. 26

9. B, p. 25
10. C, p. 26
11. A. This is a thinking question. Evolution means change rather than fixity. All the other answers do not imply any sort of change occurring.
12. C, p. 26
13. C, pp. 26-27
14. B, p. 26
15. A, pp. 27-28
16. B, p. 28
17. D, p. 28
18. C, p. 28
19. B, don't be tricked by the name Darwin. The Darwin that developed a theory of evolution by natural selection was Charles, not Erasmus. Charles Darwin is not one of the choices in the answers, p. 32.
20. D, this is Lamarck's explanation. The other answers are all statements attributable to Darwin. See pp. 32 & 33.
21. A, p. 33
22. B, p. 33
23. A, see pp. 25-27
24. C, pp. 33-34
25. D, p. 34
26. A, pp 33-34
27. B, pp. 34-35
28. B, p. 35
29. B, p. 35
30. C, p. 35. Darwin was not aware of Mendel's work. He read Lamarck and was strongly influenced by Malthus and Lyell. You will learn more about this in chapter four.
31. B, p. 40

CHAPTER 3

THE BIOLOGICAL BASIS OF LIFE

LEARNING OBJECTIVES

After reading this chapter you should be able to:
- describe the structure of a generalized cell. (pp. 42-44)
- describe the structure and function of DNA. (p. 44)
- understand the process of protein synthesis. (pp. 45-49)
- define a gene and what it does. (pp. 49-50)
- understand how a mutation occurs. (pp. 51-52)
- know the difference between autosomes and sex cells. (pp. 54-56)
- understand the importance of mitosis and meiosis and what their differences are. (pp. 57-61)
- understand why genetics is important to the study of evolution. (p. 61)

FILL-IN OUTLINE

Introduction
Human evolution and adaptation are intimately linked to life processes stemming from the genetic processes of cells, both in cell replication and in the decoding of genetic information into products usable by the organism and the transmission of this information to future generations.

I. THE CELL

    A. The cell is the basic _____ of life in all living organisms.

        1. Complex _____ life forms, such as plants and animals, are made up of billions of cells.

2. Prokaryotic cells are _____ - _____ organisms.

    a. The earliest life on earth, appearing by at least 3.7 billion years ago, were such life forms.

    b. _____ cells lack a nucleus.

3. More complex cells with a nucleus first appeared around 1.2 billion years ago.

    a These cells are called _____ cells.

    b. Multicellular organisms, which includes humans, are composed of eukaryotic cells.

B. General structure of a eukaryotic cell

    1. The type of cell studied in textbooks is a generalized or composite cell.

        a. A generalized cell contains structures known to exist in cells.

        b. On the other hand, no single cell has all the structures seen in a general cell.

    2. The _____ _____ is the outermost and functional boundary of the cell.

    3. _____ are functional structures found within the cytoplasm.

    4. The third major region of the eukaryotic cell is the _____ which is surrounded by the cytoplasm.

    5. This section of the textbook discusses organelles important for the discussion of genetics (and ultimately variation and evolution).

        a. Mitochondria

            1. These organelles produce _____ for the cell.

            2. Mitochondria also contain their own _____ which produces the proteins found in the mitochondrial membranes.

        b. Ribosomes are structures that are essential to the production of _____ .

C. There are two types of cells found in the animal body.

    1. _____ cells are the cells of the body with the exception of the sex cells.

2. Gametes are sex cells involved with _____ .

   a. Ova are egg cells produced in _____ ovaries.

   b. Sperm are sex cells produced in _____ testes.

   c. A _____ is the union between a sperm and an ovum.

II. DNA STRUCTURE

A. Cellular function and an organism's inheritance depends on the structure and function of DNA.

B. DNA is composed of _____ chains of nucleotides.

   1. A_____ consists of a sugar, a phosphate, and one of four bases.

   2. Nucleotides form long chains and the two chains are held together by bonds formed by the bases with their _____ on the other chain. This complementary phenomenon is what enables DNA to fulfill its functions. (This is sometimes called the "base pairing principle").

     a. Adenine (A) is the complement of _____ (T).

     b. Guanine (G) is the complement of _____ (C).

     c. The complementary property of the DNA bases is what enables DNA to make _____ copies of itself.

III. DNA REPLICATION

A. The most important property of DNA is that it can _____ itself.

B. The replication process

   1. Specific enzymes break the bonds between the DNA molecule.

   2. The two nucleotide chains serve as _____ for the formation of a new strand of nucleotides.

   3. Unattached nucleotides pair with the appropriate _____ nucleotide.

   4. The end result is _____ newly formed strands of DNA. Each new strand is joined to one of the original strands of DNA.

C. See Figure 3-3.

IV. PROTEIN SYNTHESIS

A. One of the most important functions of DNA is that it directs _____

synthesis within the cell.

B. Structure and function of proteins

1. Proteins are the major _____ components of the body.

2. Many proteins serve as catalysts, i.e. they initiate and enhance _____

reactions.

3. The building blocks of proteins are smaller molecules called _____

acids.

a. There are _____ biologically important amino acids.

b. What makes proteins different from one another is the number of amino acids

involved and the _____ in which they are arranged.

C. The agents of protein synthesis

1. Ribosomes are cytoplasmic organelles which help convert the genetic message

from the DNA into _____ .

2. Messenger RNA (mRNA) carries the genetic message from the cell nucleus to

the _____ .

a. RNA differs from DNA in that it is _____-_____ , has

a different type of sugar and substitutes the base uracil (U) for thymine (T).

b. mRNA has triplets (a series of three bases) called _____ which

specify a particular amino acid.

3. Transfer RNA (tRNA) is another type of RNA that is usually found in the cytoplasm.

a. tRNA binds to one specific _____ acid.

b. Each tRNA has a triplet (an anti-codon) which matches up with a codon on the

_____ strand.

  D. The process of protein synthesis

  1. Transcription

  a. A portion of the DNA unwinds and serves as a _____ for the
  formation of a mRNA strand.

  b. The process of coding a genetic message for proteins by formation of mRNA is
  called _____ .

  2. Translation

  a. The mRNA leaves the nucleus, enters the cytoplasm, and attaches to a
  _____ .

  b. tRNAs arrive at the ribosome carrying their cargoes of specific _____
  _____ .

  c. The base triplets on the _____ match up with the codons on the mRNA.

  d. As each tRNA line up according to the sequence of mRNA codons, their amino
  acids link together to form a _____ .

  e. The process in which the genetic message on the mRNA is "decoded" and
  implemented is called _____ .

V. DEFINITION OF THE GENE

  A. The sequence of DNA bases that code for a particular protein is a _____ .

  B. If the sequence of bases in a gene is altered, a _____ has
  occurred.

  a. This may interfere with the organism's ability to produce vital _____ .

  b. It may also lead to a new variety within the species and, hence, evolution.

VI. MUTATION: WHEN A GENE CHANGES

  A. A change in genetic material is called _____ .

  B. An example of a mutation: sickle-cell hemoglobin

1. Hemoglobin consists of four polypeptide chains, two alpha chains and two beta chains.

   a. A defect in the _____ chain leads to a condition called sickle-cell anemia.

      1. _____ - _____ anemia is a genetic condition in which the affected individual inherits a variant of the gene from both parents.

      2. Sickle hemoglobin is caused by the substitution of one _____ _____ (valine) for another (the normally occurring glutamic acid) on the beta chain.

         a. This substitution impairs the ability of the blood to distribute oxygen

         b. Such a substitution is called a _____ _____.

            1. In evolution point mutations are probably the most common and most important source of new _____.

            2. However, a new mutation will only have evolutionary significance if it is passed on to _____ and is selected by other evolutionary forces.

VII. CHROMOSOMES

  A. Much of a cell's existence is spent in _____.

     1. During this period, the cell is involved with normal cellular and metabolic processes.

     2. During interphase the cell's DNA exists as a substance called _____.

  B. Cell division is the process that results in the production of _____ cells. It is during cell division that DNA becomes visible under a light microscope as _____.

  C. Chromosome structure

     1. A chromosome is composed of a _____ molecule and associated proteins.

2. During interphase, chromosomes exist as _____ - _____ structures.

3. During early cell replication, chromosomes consist of _____ strands of DNA.

   a. These two strands are joined together at a constricted region called the

      _____ .

   b. The reason there are two strands of DNA is because _____

      has occurred and one strand is an exact copy of the other.

D. Each species is characterized by a specific number of _____.

   1. Humans have _____ chromosomes.

   2. Chromosomes occur in pairs and humans have 23 _____. The members of chromosomal pairs are called _____.

      a. Homologous chromosomes carry genetic information influencing the same

         _____ .

      b. However, homologous chromosomes are not genetically _____.

         1. The position a gene occupies on a chromosome is called the _____.

         2. There can be alternative versions of a gene on the homologous loci. These

            different forms are called _____ .

E. Types of chromosomes

   1. _____ carry genetic information that governs all physical characteristics except primary sex determination.

   2. The two _____ chromosomes are the X and Y chromosomes.

      a. Genetically normal mammal females have two _____ chromosomes.

      b. Genetically normal mammal males have one X chromosome and one _____ chromosome.

F. In order to function properly, a human cell must have both members of each

   chromosome _____.

VIII. KARYOTYPING

A. A photomicrograph that displays an individual's chromosomes is called a
_____ .

B. Karyotypes are constructed from photographs taken through a microscope of
chemically treated chromosomes

   1. _____ chromosomes are matched up.

   2. Chromosomes are arranged by

      a. _____ , and

      b. _____ position.

C. Technological advances now allow us to identify every chromosome on the basis of
_____ patterns

   1. Karyotypes and banding patterns enable researchers to deduce _____
relationships between different species.

   2. The chromosome patterns of humans, chimpanzees, and gorillas indicate a very
_____ relationship between these three species.

D. Karyotypes have numerous practical applications

   1. They can be used in _____ of chromosomal disorders.

   2. They can also be employed in _____ diagnosis of developing fetuses.

IX. CELL DIVISION

A. Mitosis

   1. Cell division in somatic cells is called _____.

   2. Mitosis occurs during _____ and repair/replacement of tissues.

   3. Steps in mitosis

      a. By the time that chromosomes can be seen, they have already duplicated—
hence, what we see represents two DNA molecules.

b. The 46 chromosomes line up in the center of the cell (see Fig. 3-10c).

c. The chromosomes are then pulled apart at the _____.

d. The separated chromosomes are pulled towards opposite ends of the cell; each separated chromosome is composed of _____ DNA molecule.

e. The cell membrane pinches in and two new cells now exist.

4. The result of mitosis is two identical _____ cells that are genetically _____ to the original cell.

B. Meiosis

1. Meiosis is the production of sex cells, or _____.

   a. Male sex cells are _____ , produced in the testes.

   b. _____ sex cells are eggs (ova) produced in the ovaries.

2. _____ is a reduction division.

   a. Initially the sex cells have the _____ number, or full complement, of chromosomes.

   b. After meiosis has taken place, the gametes are _____, i.e., they have half the normal complement of chromosomes.

3. Meiosis is characterized by

   a. _____ divisions,

   b. _____ haploid daughter cells, and

   c. _____, or crossing over.

      1. The _____ chromosomes form into pairs on the cell's equator.

      2. While the homologous chromosomes are together they exchange pieces of _____ material.

4. Reduction division is critical in meiosis because the fusion of two haploid gametes results in the restoration of the _____ number of chromosomes.

5. Meiosis and sexual reproduction are highly important _____ innovations.

   a. Meiosis increases genetic variation at a faster rate than _____ alone could.

   b. Offspring in _____ _____ species represent the combination of genetic information from two parents.

   c. Darwin emphasized that natural selection acted on _____ variation in all populations.

      1. _____ is the only source of new genetic variation.

      2. However, in sexually reproducing species recombination (sexual reproduction, crossing-over) produces new _____ of genetic information, providing additional material for natural selection to act on.

C. Meiosis in males and females

   1. Meiosis in human females is part of _____.

      a. The end result of meiosis is one gamete, the _____.

      b. The ovum contains 22 autosomes and an _____ chromosome.

      c. Meiosis begins before birth and is then "arrested" in an early stage of meiosis; meiosis then begins again at puberty as part of a monthly cycle

   2. Meiosis in human males is part of _____.

      a. This occurs continuously in a male who has reached reproductive age

      b. The end result of spermatogenesis is _____ sperm from every primary sex cell.

      c. In addition to the 22 autosomes, a sperm will have either an X chromosome or a _____ chromosome.

D. Problems with meiosis

    1. Meiosis must be _____ to produce a viable gamete and

        a. Must have exactly _____ chromosomes.

        b. Have only one member of each _____ pair present.

    2. Errors in meiosis may lead to spontaneous abortions, or _____.

    3. Chromosomes may fail to separate during meiosis. This is called _____.

        a. Nondisjunction may lead to an affected gamete fusing with a normal gamete.

        b. An affected gamete that contains one less chromosome and fuses with a normal gamete will produce a monosomy, i.e. the zygote will contain 45 chromosomes with one chromosome pair only represented by _____ chromosome.

        c. An affected gamete that contains an extra chromosome and fuses with a normal gamete will produce a trisomy, i.e. the zygote will contain 47 chromosomes, with one chromosome pair represented by _____ chromosomes.

    4. Examples of abnormal numbers of chromosomes

        a. Down syndrome, or trisomy 21, occurs because of three copies of

                _____ #_____.

            1. Congenital problems associated with _____ include mental retardation, heart defects, and increased susceptibility to respiratory infections.

            2. Trisomy 21 is associated with _____ _____ _____ (over 35 years of age).

        b. Nondisjunction may also occur in _____ chromosomes resulting in impaired mental function, sterility, or death.

KEY TERMS

amino acids: small molecules that are the basic building blocks of proteins.

autosomes: one of the pairs of chromosomes that determines traits other than sex.

cell (plasma) membrane: the living boundary of an animal cell.

chromosome: structures that are composed of DNA and protein, found in the nucleus of the cell, and are only visible during cell replication.

codon: three nitrogeneous bases (i.e., a triplet) found on the mRNA which complements three bases on a tRNA carrying a specific amino acid.

complementarity, principle of: the rule that certain bases in DNA and RNA always bind together. Cytosine always pairs with guanine and, in DNA adenine always pairs with thymine. In RNA uracil replaces thymine and pairs with adenine. Sometimes referred to as the "base-pairing principle."

cytoplasm: the region of a cell that is contained within the cell membrane, excluding the nucleus.

diploid: the full complement of chromosomes of a species.

DNA (deoxyribonucleic acid): a double-stranded molecule that contains the genetic information.

eukaryote cell: cells of organisms in which the DNA is enclosed by membranes forming a nucleus

gametes: sex cells, viz. ova (eggs) and sperm.

gene: a sequence of DNA nucleotides that code for a particular polypeptide chain.

generalized cell: a eukaryotic cell that has all of the structures known to exist in cells; also referred to as a composite cell. The generalized cell is a teaching device. Most cells are specialized and may not have some of the structures of a generalized cell. For example, mature red blood cells do not have a nucleus.

genetics: the discipline within biology that studies the inheritance of biological characteristics.

haploid: half the normal complement of chromosomes of a species. The haploid condition is characteristic of animal sex cells.

homologous: the pair of chromosomes that carry genes for the same traits.

karyotype: the chromosomal complement of an individual or that typical for a species. Usually displayed as a photomicrograph, often using special stains to highlight the bands or centromeres.

meiosis: specialized cell division in the reproductive organs which produce gametes. The gametes are haploid and are not identical.

messenger RNA (mRNA): a form of RNA, formed on one strand of the DNA, that carries the DNA code from the nucleus to the cytoplasm where protein synthesis takes place.

mitochondria: organelles found in the cytoplasm which produce cellular energy.

mitosis: cell division in somatic cells.

monosomy: the absence of a member of a chromosome pair.

mutation: a change in the sequence of bases coding for the production of a protein.

nondisjunction: the failure of homologous chromosomes to separate during meiosis.

nucleotide: the basic unit of DNA. A nucleotide consists of one of four nitrogeneous bases, plus a sugar and a phosphate.

nucleus: a structure found in eukaryotic cells which contains chromosomal DNA.

organelle: a structure found in the cytoplasm that performs some physiological function.

point mutation: a mutation that results from the substitution of one nitrogenous base by another.

prokaryote cell: a single-celled organism that lacks a nucleus.

proteins: three-dimensional molecules composed of amino acids that serve as structural components of animal bodies and as catalysts for biochemical reactions.

protein synthesis: the process by which proteins are produced from amino acids.

ribosome: a cytoplasmic organelle, made up of RNA and protein, where protein synthesis takes place.

RNA (ribonucleic acid): a single-stranded molecule, similar in structure to DNA. The three types of RNA are essential to protein synthesis.

sex chromosomes: in animals, those chromosomes involved with primary sex determination. The X and Y chromosomes.

sickle-cell anemia: a severe inherited disease that results from a double dose of a mutant allele, which in turn results from a point mutation.

somatic cells: the cells of the body, excluding the cells involved with primary reproduction.

transcription: the formation of a messenger RNA molecule from a DNA template.

transfer RNA (tRNA): the form of RNA that binds to a specific amino acid and, during translation, transports them to the ribosome in sequence.

translation: the process of sequencing amino acids from a messenger RNA template into a functional protein or a portion of a protein.

triplet: a set of three nitrogenous bases on the DNA molecule.

trisomy: the present of three members of a chromosome pair instead of the usual two.

zygote: a cell resulting from the fusion of a sperm and an egg (ovum).

Now take the Fill-in and Multiple Choice tests. Do not guess. Following completion of the tests, correct them. The correct answers and textbook page references are at the end of this study guide chapter. Note your strong areas and your weak areas to guide you in your continuing study.

FILL-IN QUESTIONS

1. _____ is the study of how traits are transmitted from one generation to the next.

2. DNA is found within the _____ of an eukaryotic cell.

3. The structures found in the cytoplasm that are responsible for energy production are the

   _____ .

4. Some antibiotics interfere with a bacterium's ability to synthesize proteins. The organelles damaged in the bacterial cytoplasm by these antibiotics must be the _____.

5. The sole function of a gamete is to unite with a gamete from another individual to form

   a _____.

6. An individual _____ consists of one deoxyribose sugar, one phosphate, and one of four nitrogenous bases.

7. Two long strands of nucleotides, formed into a double helix, describes the _____ molecule.

8. In the following illustration, DNA is replicating. Put in the letter of the nitrogeous bases of the new strand of DNA in accordance with the principle of complementarity.

$$A - A - C - G - T - A$$
$$\_ - \_ - \_ - \_ - \_ - \_$$

9. _____ are a group of substances that function in a myriad of ways, serving as structural components, as well as initiating and enhancing chemical reactions in the body.

10. In order for a protein to function properly its _____ _____ must be arranged in the proper sequence.

11. In the DNA instructions, a _____ , or group of three bases, codes for a particular amino acid.

12. The genetic instructions for producing a protein are carried into the cytoplasm by a _____ _____ molecule.

13. The process in which a mRNA molecule is formed from DNA is called _____.

14. The cytoplasmic organelles to which mRNAs attach are the _____.

15. The molecule which carries a specific amino acid and has a triplet which matches one of the mRNA codons is called _____ _____.

16. A gene is a particular sequence of nucleotides along part of a chromosome that codes for the production of a _____ _____.

17. A change in the sequence of nucleotides of a gene results in a _____.

18. Individuals who have only one HbS allele are said to have _____ - _____ _____.

19. A mutagen results in the substitution of an adenine in a gene. That substitution results in a different amino acid in the polypeptide chain produced by the gene. Such an event is called a _____ _____.

20. The structures to the right are _____ .

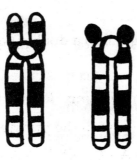

21. The reason that there are two strands of DNA when chromosomes become visible is because the DNA molecules have _____ .

22. Alternate forms of a gene are called _____ .

23. A researcher has identified a position that is designated SDR on the Y chromosome. The series of nucleotides appears to be the gene that codes for testosterone. This position is properly referred to as a _____ .

24. Chromosomes that determine an individual's sex are referred to as _____ chromosomes.

25. The illustration below is a _____ .

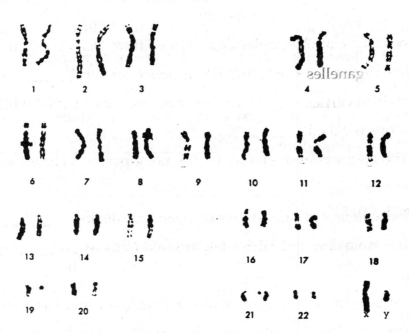

26. The illustration of homologous chromosomes above has been arranged according to size and position of the _____ .

27. Cell division in which the end result is two identical daughter cells with the full genetic complement of the species, from one parent cell, is called _____ .

28. In meiosis, the end result is four gametes with the _____ number of chromosomes.

29. What process is occurring in the illustration below? _____

30. The random distribution of chromosomes to daughter cells during meiosis is called _____ _____ .

31. The type of cell division that has the most importance for evolution is _____ .

32. A boy is born with three 21st chromosomes. This is a condition known as trisomy 21 or Down Syndrome. The cause of this condition is the failure of the 21st chromosome to separate normally during meiosis in one of the parent's gametes. This failure to separate properly is called _____ .

33. Human genes can be inserted into bacteria in order to produce human protein products such as insulin. This procedure is called _____ technology.

MULTIPLE CHOICE QUESTIONS

1. The discipline that links or influences the various subdisciplines of physical (biological) anthropology is
   A. genetics.
   B. cell biology.
   C. paleontology.
   D. primatology.

2. A cell that has its DNA enclosed by a nucleus is called a
   A. karyote cell.
   B. prokaryote cell.
   C. eukaryote cell.
   D. prion.

3. The two nucleic acids that contain the genetic information that controls the cell's functions are
   A. ribosomes and Golgi apparati.
   B. mitochondria and desmosomes.
   C. the endoplasmic reticulum and ribosomes.
   D. DNA and RNA.

4. The organelles found in the cytoplasm that contains its own DNA are the
   A. ribosomes.
   B. mitochondria.
   C. lysosomes.
   D. vacuoles.

5. Which of the following is **not** a sex cell?
   A. gamete
   B. ovum
   C. sperm
   D. skin cell

6. A cell formed by the union of an egg and a sperm is called a
   A. gamete.
   B. zygote.
   C. neuron.
   D. ovum.

7. The smallest unit of DNA consists of one sugar, one phosphate, and one of four bases. This unit is called a
   A. sperm.
   B. nucleotide.
   C. nucleus.
   D. ribosome.

8. Researchers found that certain bases of the DNA macromolecule always pair. These bases are referred to as
   A. independently assorted.
   B. segregated.
   C. in equilibrium .
   D. complementary.

9. A parental chain of DNA provides the following template: AAT CGA CGT. Which of the following sequences of free nucleotides would pair with the parental template?
    A. TTA GCT GCA
    B. AAT CGA CGT
    C. GGC TAG TAC
    D. UUA GCU GCA

10. The end result of DNA replication is
    A. two new strands of DNA.
    B. the fusion of the mother's DNA with the father's DNA.
    C. the formation of a mRNA molecule.
    D. the production of an amino acid molecule.

11. A type of protein which helps to enhance chemical reactions in the body is
    A. bone.
    B. muscle.
    C. enzymes.
    D. hemoglobin.

12. Proteins consist of chains of
    A. triglycerides.
    B. monosaccarides.
    C. amino acids.
    D. fatty acids.

13. Which of the following is **not** true of RNA?
    A. It is single stranded.
    B. Some forms of RNA are involved with protein synthesis.
    C. It has a different type of sugar than DNA has.
    D. It contains the base thymine.

14. The formation of a mRNA molecule from DNA is called
    A. transcription.
    B. translation.
    C. translocation.
    D. transformation.

15. The reading of mRNA by a ribosome to produce protein is called
    A. transcription.
    B. translation.
    C. translocation.
    D. transforamation.

16. A portion of a mRNA molecule that determines one amino acid in a polypeptide chain is called a
    A. nucleotide.
    B. gene.
    C. codon.
    D. nucleoside.

THE BIOLOGICAL BASIS OF LIFE 49

17. In protein synthesis, all of the following occur **except**
    A. amino acids are initially bonded to specific tRNA molecules.
    B. amino acids are transported to the nucleus to bond with DNA molecules.
    C. the sequence of amino acids is determined by the codon sequence in mRNA.
    D. amino acids are bonded together to form a polypeptide chain.

18. What is the name of the molecule that amino acids bind to?
    A. messenger RNA (mRNA)
    B. ribosomal RNA (rRNA)
    C. transfer RNA (tRNA)
    D. mitochondral DNA (mtDNA)

19. The following segment of mRNA contains the bases UUA CGC UGA. Which triplets on three different tRNAs will line up in order during translation?
    A. UUA CGC UGA
    B. AAT GCG ACT
    C. AGU CGC AUU
    D. AAU GCG ACU

20. A series of DNA bases on the chromosome that code for a particular polypeptide chain is a(n)
    A. ribosome.
    B. amino acid.
    C. gene.
    D. polypeptide chain.

21. Which of the following is **not** true regarding the DNA code?
    A. The code is universal.
    B. The code is continuous.
    C. The code accommodates 24 different amino acids.
    D. The code is redundant.

22. A severe hemoglobin disorder in which oxygen-deprived red blood cells collapse, that results from a single base substitution at the DNA level, is
    A. sickle-cell anemia.
    B. Tay-Sachs disease.
    C. cystic fibrosis.
    D. hemolytic disease of the newborn.

23. A change in one base of a codon may produce a change in the hereditary information. This is called a
    A. point mutation.
    B. chromosomal reversal.
    C. chromosomal inversion.
    D. synapsis.

24. What is the characteristic number of chromosomes in human somatic cells?
    A. 23
    B. 46
    C. 48
    D. 78

25. A genetically normal human female has
    A. 23 pairs of autosomes.
    B. 23 pairs of autosomes and two X chromosomes.
    C. 22 pairs of autosomes and two X chromosomes.
    D. 22 pairs of autosomes, one X chromosome, and one Y chromosome.

26. Pregnant women can have a procedure done called amniocentesis. In this procedure some of the fetal cells are obtained and photomicrographs are produced illustrating the fetus's chromosomes. Such a photomicrograph is called a
    A. banding pattern.
    B. CT scanning.
    C. karyotype.
    D. PET Imaging.

27. The end result of mitosis in humans is
    A. two identical "daughter" cells.
    B. four haploid cells.
    C. two cells with 23 chromosomes.
    D. two cells with mutations.

28. Which of the following is **true** for meiosis?
    A. It has only one division which duplicates the parent cell exactly.
    B. It produces gametes.
    C. When a mutation occurs, it affects only the individual.
    D. It has no effect on evolution.

29. Crossing-over is a process in which
    A. segments of DNA are exchanged between homologous chromosome arms.
    B. two different chromosomes are fused together.
    C. a mutation occurs.
    D. two strands of DNA from two different species are allowed to combine.

30. The end result of meiosis in human females is
    A. four sperm.
    B. four ova (eggs).
    C. one ovum (egg).
    D. one ovum and three polar bodies.

31. If chromosomes or chromosome strands fail to separate during meiosis, serious problems can arise. This failure to separate is called
    A. Turner's syndrome.
    B. nondisjunction.
    C. a monosomy.
    D. random assortment.

ANSWERS TO FILL-IN OUTLINE

I. THE CELL
  A. unit
    1. multicellular
    2. single-celled
      b. prokaryote (the word prokaryote actually means "before a nucleus")
    3. a. eukaryote (this word means "true nucleus")
  B. 2. cell membrane
    3. organelles
    4. nucleus
    5. a. 1. energy
         2. DNA
      b. proteins
  C. 1. somatic
    2. reproduction
      a. female
      b. male
      c. zygote

II. DNA STRUCTURE
  B. two
    1. nucleotide
    2. complements
      a. thymine (T)
      b. cytosine (C)
      c. exact

III. DNA REPLICATION
  A. replicate
  B. 2. templates
    3. complementary
    4. two

IV. PROTEIN SYNTHESIS
  A. protein
  B. 1. structural
    2. chemical
    3. amino
      a. 20
      b. sequence
  C. 1. proteins
    2. ribosome
      a. single-stranded
      b. codons
    3. a. amino
      b. mRNA

D. 1. a. template
     b. transcription
  2. a. ribosome
     b. amino acids
     c. tRNA
     d. protein
     e. translation

V. DEFINITION OF THE GENE
  A. gene
  B. mutation
    a. proteins

VI. MUTATION: WHEN A GENE CHANGES
  A. mutation
  B. 1. a. beta
         1. sickle-cell
         2. amino acid
      b. point mutation
         1. variation
         2. offspring

VII. CHROMOSOMES
  A. interphase
    2. chromatin
  B. new; chromosomes
  C. 1. DNA
    2. single-stranded
    3. two
      a. centromere
      b. replication
  D. chromosomes
    1. 46
    2. pairs; homologous
      a. traits
      b. identical
         1. locus
         2. alleles
  E. 1. autosomes
    2. sex
      a. X
      b. Y
  F. pair

VIII. KARYOTYPING CHROMOSOMES
  A. karyotype
  B. 1. homologous
    2. a. size
      b. centromere

C. banding
   1. evolutionary
   2. close
D. 1. diagnosis
   2. prenatal

IX. CELL DIVISION
  A. 1. mitosis
     2. growth
     3. c. centromere
       d. one
     4. daughter; identical
  B. 1. gametes
      a. sperm
      b. female
     2. meiosis
      a. diploid
      b. haploid
     3. a. two
      b. four
      c. recombination
        1. homologous
        2. genetic
     4. diploid

5. evolutionary
  a. mutation
  b. sexually reproducing
  c. genetic
    1. mutation
    2. arrangements (or combinations)
  1. oogenesis
    a. ovum
    b. X
  2. spermatogenesis
    b. four
    c. Y
D. 1. exact
    a. 23
    b. chromosome
  2. miscarriages
  3. nondisjunction
    b. one
    c. three
  4. a. chromosome #21.
      1. trisomy 21
      2. advanced maternal age
    b. sex

ANSWERS & REFERENCES TO FILL-IN QUESTIONS

1. genetics, p. 42
2. nucleus, p. 42
3. mitochondria, p. 43
4. ribosomes, p. 43
5. zygote, p. 43
6. nucleotide, p. 44, see also Fig. 3-2
7. DNA, p. 44
8. T-T-G-C-A-T, p. 44 & Fig. 3-2
9. proteins, pp. 45, 47
10. amino acids, p. 47
11. triplet, p. 47
12. messenger RNA, p. 48
13. transcription, p. 48, Fig. 3-4
14. ribosomes, p. 48
15. transfer RNA, p. 48
16. polypeptide chain, p. 49
17. mutation, p. 50
18. sickle-cell trait, p. 51
19. point mutation, p. 52
20. chromosomes, see Figs. 3-7 & 3-8, pp. 54-55

21. replicated, pp. 52-53
22. alleles, p. 54
23. locus, p. 53
24. sex, p. 54
25. karyotype, p. 56, see Fig. 3-9
26. centromere, p. 56
27. mitosis, p. 57
28. haploid, p. 58
29. recombination (crossing-over) in which bits of genetic material are exchanged between homologous chromosomes, p. 60, see Fig. 3-11
30. random assortment, p. 61
31. meiosis; this is because meiosis has the potential to affect future generations, whereas, mitosis affects only the individual in which mitosis is occurring, p. 60
32. nondisjunction, p. 62
33. recombinant DNA, p. 67

ANSWERS & REFERENCES TO MULTIPLE CHOICE QUESTIONS

1. A, p. 42
2. C, p. 42
3. D, p. 43
4. B, p. 43
5. D, p. 43
6. B, pp. 43-44
7. B, p. 44
8. D, p. 44
9. A, p. 44
10. A, p. 45
11. C, p. 47

12. C, p. 47
13. D, p. 47
14. A, p. 48
15. B, p. 48
16. C, p. 48
17. B, pp. 48-49
18. C, p. 48
19. D, p. 48 & see Fig. 3-5 & Table 3-1
20. C, p. 49
21. C, p. 51 (Box 3-1)

22. A, p. 51
23. A, p. 52 & see Fig. 3-6
24. B, p. 53 & see Table 3-2)
25. C, pp. 54, 56
26. C, p. 56
27. A, p. 57
28. B, p. 57
29. A, p. 60
30. D, p. 61
31. B, p. 62

CHAPTER 4

HEREDITY AND EVOLUTION

LEARNING OBJECTIVES

After reading this chapter you should be able to:
- discuss Mendel's principles of segregation and independent assortment. (pp. 71-75)
- perform simple matings using a Punnett square. (p. 74)
- analyze a simple genealogy by pedigree analysis. (pp. 78-84)
- recognize the patterns of inheritance for autosomal dominant and recessive traits and sex-linked traits. (pp. 80-83)
- describe the difference between Mendelian traits and polygenic traits. (p. 84-86)
- understand the complexity involved between genetic and environmental factors. (p. 86-87)
- define biological evolution. (pp. 87-89)
- describe the agents that are responsible for generating and distributing variation. (pp. 89-93)
- discuss the role natural selection plays in the direction of evolution. (pp. 93-94)
- distinguish between the roles of individuals and of populations in evolution. (pp. 95-97)

FILL-IN OUTLINE

Introduction
In the last chapter the structure and function of DNA was presented. This chapter examines the principles of heredity, originally studied by Gregor Mendel. Also discussed is the synthesis of Darwinism, Mendelianism, and genetics into the comprehensive modern theory of biological evolution.

I. GREGOR MENDEL'S EXPERIMENTS WITH GARDEN PEAS

A. Introduction

1. _____ (1822-1884) discovered the basic principles of heredity.

2. Mendel crossed different strains of purebred plants and studied their _____.

B. Crosses between plants: single traits

1. Mendel crossed purebred plants that differed in one trait.

   a. The plants used in this first cross were designated the _____,

   or P generation.

   b. One of the traits disappeared in the _____ offspring.

   c. The trait that was present in the F_1 generation was not _____

   between the two traits as would be the case if _____

   _____ was valid.

   d. When the F_1 generation self-fertilized, the missing trait _____

   in the F_2 generation.

   e. Mendel obtained a constant ratio of _____ dominants to _____ recessive in

   the F_2 generation.

2. Mendel's results could be explained if:

   a. The trait was the result of _____ units.

   b. These two factors _____ during gamete formation.

   c. The idea that traits are controlled by two discrete units, which separate into

   different sex cells, was Mendel's principle of _____ .

   d. Today we know that _____ explains Mendel's principle of segregation.

3. Mendel's terms

   a. Mendel called the trait that disappeared in the F_1 generation, but reappeared

   in the F_2 generation, _____.

   b. Mendel called the trait that was expressed in the F_1 generation _____.

   c. When two copies of the same allele are present the individual is _____

   for that trait.

d. When there are two different alleles at a locus the individual is _____.

4. Mendel's results can be illustrated by a Punnett square (see Fig. 4-3).

a. The Punnett square shows the _____ of offspring with specific genotypes.

b. The Punnett square does not show the actual _____ of offspring with a specific genotype.

c. The Punnett square is useful for predicting the proportions of _____ generation genotypes.

C. Crosses between plants: two traits together

1. Mendel next crossed two different characters which he considered _____.

2. The F_1 generation expressed only the _____ traits.

3. The _____ generation contained combinations of traits not present in either of the plants of the P generation.

4. Mendel deduced that these traits were inherited _____ of one another.

5. Mendel's second principle of inheritance is the principle of _____ _____.

II. MENDELIAN INHERITANCE IN HUMANS

A. More than _____ traits are known to be inherited by simple Mendelian principles.

B. The human _____ blood system is an example of a simple Mendelian inheritance.

1. The A and B alleles are _____ to the O allele.

2. Neither the A or B allele are dominant to one another; they are _____ and both traits are expressed.

C. Genetic disorders can be inherited as dominant or recessive traits.

   1. Dominant disorders are inherited when _____ copy of a dominant allele is present. Such disorders include achondroplasia, brachydactyly, and familial hypercholesterolemia

   2. Recessive disorders require the presence of _____ copies of the recessive allele.

     a. Heterozygotes for such disorders are not affected, but because they carry one copy of the recessive allele, they are _____.

     b. Some recessive conditions that affect humans are _____, _____ _____ , _____-_____ _____, and _____-_____ _____.

D. The principle technique that has been used in human inheritance studies is the construction of pedigrees.

   1. _____ analysis helps determine if a trait is Mendelian.

   2. Pedigree analysis helps determine the mode of inheritance; six different modes of Mendelian inheritance are recognized. The three most important are:

     a. _____ _____.

     b. _____ _____ .

     c. ___-_____ _____ .

   3. In pedigree charts _____ represent males and _____ represent females.

E. Autosomal dominant traits

   1. These traits are governed by _____ on autosomes.

   2. Because these traits are dominant, anyone who inherits a dominant allele will express the trait and almost all affected individuals are _____.

3. pattern of inheritance

   a. Each affected individual has at least one _____ parent.

   b. Autosomal dominant traits _____ _____ _____ generations.

   c. There is no _____ bias in autosomal dominant traits; equal numbers of males and females are affected.

   d. Another characteristic of autosomal dominance is that about _____ - _____ of the offspring of an affected parent are also affected.

F. Autosomal recessive traits

  1. These traits are also controlled by loci located on the _____.

  2. Because these traits are recessive, there must be _____ alleles present in an affected person.

  3. pattern of inheritance

   a. Recessive traits often appear to _____ generations.

   b. Affected individuals often have two _____ parents who are carriers.

   c. Affected individuals occur less often than with dominant traits; because they are often the result of two heterozygous parents roughly _____ of the offspring express the trait.

G. Sex-linked traits

  1. The loci for sex-linked traits are found on the _____ chromosomes.

  2. Almost all of the known sex-linked traits are on the _____ chromosome.

  3. One of the best known sex-linked traits is _____ (see pedigree, Fig. 4-10).

  4. Because males are _____ for the X chromosome, any allele on that chromosome is expressed.

III. POLYGENIC INHERITANCE

A. Mendelian traits are discrete traits.

    1. _____ traits fall into clear categories.

    2. Because discrete traits are discontinuous, there are no _____

       forms between discrete traits.

    3. Mendelian traits are governed by _____ genetic locus.

B. Polygenic traits are continuous traits governed by alleles at more than one genetic

   locus.

    1. Continuous traits show _____ .

       a. There is a series of _____ intermediate forms between the

         two extremes.

       b. The gradations formed by continuous traits produce a bell curve graphically

    2. Each locus in a polygenic trait contributes to the _____.

    3. A well-known example of a polygenic trait is human _____ _____,

       governed by perhaps 6 loci and at least 12 alleles.

C. Because polygenic traits are continuous, they can be treated _____.

    1. The _____ is a summary statistic which gives the average of a sample

       or population.

    2. A standard deviation measures _____ - _____ _____.

    3. Researchers are able to _____ continuous traits between different

       populations and to see if there are significant differences statistically.

D. Mendelian characteristics are not as amenable to statistical analysis as polygenic

   characters are. However,

    1. Mendelian characteristics can be described in terms of _____

       within populations and compared between populations.

2. Mendelian characters can be analyzed for mode of inheritance from

   _____ data.

3. Mendelian characters are valuable because the approximate or exact

   _____ ___ _____ _____ for them is known.

IV. GENETIC AND ENVIRONMENTAL FACTORS

A. The terms genotype and phenotype have both a narrow and broad definition.

   1. On the narrow level they both may be used in reference to a single trait, e.g., the genetic and physical expression of purple flowers vs. white flowers that Mendel studied on pea plants.

   2. At a broader level these two terms may refer to the individual's _____ genetic makeup and all of its observable characteristics.

B. The genotype sets limits and potentials for development.

   1. The genotype also interacts with the organism's _____.

   2. Many aspects of the _____ are influenced by the genetic/environmental interaction.

C. Many _____ traits, such as height, are influenced by the environment.

D. Mendelian traits are _____ likely to be influenced by the environment.

E. Even though polygenic traits are controlled by several loci and are more amenable to the environment, they still obey _____ principles at the individual loci.

V. MODERN THEORY OF EVOLUTION

A. Darwin and Mendel each discovered essential mechanisms for how evolution worked.

   1. Those who followed saw the work of these two men incompatible for explaining evolution.

   2. By the 1930s, biologists realized that Darwinian selection and Mendelian genetics were complementary factors that explained evolution—the fusion of these two ideas was called the _____ _____.

B. The modern synthesis partitioned evolution into two stages:

1. small new changes in the genetic material were _____ by Mendelian principles and resulted in variation.

2. the genetic variation was acted on by _____ _____.

VI. DEFINITION OF EVOLUTION

A. The modern definition of evolution is a _____ ___ _____ _____ _____ _____ _____ _____ _____ _____.

B. Allele frequencies are numerical indicators of the genetic makeup of a _____.

C. Only populations _____, individuals do not evolve, over time.

D. _____ consists of small, short-term inherited changes that occur over a short period within a species.

E. _____ are major evolutionary changes that occur over geological time and may result in new species.

VII. FACTORS THAT PRODUCE AND REDISTRIBUTE VARIATION

A. Mutation

1. An actual molecular alteration in genetic material is called _____.

2. For a mutation to have any evolutionary significance it must occur in a _____ _____.

3. Mutation rates for any given trait are quite _____.

4. Mutation is the only way to produce "new" _____; hence, mutation is the basic creative force in evolution.

B. Gene Flow

1. Gene flow is the movement of _____ from one population to another.

2. Gene flow has been a consistent feature of hominid evolution and explains why speciation has been _____ in humans.

C. Genetic Drift

   1. Genetic drift is a _____ factor that is due mainly to sampling phenomena.

     a. Genetic drift is directly related to the _____ of the population.

     b. _____ populations are more prone to randomness in evolution, i.e., gene drift.

   2. A special case of genetic drift is _____ _____ (Sewell Wright effect).

     a. In founder effect only a very small proportion of a population contributes _____ to the next generation.

     b. Founder effect can result when a small group _____ and founds a new population.

     c. Through founder effect an individual who carries an allele, rare in the parent population, can make a _____ genetic contribution to the next generation.

   3. Genetic drift has probably played an _____ role in human evolution.

D. Recombination

   1. _____ reproduction is, in itself, a recombination, or reshuffling, of genetic material coming from two different parents.

   2. The reshuffling of chromosomes, including crossing-over, during _____ can produce trillions of gene combinations.

VIII. NATURAL SELECTION ACTS ON VARIATION

A. Without natural selection there is no long-term _____ to evolution.

   1. Mutation, gene flow, genetic drift, and recombination produce _____.

   2. _____ _____ acts on the variation and provides direction.

B. Selection acting on variation enables populations to adapt.

1. Selection results in a change in allele frequency relative to specific

   _____ factors.

2. If the environment changes, _____ pressures change also.

IX. NATURAL SELECTION IN HUMANS

A. Humans are a long-lived, slow-reproducing species which are not amenable to
controlled laboratory experiments; obtaining _____ data on
natural selection, comparable to other species, has been difficult.

B. _____-_____ trait is the only well documented case of natural selection
in humans.

   1. Hb^s is the result of a _____ _____ in the gene coding for
   the hemoglobin beta chain.

   2. Inheriting two copies of the Hb^s allele results in _____.

   3. Nevertheless, Hb^s allele is frequent in some populations, especially in west and
   central _____.

      a. It is associated with higher frequencies of Hb^s is the presence of _____.

      b. An experiment was done in the 1950s in which _____
      and individuals homozygous for normal hemoglobin were compared in their
      response to infection by malaria.

         1. Heterozygotes were _____ resistant to malaria.

            a. Heterozygote _____ _____ _____ do not provide a
            conducive environment for the malarial parasite to reproduce.

            b. Hence, the parasite often dies before infecting the body of a _____.

         2. "Normal" individuals were more likely to have their reproductive success
         _____ due to malarial infections.

X. REVIEW, GENETICS AND EVOLUTIONARY FACTORS

A. The different levels at which evolutionary factors operate are all _____ and _____.

B. Evolution works on a _____; it is the population that will, or will not, change over time.

C. If the _____ frequencies in a population have changed, then evolution has occurred.

D. If evolution has occurred, why has it occurred?

   1. A new allele can only arise through _____.

   2. Mutations must spread; this could occur in a small population through _____ _____.

   3. Long-term evolutionary trends can only occur due to _____ _____.

KEY TERMS

allele: the alternative form of a gene.
allele frequency: the proportion of a particular allele to all the other alleles at a given locus in a population.
autosome: any of the chromosomes excluding the two sex chromosomes.
carrier: an individual who is a heterozygote for a recessive genetic disorder; the individual is unaffected.
codominance: a condition in which both alleles are expressed in the phenotype.
continuous traits: traits which have measurable gradations between the two end points, such as height in humans.
discrete traits: traits which fall into clear categories, such as a purple flower versus a white flower in a garden pea.
dominant: the genetic trait that is expressed in the heterozygous state.
evolution (biological): a change in allele frequencies between generations.
F$_1$ generation: the hybrid offspring of purebreeding parents.
gene flow: exchange of genes between different populations of a species.
genetic drift: evolutionary changes in the gene pool of a small population due to chance (random factors).
gamete: a sex cell, in humans these are ova (eggs) and sperm.
genotype: the genetic makeup of an organism.

hemizygous: condition where there is only one allele present (on the X chromosome) instead of two.

heterozygous: the presence of two different alleles for a given genetic trait in an individual.

hybrid: parents who are in some ways genetically dissimilar. This term can also be applied to heterozygotes.

homozygous: the presence of the same alleles for a given genetic trait in an individual.

mean: a summary statistic which gives the average of a sample or of a population.

macroevolution: evolutionary changes on a large scale, encompassing many generations, and involving change above the species level.

Mendelian traits: traits that are inherited at a single locus on a single chromosome.

microevolution: small, short-term changes in the gene pool of a population occurring over just a few generations.

mutation: an alteration in the genetic material (a change in the base sequence of DNA).

natural selection: the evolutionary factor that causes changes in the allele frequencies in populations due to differential net reproductive success of individuals. The force of evolution that gives direction in response to environmental factors.

phenotype: the physical expression of an organism's genotype.

phenotypic ratio: the proportion of one phenotype to other phenotypes.

population: a community of individuals, all of the same species, that occupy a particular area and breed among themselves.

polygenic: referring to traits that are influenced by genes at two or more loci.

principle of independent assortment: Mendel's principle that states that alleles for different traits sort independently during gamete formation.

principle of segregation: the principle expounded by Mendel that alleles occur in pairs which separate (segregate) during gamete formation. At fertilization the full number of alleles is restored.

recessive: the genetic trait that is not expressed in a heterozygous state.

sex chromosome: the chromosomes that determine sex. In humans these are the X and Y chromosomes.

sickle-cell trait: a condition resulting from a point mutation of the gene coding for production of the beta-chain hemoglobin. A red blood cell with this trait is subject to collapse during periods of extreme stress or low blood oxygen levels.

standard deviation: a summary statistic which measures within-group variation.

variation (genetic): inherited differences between individuals. The basis of all evolutionary change.

Now take the Fill-in and Multiple Choice tests. Do not guess. Following completion of the tests, correct them. The correct answers and textbook page references are at the end of this study guide chapter. Note your strong areas and your weak areas to guide you in your continuing study.

FILL-IN QUESTIONS

1.   The scientist who first described the basic principles of inheritance, based on his work with

the common garden pea, was _____ .

2.   A key characteristic of the different strains of pea plants that Mendel began his experiments with were that they always produced offspring that had the same traits as the parents. These are known as _____ plants.

3.   When Mendel allowed the F_1 generation to self-pollinate he obtained a ratio of _____ dominant traits for _____ recessive trait.

4.   Mendel's principle that any particular trait is governed by two different factors (alleles) which separate during the formation of gametes is called _____.

5.   Using the Punnett square provided below, mate a heterozygous tall pea plant with a dwarf pea. The phenotypic ratios for this cross are _____:_____ .

6.   What does Mendel's principle of independent assortment state? _____
     _____.

7.   Mr. and Mrs. Blutrot both have type A blood. What are the possible phenotypes for blood groups that the offspring of Mr. and Mrs. Blutrot could produce? _____.

8.   The **expression** of two different alleles for a trait, such as blood types AB and MN is called _____ .

9.   Genetic disorders such as achondroplasia are expressed in the heterozygotes. This type of disorder is inherited as a _____ trait; other genetic disorders, often associated with the lack of an enzyme that blocks a metabolic pathway, requires both harmful alleles to be expressed—these are _____ traits.

10. What tool is used to help analyze human inheritance? _____ .

11. In pedigree analysis, circles represent _____, while squares represent _____.

12. A genetic trait that is governed by one copy of an allele that is **not** on one of the sex chromosomes is a(n) _____ _____.

13. A genetic trait that requires two copies of the allele to be expressed and is **not** on one of the sex chromosomes is a(n)_____ _____.

14. Perform a mating in the Punnett square below between two normally pigmented individuals who each have a parent who is an albino. Of four children, what can we expect in terms of genotype? _____ What is the probability of albino offspring? _____

15. The genetic condition in which blood clotting factor is not operating is called _____. This condition is inherited as a(n) _____.

16. Perform a mating in the Punnett square below between a mother whose father suffers from hemophilia and a normal man who has no history of hemophilia in his family? What can we expect from such a mating? _____

17. Traits that are influenced by genes at two or more loci are called _____ traits.

18. Traits that fall into clearly defined categories are said to be _____ traits.

19. Polygenic traits are more likely to interact with the _____ than are discrete traits.

20. Even though polygenic traits are influenced by several loci, _____ principles still apply at the individual loci.

21. The fusion of Darwinian selection with Mendelian genetics was termed the _____ _____ .

22. A change in allele frequencies from one generation to the next is the definition of _____ .

23. Everyone in your class has had their blood typed. Your lab instructor has tallied up the results and put them into the following categories: type A = .5, type B = .4, type O = .1. This proportion of each of these types represents the _____ for this population.

24. The modern British population has a slight overbite. Anthropologists studying skeletons of Britons living six hundred years ago do not. Assuming that the modern British population is directly descended from this earlier population, this short-term effect is called _____ .

25. If one allele changes into another, a _____ has occurred.

26. The African American gene pool in the northern United States is estimated to contain around 20% European alleles. This is an example of _____ .

27. The force of evolution that is more likely to affect a small population rather than a large population is _____ .

28. When plague hit Europe in the fourteenth century, large populations were reduced to small remnants. Genetically these survivors represented a _____ population.

29. Sickle-cell trait in humans is a good example of _____ .

30. An anthropologist obtains records of allele frequencies for type MN blood at the Red Lake Ojibwa Reservation. In 1955 type M blood had an allele frequency of .6, type N blood had an allele frequency of .4. The anthropologist takes samples from the current residents of

Red Lake and obtains allele frequencies of .5 for both blood types. What has happened?

_____

_____

MULTIPLE CHOICE QUESTIONS

1. In a cross between two purebreeding strains of garden peas Mendel found that in the offspring
    A. both traits were represented in the F_2 generation.
    B. they were homozygous for the traits being studied.
    C. one of the traits disappeared.
    D. the traits were intermediate between the two parental traits.

2. Mendel used the term dominant for
    A. plants that were larger than others of the same variety.
    B. a trait that prevented another trait from appearing.
    C. a variety of pea plants that eliminated a weaker variety.
    D. a trait that "skipped" generations.

3. When Mendel crossed peas with Rr and Rr genotypes, the phenotypic ratio of the offspring was _____ and the genotypic ratio was _____. (Note: you may want to use a Punnett square to figure this out.)
    A. 1:1, 3:1
    B. 3:1, 1:2:1
    C. 1:2:1, 3:1
    D. 3:1, 1:1

4. Genes exist in pairs in individuals; during the production of gametes, the pairs are separated so that a gamete has only one of each kind. This is known as the
    A. principle of segregation.
    B. principle of independent assortment.
    C. mitosis.
    D. unification theory.

5. What physiological process explains Mendel's principle of segregation?
    A. mitosis
    B. meiosis
    C. metamorphosis
    D. metastasis

6. Which of the following is characteristic of dominant alleles?
    A. Dominant alleles are expressed in heterozygous genotypes.
    B. Dominant alleles are the alleles which are most common in a population.
    C. Dominant alleles always cause more serious defects than recessive alleles.
    D. Dominant alleles drive recessive alleles out of a population.

7. A trait which is inherited as a recessive is expressed in the
    A. homozygous recessive individual.
    B. homozygous dominant individual.
    C. heterozyous individual.
    D. codominant individual.

8. An alternative form of a gene is called a(n)
    A. nucleotide.
    B. locus.
    C. allele.
    D. epistasis.

9. Homozygous means that an individual has
    A. two different alleles of the same gene.
    B. the same alleles of the same gene.
    C. the same alleles of different genes.
    D. two different alleles of different genes.

10. The principle of independent assortment states that
    A. a pair of genes segregate during the production of gametes.
    B. genes recombine in a predetermined way.
    C. the distribution of one pair of genes does not influence the distribution of other pairs of genes on other chromosomes.
    D. mutations come from independent sources.

11. A heterozygous genotype would be written as
    A. AA.
    B. Aa.
    C. aa.
    D. AA and aa.

12. Mendelian traits are
    A. also known as traits of simple inheritance.
    B. controlled by alleles at more than one genetic locus.
    C. the product of several alleles on different chromosomes.
    D. only known for about 160 human traits.

13. When there are two different alleles present in a heterozygote and both of these alleles are expressed, this condition is called
    A. recessive.
    B. dominance.
    C. codominance.
    D. sex-linked.

14. Geneticists call a family tree that shows the matings that have taken place in a family, going back several generations, a
    A. karyotype.
    B. pedigree.
    C. genotype.
    D. syndrome.

15. The trait shown in this pedigree is most likely inherited as a
    A. autosomal recessive.
    B. autosomal dominant.
    C. sex-linked recessive.
    D. Y-linked recessive.

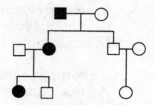

16. A certain form of albinism is inherited as an autosomal recessive. An albino and a normally pigmented person marry and have a child. This child meets and marries a person with the same background, i.e., an albino parent and a normally pigmented parent. What is the probability that the first offspring of the F_2 generation will be an albino?
    A. 0
    B. 0.25
    C. 0.50
    D. 0.75

17. Mr. and Mrs. Stargazer visit a genetic counselor. They want to have children who can become astronauts, but red-green color blindness disqualifies individuals from becoming astronauts. Mrs. Stargazer is adamant that she does not suffer from red-green color blindness, even though her father did. However, she is concerned about her husband's side of the family. Her husband is not color blind. What can we predict will result from four matings of this couple?
    A. 2 daughters who are color blind, no sons that are color blind
    B. 2 sons who are color blind, 2 daughters who are carriers
    C. 1 color blind daughter, 1 color blind son, 1 carrier daughter, 1 carrier son
    D. 1 color blind son, 1 carrier daughter, 1 normal daughter, 1 normal son

18. Males have only one X chromosome. This condition is called
    A. heterozygous.
    B. homozygous.
    C. hemizygous.
    D. autozygous.

19. The individual designated "A"
    A. is the carrier of a dominant autosomal allele.
    B. is a carrier of a recessive X-linked allele .
    C. expresses an autosomal recessive trait.
    D. expresses a recessive X-linked trait.

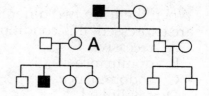

20. In many polygenic traits the various loci each influence the phenotype producing
    A. a discrete trait.
    B. a discontinuous trait.
    C. an additive effect.
    D. a new allele.

21. The modern synthesis integrates Darwinian natural selection with
    A. paleontology.
    B. embryology.
    C. genetics.
    D. ecology.

22. The most complete definition of biological evolution is
    A. change.
    B. a change in allele frequency from one generation to the next.
    C. mutation.
    D. survival of the fittest.

23. The only source for a new allele for a species gene pool is
    A. mitosis.
    B. natural selection.
    C. mutation.
    D. recombination.

24. When alleles are introduced into a population from another population it is a case of
    A. genetic drift.
    B. gene flow.
    C. founder effect.
    D. bottleneck effect.

25. An example of gene flow would be
    A. the Amerasian children of Vietnam.
    B. the isolated Amish of Pennsylvania.
    C. the American colonization of Antarctica.
    D. a small hunting and gathering society in Siberia with little outside contact.

26. The force of evolution which is significant when small human populations become isolated is
    A. gene flow.
    B. mutation.
    C. genetic drift.
    D. random mating.

27. In tenth century Norway, Eric the Red and his followers were banished for murders and general rowdiness (even by Viking standards). This small group, which had a higher representation of the red-hair allele than the rest of the population of Norway, sailed west and established a colony on Iceland. Within several centuries the colony had a population of several thousand. This would best be explained as
    A. gene flow.
    B. natural selection.
    C. mutation.
    D. founder effect.

28. In any sexually reproducing species both parents contribute genes to the offspring. This is
    A. mutation.
    B. genetic drift.
    C. recombination.
    D. natural selection.

29. A genetic trait which gives an advantage to a heterozygote for this trait in a malarial environment is
    A. hemophilia.
    B. sickle-cell trait.
    C. brachydactyly.
    D. albinism.

30. The unit of evolutionary change is the
    A. family.
    B. individual.
    C. population.
    D. pedigree.

ANSWERS TO FILL-IN OUTLINE

I. GREGOR MENDEL'S EXPERIMENTS WITH GARDEN PEAS
A. 1. Mendel
   2. progeny
B. 1. a. parental
      b. hybrid (F_1)
      c. intermediate; blending inheritance
      d. reappeared
      e. 3: 1
   2. a. two
      b. segregate (separate)
      c. segregation
      d. meiosis
   3. a. recessive
      b. dominant

c. homozygous
d. heterozygous
   4. a. proportions
      b. numbers
      c. F_2
C. 1. simultaneously
   2. dominant
   3. F_2
   4. independent
   5. independent assortment

II. MENDELIAN INHERITANCE IN HUMANS
A. 4,000
B. ABO
   1. dominant
   2. codominant

C. 1. one
   2. two
      a. carriers
      b. phenylketonuria, cystic fibrosis, Tay-Sachs disease, and sickle-cell anemia
D. 1. pedigree
   2. a. autosomal dominant
      b. autosomal recessive
      c. X-linked recessive
   3. squares; circles
E. 1. loci
   2. heterozygotes
   3. a. affected
      b. do not skip
      c. sex
      d. one-half
F. 1. autosomes
   2. two
   3. a. skip
      b. unaffected
      c. one-fourth, see Fig. 4-9
G. 1. sex
   2. X
   3. hemophilia
   4. hemizygous

III. POLYGENIC INHERITANCE
   A. 1. discrete or discontinuous
      2. intermediate
      3. one
   B. 1. gradations
         a. measurable
      2. phenotype
      3. skin color
   C. statistically
      1. mean
      2. within-group variation
      3. compare
   D. 1. frequencies
      2. pedigree
      3. position of genetic loci

IV. GENETIC AND ENVIRONMENTAL FACTORS
   A. 2. entire
   B. 1. environment
      2. phenotype
   C. polygenic
   D. less
   E. Mendelian

V. MODERN THEORY OF EVOLUTION
   A. 2. "modern synthesis"
   B. 1. transmitted
      2. natural selection

VI. DEFINITION OF EVOLUTION
   A. change in allele frequency from one generation to the next
   B. population
   C. evolve
   D. microevolution
   E. macroevolution

VII. FACTORS THAT PRODUCE AND REDISTRIBUTE VARIATION
   A. 1. mutation
      2. sex cell
      3. low
      4. variation
   B. 1. genes
      2. rare
   C. 1. random
         a. size
         b. small
      2. founder effect
         a. alleles
         b. migrates
         c. disproportionate
      3. important
   D. 1. sexual
      2. meiosis

VIII. NATURAL SELECTION ACTS ON VARIATION
   A. direction
      1. variation
      2. normal selection
   B. 1. environmental
      2. selection

IX. NATURAL SELECTION IN HUMANS
   A. rigorous
   B. sickle-cell
      1. point mutation
      2. death
      3. Africa
         a. malaria
         b. carriers (heterozygotes)
            1. more
               a. red blood cells
               b. heterozygote
            2. lowered

X. REVIEW, GENETICS AND EVOLUTIONARY
    FACTORS
    A. related and integrated
    B. population
    C. allele
    D. 1. mutation
        2. genetic drift
        3. natural selection

ANSWERS & REFERENCES TO FILL-IN QUESTIONS

1. Gregor Mendel, p. 70
2. purebred; genotypically a purebred is homozygous for the allele of the trait in question. For example, both alleles in a purebred tall pea plant would be the same, designated by Mendel as TT. A purebred dwarf pea plant would also be homozygous for this trait, tt, p. 71.
3. The heterozygous pea plant has a genotype of Tt and produces gametes that contain either T or t. The dwarf pea plant has a homozygous recessive genotype, tt. It produces gametes that only have a t. When these two plants are mated they produce two pheno-types, tall and dwarf, and two genotypes, Tt and tt. The phenotypic ratio is 1:1, p. 72
4. principle of segregation, p. 72
5. a tall heterozygous pea plant has the genotype Tt, the dwarf pea plant is true breeding and is tt. This exercise is actually one of Mendel's test crosses and the phenotypic result is 1:1. See p. 74, Fig 4-3, for the explanation on how to use a Punnett square.
6. Mendel's units (genes) that code for different traits assort independently of each other during gamete formation, p. 75
7. Blood type A and, if they both have AO genotypes, type O, p. 74, see Fig. 4-3.
8. codominance, p. 77
9. dominant, recessive. A dominant trait requires only one of the alleles to be expressed. Heterozygotes have one of the dominant alleles and, thus, express the trait. Because only one allele is needed to express a dominant trait most individuals affected with a dominant genetic disorder are heterozygous for that trait, p. 77
10. pedigree charts, p. 78
11. females, males, p. 80
12. autosomal dominant, p. 80
13. autosomal recessive, p. 81
14. Each individual has an albino parent. This means that the mating between their parents would have been A_ X aa = Aa. (We do not know what the second allele was on the first parent, but because these two individuals are normal their genotype has to be Aa). Aa X Aa produces the genotype ratio of 1AA : 2Aa : 1aa. Phenotypically we can expect one albino child out of four, i.e., a 25% probability, p. 81, see Fig. 4-9, p. 82.
15. hemophilia; sex-linked recessive, p. 82
16. .5 probability that sons will express hemophilia, .5 probability that daughters will be carriers, p. 83
17. polygenic, p. 84

18. discrete. Some examples in humans include blood types A, B, and O and the M and N blood types. There are no gradations in discrete traits. An individual either has the trait or does not have the trait, p. 84.

19. environment. Some examples in humans include height (influenced by nutrition) and intelligence (influenced by experience), p. 86.

20. Mendelian. If six loci help determine a trait, alleles at the individual locus still behave in a Mendelian fashion, i.e. there are alleles that are dominant and alleles that are recessive and, in some cases, alleles that are codominant at each locus, p. 87.

21. the modern synthesis. Prior to the 1930s, Mendelians believe that the driving force behind evolution was mutation and that evolution proceeded by the development of a mutation in an organism which resulted in a "leap" from one species to another. This latter idea was called saltation. The Darwinists saw natural selection as the driving force behind evolution and that it occurred very slowly over many generations. This idea is called gradualism, p. 87.

22. biological evolution, p. 88

23. allele frequencies, p. 89

24. microevolution. Short-term changes over several generations represent microevolution. Microevolution is generally at, or below, the species level. Macroevolution, on the other hand, is above the species level, results in great changes, and occurs over much longer periods of time, p. 89.

25. mutation. A mutation is defined as an alteration in the genetic material. p. 90

26. gene flow. Gene flow is the exchange of alleles between populations. The United States population as a whole is an example of gene flow, p. 90

27. genetic drift. Large populations are fairly immune to genetic drift; it is only in small populations where the increase or decrease of a few alleles can be reflected in dramatic changes in allele frequencies. Because most of human evolutionary history was spent as small hunter-gatherer bands genetic drift may have played a very important role during the course of human evolution, pp. 91 and 92.

28. founding. Founder populations are often thought of as "colonists" that settle a new area. However, when a catastrophe decimates a population, the survivors become the new founder population, p. 92.

29. natural selection, p. 94

30. evolution (technically microevolution) has occurred. Recall that evolution is a change in allele frequencies between generations. There has been a change in both allele frequencies, p. 88

ANSWERS & REFERENCES TO MULTIPLE CHOICE QUESTIONS

1. C, pp. 71-72
2. B, p. 72
3. B, p. 74
4. A, p. 72
5. B, p. 72
6. A, p. 72
7. A, p. 72
8. C, p. 72
9. B, p. 72

10. C, p. 75
11. B, p. 74
12. A, p. 75
13. C, p. 77
14. B, p. 78
15. B, note that the trait shows up in each generation which is typical of the autosomal dominant pattern, p. 80
16. B because each of these individuals has an albino parent they must be heterozygotes. Therefore, roughly one-fourth of their offspring will be albinos, pp. 82-83 & Fig. 4-9.
17. D, the fact that Mrs. Stargazer's father was color blind means that she carries the allele for color blindness on one of her X chromosomes. There is a fifty percent probability that she will contribute an X chromosome with the allele for color blindness to any son she bears. Her husband can only contribute Y chromosomes to his sons, so even if he was color blind he would have no effect on sons, p. 83; also see Table 4-5.
18. C, p. 83
19. Individual A has an affected parent and she also produces an affected offspring. In order to do this she must be a heterozygote, as is her mate, B, p.83.
20. C, p. 85
21. C, p. 87
22. B, p. 88
23. C, p. 90
24. B, p. 90
25. A, gene flow is the movement of alleles from one population into another. This is the case with the Amerasian children of Vietnam. Their fathers contributed alleles to the Vietnamese population. Note that the contributors do not have to become a part of the population to which they contributed their alleles. The American colonization of Antarctica did not involve a movement of alleles from the American population to the Antarctic population. While this colonization could be viewed as a movement of individuals, it did not involve any movement of alleles. pp. 90-91
26. C, p. 91
27. D, p. 92
28. C, p. 93
29. B, p. 94
30. C, p. 96

CHAPTER 5

MICROEVOLUTION IN MODERN HUMAN POPULATIONS

LEARNING OBJECTIVES

After reading this chapter you should be able to:
- explain what a population is and the evolutionary dynamics that lead to populations. (pp. 104-105)
- name the assumptions of the Hardy-Weinberg theory of genetic equilibrium. (p. 105)
- calculate a simple Hardy-Weinberg example. (pp. 106-108)
- discuss the different polymorphisms and understand why they are studied. (pp. 110-118)
- discuss how human cultural activities have influenced human evolution. (pp. 119-122)
- cite at least two instances of human biocultural evolution. (pp. 119-122)

FILL-IN OUTLINE

Introduction
In this chapter we will not only see how genetic principles lie at the very foundation of the evolutionary process, but how these processes interact to produce evolutionary change in living human populations. Humans are unusual in the natural world because cultural activities can influence their evolution. Finally we look at the pattern of human genetic diversity.

I. HUMAN POPULATIONS

    A. A population is a group of _____ individuals.

        1. Populations contain a degree of relatedness and, thus, share a _____ _____.

        2. The largest population of *Homo sapiens* that could be described is the entire

        _____.

      a. All members of a species are _____ capable of interbreeding, but are incapable of fertile interbreeding with members of other species.

      b. A species such as ours is a _____ _____ system.

  B. Breeding isolation

    1. Geography, by isolating populations through barriers such as bodies of water or mountains, causes the formation of _____ _____ .

    2. However, _____ rules can also play a role by prescribing who is most appropriate among those potentially available.

      a. Human populations tend to mate within their own group; this is called _____.

      b. However, human populations are not completely closed and individuals may choose mates from outside of their group; this is called _____ .

II. POPULATION GENETICS

  A. The _____-_____ theory of genetic equilibrium is a mathematical model that helps researchers to determine if evolution is occurring at any particular genetic locus.

  B. The Hardy-Weinberg equilibrium postulates a set of conditions in an idealized, hypothetical population in which no _____ is occurring.

    1. The Hardy-Weinberg equilibrium makes the following assumptions:

      a. The population is infinitely _____. This eliminates gene drift as a factor.

      b. There is no _____ ; therefore, no new variation is added at the molecular level of the gametes.

      c. There is no _____ flow, i.e., there are no new alleles coming into the population from another population.

      d. Natural selection is _____ _____. Specific alleles confer no advantage over others that might influence reproductive success.

    e. Mating is _____ . Each adult member of one sex has an equal chance of mating with any adult member of the opposite sex.

2. If the above conditions are met, allele frequencies will not change from one generation to the next, i.e., ____ _____ will take place.

3. By setting the conditions that would exist if no evolution were occurring, the Hardy-Weinberg equilibrium can be used to predict the _____ frequencies for the next generation.

    a. Expected (predicted) allele frequencies can be _____ to observed allele frequencies.

    b. This makes the Hardy-Weinberg equilibrium testable.

        1. The _____ hypothesis is that no evolution is occurring.

        2. If observable allele frequencies differ significantly from expected allele frequencies, the null hypothesis is _____. This would mean that evolution has occurred at the locus in question.

C. For a simple Mendelian trait, the Hardy-Weinberg equation is:
$$p^2 + 2pq + q^2$$

1. where p = the _____ of the dominant allele (when there is one)

2. where q = the frequency of the _____ allele

   (See Box 5-1 for a step-by-step example of allele frequency calculation.)

3. p + q always equals ____ , as does the sum of the products of $(p + q)^2$

4. When the allele frequencies p and q are squared, the resulting term represents the _____ frequencies. In the textbook example,

    a. ____ = the frequency of AA (homozygous dominant)

    b. 2pq = the frequency of Aa (_____)

    c. q^2 = the frequency of ____ (homozygous recessive)

III. EVOLUTION IN ACTION: MODERN HUMAN POPULATIONS

A. A number of factors initiate changes in allele frequencies. In addition to such factors that appear to work in a random fashion, nonrandom factors must also be taken into account.

B. Nonrandom Mating

1. Any consistent bias in _____ patterns can alter the genotypic proportions.

2. There are different types of nonrandom mating.

   a. Positive assortative mating

      1. occurs when individuals who are phenotypically alike mate with each other _____ often than expected.

      2. results in an increase in _____.

   b. Negative assortative mating

      1. occurs when individuals choose mates phenotypically _____ from themselves more often than expected.

      2. results in an increase in _____ .

   c. Inbreeding

      1. occurs when _____ mate among themselves more often than expected.

      2. results in an increase in homozygosity and a decrease in _____.

      3. almost all societies have taboos against _____ (matings between parent and child, and brother and sister).

      4. in some societies however, mating between close relations such as cousins is _____; however, most human groups work hard at maintaining _____ .

IV. HUMAN POLYMORPHISMS

    A. Simple Polymorphisms

        1. _____ traits are those traits governed by a locus with more than one allele and found at frequencies greater than accounted for by mutation.

           a. Simple Mendelian traits, linked to _____ locus, are polymorphic traits.

           b. Simple Mendelian polymorphic traits are much more straight forward than the _____ traits (traits governed by more than one locus) usually associated with human variation.

        2. Polymorphic traits are useful in studying the genetic differences between different _____.

           a. Genetic differences between human populations demand _____ explanations.

           b. By comparing allele _____ evolutionary events can be reconstructed.

    B. ABO blood system

        1. The ABO system is a polymorphic trait with three different alleles, ____ , ____, and ____ .

        2. The phenotypes associated with this system are expressed by antigens (proteins) found on _____ _____ _____.

        3. The frequencies of the three alleles vary tremendously, with most human groups being polymorphic for all three alleles.

           a. One exception is blood type O among South American Indians, where the allele frequency for O is 100%. This is referred to as being "_____" in the population.

           b. The ___ allele is the rarest of the three alleles.

           c. The A allele has two peaks.

1. The North American _____ have frequencies over 50%.

2. A also occurs in high frequencies in central _____.

3. These two peaks illustrate the point that the distribution of alleles for a single trait do not conclusively demonstrate _____ relationships between populations; to understand _____ of population relationships the allele frequencies for several traits must be considered simultaneously.

C. Rh system

1. The Rh system is another group of _____ found on red blood cells.

2. The two phenotypes are Rh _____ (antigen present) and Rh negative (antigen absent).

   a. The phenotypes are accounted for by three genotypes: _____, _____, _____.

   b. The actual genetics is more complicated and several loci appear to be involved that act as large genes.

3. The distribution of Rh allele combinations _____ considerable among human populations.

D. MN blood group

1. The MN blood system is a preferred research tool because the pattern of inheritance is very straightforward.

2. All three genotypes, _____, _____, and _____ are observable through the use of antisera.

3. Almost all human groups are _____ for the MN system, although the allele frequencies vary tremendously.

E. Polymorphisms in white blood cells

1. The _____ (human lymphocyte antigen) system is an antigen system found on white blood cells (lymphocytes).

a. The HLA system is very complex and there is a potential of at least _____ _____ genotypes.

b. This system is composed of a number of loci on chromosome 6 which act as a "_____."

    1. Some of these loci control for other factors in the _____ response.

    2. Together this whole system is called the _____ _____ _____ (MHC).

2. The geographical distribution of HLA is not yet well known; however, because HLA is involved with the immune response, there is some suggestion that _____ _____ may be major factors that play a role in the distribution of HLA alleles.

F. Miscellaneous polymorphisms

  1. PTC Tasting

    a. PTC is a _____ chemical which individuals can either taste, or not taste.

    b. PTC is inherited by a simple _____ transmission.

    c. As with other polymorphic traits in this chapter, the _____ of phenotypes and alleles varies between populations.

    d. The ability to _____ PTC by humans may have resulted from selection to taste bitter (and toxic) plants.

  2. Earwax (cerumen)

    a. The two phenotypes are _____ and _____, and gray and dry.

    b. This trait is also inherited as a _____ Mendelian transmission.

G. Recent advances in technology have permitted the study of polymorphisms at the DNA level.

  1. mitochondral DNA (mtDNA)

a. Mitochondria (organelles involved with energy production for the cell) have their own _____ .

b. mtDNA is considerably _____ than nuclear DNA.

c. The smaller length of mtDNA has enabled researchers to work out the mtDNA genome.

   1. Variation of the mtDNA genome in humans is much _____ pronounced than is the case for other species.

   2. The small degree of variation in the human mtDNA genome suggests that all modern humans have a _____ origin from a restricted ancestral population base.

2. Nuclear DNA

a. By using _____ enzymes considerable insight has been gained regarding human variation directly at the DNA level.

b. Researchers have observed great variation in the length of the DNA fragments at numerous DNA sites. These genetic differences are called

_____ _____ _____

_____ (RFLPs).

V. HUMAN BIOCULTURAL EVOLUTION

A. _____ is the human strategy of adaptation.

B. Culture, evolution, and malaria

1. Before the advent of agriculture humans rarely lived near mosquito breeding areas.

a. About 2,000 years ago slash-and-burn agriculturists penetrated and cleared forested areas in Africa.

b. A result of deforestation was the creation of stagnant pools of water which served as prime breeding areas for _____, the vectors for malaria.

2. Malaria has served as a powerful _____ force.

   a. Sickle-cell trait is a _____ adaptation to malaria.

   b. There is an advantage for carriers of sickle-cell, but only in _____ environments.

3. After WWII, extensive spraying of DDT eliminated large numbers of mosquito breeding grounds.

   a. Malaria _____, as did the sickle-cell allele.

   b. During the intervening years, mosquitoes, also subject to natural selection, have developed DDT-resistant strains with the result that _____ is again on the rise.

4. Sickle-cell trait, in which the heterozygote has an advantage in a specific environment, is an example of natural selection in humans; the precise evolutionary mechanism in sickle-cell is called a _____ _____.

   a. As defined earlier, a polymorphism is a trait with more than one allele in appreciable frequencies.

      1. Sickle-cell allele is found at a frequency of 10 percent, which can not be accounted for by _____ alone.

      2. A fuller evolutionary explanation is needed, and that explanation is

      _____ _____.

   b. "Balanced" refers to the interaction of selective pressures to maintain both alleles in appreciable frequencies. This is due to the selective advantage of the _____ who pass on both alleles.

5. Two other traits that may be influenced by malaria as a selective agent are G-6-PD deficiency and _____ .

C. Lactose Intolerance

1. _____ is a sugar found in milk which is broken down by the enzyme lactase.

   a. In adult mammals, the gene coding for lactase is "switched off."

   b. In most adult _____ (including humans and cats), lactose in milk that is ingested is not broken down and ferments in the large intestine. This results in diarrhea and gastrointestinal distress.

   c. Many African and Asian populations, _____ of the world's population, are intolerant of milk.

   d. This inability to digest milk is called _____ _____.

2. Why can the majority of adults in some populations tolerate milk?

   a. Peoples whose ancestors were _____ (such as modern Europeans and African peoples like the Tutsi and Fulani) probably drank large quantities of milk.

   b. In a cultural environment where milk was consumed, strong selection pressures would act to _____ allele frequencies in the direction of more lactose tolerance.

   c. Some populations rely on dairying, but consume milk products as fermented dairy products such as cheese and yogurt. These populations have _____ developed a tolerance for lactose.

3. This interaction of human cultural environments and changes in lactose tolerance is another example of _____ evolution.

VI. PATTERNS OF HUMAN POPULATION DIVERSITY

A. A simple approach to understanding human genetic diversity is to look at _____ polymorphic trait at a time.

   1. In this approach, allele frequencies for one trait can be geographically mapped into _____.

2. Clinal distributions are believed to reflect _____ influences of natural selection and/or gene flow.

3. Utilizing single traits has _____ when we try to sort our population relationships.

B. _____ approaches consider several traits simultaneously.

1. R. D. Lewontin analyzed human diversity using a multivariate approach.

   a. Lewontin considered 17 polymorphic traits for seven geographical areas ("races").

   b. After breaking down his seven geographical groups into subgroups, Lewontin could only account for about 15% of human genetic diversity as being due to "_____."

   c. Most human _____ appears to be explained in terms of differences from one village to another, one family to another, and even between one individual to another (even within the same family!).

   d. Superficially, visible traits that stand out suggest that human races exist.

      1. However, those traits used to form races may produce a _____ sample and not give an accurate picture of the actual pattern of genetic variation.

      2. Lewontin's final conclusion is that human racial classification, shown to have no genetic or taxonomic significance, should be _____.

2. Other geneticists have conducted multivariate studies.

   a. Cavalli-Sforza, et al., analyzed 44 different polymorphisms from 42 different populations.

      1. This analysis led to a genetic "_____" (dendogram).

      2. This genetic tree depicted the _____ of the populations under study (see Fig. 5-4).

b. Stoneking analyzed populations using mitochondrial DNA.

    1. mtDNA is inherited solely through the _____ line; however, because it acts like a single large locus, it must be supplemented with other genetic data.

    2. mtDNA analysis shows that the greatest genetic diversity exists among _____ populations.

c. Comparative studies from nuclear DNA suggest that the vast majority of variation occurs within populations at the _____ level.

KEY TERMS

ABO blood group system: a polymorphism based on the presence (or absence) of two antigens found in the cell membrane of red blood cells.

balanced polymorphism: the maintenance of two or more alleles in a population due to the selective advantage of the heterozygote.

breeding isolates: a population that is distinctly isolated geographically and/or socially from other breeding groups.

cline: a gradient of genotypes (usually measured as allele frequencies) over geographical space.

endogamy: mating with individuals from the same group.

exogamy: mating with individuals from other groups.

gene pool: the total complement of alleles shared by the reproductive members of a population.

genome: the full genetic complement of an individual or species.

Hardy-Weinberg theory of genetic equilibrium: the mathematical relationship expressing, under ideal conditions, the predicted distribution of genes in populations; the central theorem of population genetics.

Human Genome Project: a multinational effort designed to map, and ultimately sequence, the complete genetic complement of *Homo sapiens*.

Human Lymphocyte Antigen (HLA): antigens found on the surface of an individual's cell surfaces which provide a way for the immune system to identify "self." "Non-self" antigens are attacked. HLA is a very complex genetic system and provides a rich ground for anthropologists to study human genetic relationships.

inbreeding: a type of nonrandom mating in which relatives mate more often than predicted under random mating conditions.

incest taboo: the rule found in almost every human society that prohibits sexual relationships between parents with offspring and siblings with each other.

lactose intolerance: the inability to digest fresh milk products, caused by the discontinued production of lactase, the enzyme that breaks down lactose, or milk sugar.

mitochondrial DNA (mtDNA): circular DNA found in the mitochondria and inherited through the maternal line.

MN blood group system: a blood polymorphism based upon the presence of the two alleles, which are codominant.

negative assortative mating: a type of nonrandom mating in which individuals of different phenotypes mate more often than predicted under random mating conditions.

polymorphism: genetic trait governed by a locus with more than one allele in appreciable frequencies.

population: a group of individuals of the same species that regularly interbreed with one another.

positive assortative mating: a type of nonrandom mating in which individuals of like phenotype mate more often than predicted under random mating conditions.

PTC Tasting: refers to the ability to taste, or not to taste, the chemical phenylthiocarbamide (PTC).

restriction fragment length polymorphisms (RFLPs): variation among individuals in the length of DNA fragments produced by enzymes that break the DNA at specific sites.

Rh system: a blood polymorphism with two phenotypes, Rh+ and Rh-. This system is clinically important because of its involvement with hemolytic disease of the newborn.

tawny hair: a reddish-blonde hair color found among the aboriginal populations of central Australia.

Now take the Fill-in and Multiple Choice tests. Do not guess. Following completion of the tests, correct them. The correct answers and textbook page references are at the end of this study guide chapter. Note your strong areas and your weak areas to guide you in your continuing study.

FILL-IN QUESTIONS

1. A _____ is a group of interbreeding individuals.

2. In an Indian village, a marriage is arranged between two first cousins. This mating pattern is called _____.

3. Among the Inuit, males must find a mate from a distant village. This mating pattern is called _____.

4. The mathematical model used by population geneticists to compare observed allele frequencies with predicted allele frequencies is the _____-_____ theory of genetic equilibrium.

5. The population for which the Hardy-Weinberg model postulates a set of conditions is an idealized, _____ population.

6. If the observed allele frequencies for a locus under study differ from the allele frequencies predicted from the Hardy-Weinberg model, what can we say? _____

   _____

   _____

7. When the frequencies of alleles used in the Hardy-Weinberg model are summed, p + q, they add up to _____.

8. In the Hardy-Weinberg model, the term q^2 represents the frequency of the homozygous recessive _____ (aa was the example in the text).

9. We can ascertain the exact allele frequencies for the MN blood group because these two alleles are _____.

10. Individuals who mate with those whose phenotype is more like their own, more often than would be expected by chance, are practicing _____ _____ mating.

11. It has been suggested that redheaded people tend to pick mates who do not have red hair. This is an example of _____ _____ mating.

12. In most human societies, people avoid mating with close relatives (parents or siblings). This is called a(n) _____ _____.

13. A genetic trait that is governed by more than one allele in which both alleles occur in appreciable frequencies is called a(n) _____ trait.

14. An individual's blood reacts with A antiserum, but not with B antiserum. This individual is blood type _____.

15. A blood antigen system which can cause serious clinical problems when the mother does not have the antigen, but the fetus does, is the _____ system.

16. The problem of Rh incompatibility arises only if the mother is _____ and her fetus is _____.

17. The pattern of inheritance for the MN blood system is codominant. This means that if there is a M allele present and a N allele present in the individual's genotype, the N allele will be _____.

18. An important polymorphic trait found in white blood cells is _____.

19. HLA patterns among the Lapps, Sardinians, and Basques show deviations from other _____ populations.

20. If you were given a strip of PTC paper, which you placed on your tongue, and you tasted a bitter taste, you would be a PTC _____.

21. PTC tasting varies in different human populations, but in most populations the majority of individuals are _____.

22. Cerumen is most commonly known to most people as _____.

23. The sticky cerumen allele is _____ to the dry cerumen allele.

24. In addition to the DNA enclosed by the cell's nucleus, DNA is also found in cytoplasmic organelles, the _____.

25. The multinational effort to map the complete genetic complement of humans is called the

_____ _____ _____.

26. The persistence of the sickle-cell allele seems to be correlated with a human activity, _____-_____-_____ agriculture.

27. The maintenance of two or more alleles in a population due to the selective advantage of the heterozygote is called a _____ _____.

28. The inability to digest fresh milk due to the discontinued production of the enzyme lactase is called _____ _____.

29. _____ hair is a polymorphism that can be followed by clines from central Australia (where it probably arose as a mutation).

30. Comparative data indicate that most human variation occurs _____ populations at the _____ level.

MULTIPLE CHOICE QUESTIONS

1. The total complement of genes shared by reproductive members of a population, is that population's
    A. gene flow.
    B. gene drift.
    C. gene pool.
    D. bottleneck effect.

2. Which of the following is **not** a factor that influences mate choice?
    A. geography
    B. ecology
    C. social
    D. genetic diversity

3. Which of the following is **not** an assumption of the Hardy-Weinberg theory of genetic equilibrium?
    A. The population is infinitely large.
    B. Mating is nonrandom.
    C. No mutation is occurring.
    D. There is no natural selection occurring.

4. Random mating means
    A. every adult individual of one sex has an equal opportunity to mate with any other mature individual of the opposite sex.
    B. every individual of one sex can mate with any individual of the opposite sex, except close family members.
    C. that people may have as many spouses of the opposite sex as they please.
    D. that adults may mate only with those individuals from the same social standing as they are.

5. You have taken blood samples from 100 individuals. You want to know what the allele frequencies for the MN blood group is in this population. You find that 70 individuals have type M blood, 20 have type MN blood, and 10 have type N blood. What are the allele frequencies for blood types M and N?
    A. M = .7, N = .3
    B. M = .7, N = .2
    C. M = .8, N = .2
    D. M = .9, N = .1

6. You find in a population, while taking blood samples and looking at the MN blood group, that the M allele is present at a frequency of 0.7. Using the Hardy-Weinberg formula predict the genotypic frequencies for the next generation.
    A. .64(MM) + .32(NN) + .04(NN)
    B. .36(MM) + .48(MN) + .16(NN)
    C. .49(MM) + .42(NN) + .09(NN)
    D. .25(MM) + .5 (MN) + .25(NN)

7. If significant deviations are shown from Hardy-Weinberg expectations, this may suggest
   A. equilibrium.
   B. evolution.
   C. the locus in this population is not evolving.
   D. a balanced polymorphism.

8. When allele frequencies do not change between generations and it appears that our population is in equilibrium conditions, what does it mean?
   A. Evolution is occurring for the trait in question.
   B. Evolution does not appear to be occurring for this trait.
   C. We cannot reject the null hypothesis.
   D. Both B and C are correct.

9. The most consistent mating bias documented in the United States is
   A. stature.
   B. hair color.
   C. IQ.
   D. Both A and C are correct.

10. The result of positive assortative mating and inbreeding is to
    A. increase homozygosity.
    B. decrease homozygosity.
    C. increase heterozygosity.
    D. increase gene flow.

11. Mating with relatives more often than would be expected by chance is called
    A. positive assortative mating.
    B. negative assortative mating.
    C. inbreeding.
    D. incest avoidance.

12. When humans, such as first cousins, produce offspring there is a danger of
    A. gene flow.
    B. genetic disorders.
    C. mutations occurring.
    D. Both A and C are correct.

13. Most human populations are polymorphic for the ABO system, but one notable exception is the fixed O allele among
    A. Australian Aborigines.
    B. the peoples of central Asia.
    C. South American Indians.
    D. Blackfeet Indians.

14. The rarest allele in the ABO system is
    A. A.
    B. B.
    C. O.
    D. AB.

15. The highest frequencies of type A blood is found among
    A. Australian Aborigines.
    B. the peoples of central Asia.
    C. South American Indians.
    D. Blackfoot Indians.

16. Which of the following is a true statement?
    A. Polygenic traits are usually more straightforward than polymorphic traits.
    B. Comparing allele frequencies between populations can tell us nothing about evolutionary events.
    C. Distributions of alleles for a single genetic trait do not conclusively demonstrate genetic relationships between populations.
    D. The best way to understand patterns of population relationships is to follow a single polymorphic trait.

17. It has been suggested that type O individuals are more likely to be bitten by mosquitoes. If this is true, which of the following would be an important selective factor against type O blood?
    A. infectious diseases
    B. cancers
    C. pernicious anemias
    D. ability of an individual tracked by a cloud of insects to find a mate

18. Which of the following is **not** a clinically important genetic trait?
    A. type A blood
    B. type B blood
    C. Rh+ factor
    D. MN blood group

19. The most genetically complex blood polymorphism yet discovered is the
    A. ABO blood group.
    B. HLA system.
    C. MN blood system.
    D. Rh system.

20. It has been observed that higher rates of PTC tasters are found among peoples who gather a great deal of vegetable matter. Among people who eat mostly meat or cook their food the percentage of PTC tasters is low. This suggests PTC tasting is adaptive for peoples
    A. consuming large amounts of meat.
    B. eating uncooked vegetables which may contain toxins.
    C. who cook vegetables in which the toxins are leeched out.
    D. that are strictly carnivorous.

21. Which of the following is **not** a blood polymorphism?
    A. ABO
    B. Rh factor
    C. MN
    D. cerumen

22. One of the results of mitochondrial DNA research has been.
    A. the variation of mtDNA within *Homo sapiens* is much less than found in other species.
    B. the variation of mtDNA within *Homo sapiens* is much more than found in other species.
    C. chimpanzees have much less variation in their mtDNA than humans do.
    D. the length of the mtDNA is as long as nuclear DNA, about 3 billion nucleotides.

23. The surprising results of mtDNA analysis (refer to question 22) can be explained if
    A. the common ancestor of humans and chimps separated 3 million years ago.
    B. the last common ancestor of modern humans was in east Africa about 2 million years ago.
    C. all modern humans have a fairly recent common ancestor.
    D. the common ancestor for modern humans goes back before the first hominids.

24. DNA can actually be "cut" at particular points by
    A. lipids.
    B. enzymes.
    C. phospholipids.
    D. nanosaws.

25. The sickle-cell allele is maintained at relatively high frequencies in some populations by
    A. the selective advantage of the heterozygote in malarial areas.
    B. mutation.
    C. positive assortative mating.
    D. the susceptibility of the heterozygote to malarial infection.

26. Which of the following is not a way that humans have adapted to living in malarial environments?
    A. sickle-cell trait
    B. G-6-PD deficiency
    C. thalessemia
    D. lactose

27. Many individuals have difficulty digesting milk because
    A. they have an Rh antigen producing an immune response to milk.
    B. they don't have enough lactose in their cardiovascular system.
    C. they cannot process the lipoproteins in the milk.
    D. as adults, they lack the enzyme lactase.

28. A gradual distribution of allele frequencies over space is called a
    A. race.
    B. phenotypic grade.
    C. cline.
    D. Hardy-Weinberg equilibrium.

29. Multivariate population genetics studies seek
    A. to prove races exist.
    B. to study one genetic trait at a time.
    C. to describe the pattern of several traits at one time.
    D. to find non-adaptive traits that can be used to describe groups.

30. In Lewontin's multivariate computer study of race, he concluded that
    A. there is more variation between races than is found within any one specific race.
    B. the seven "geographic" races cluster independently, indicating that they are true races.
    C. there is more variation within any one race than there is between races.
    D. the idea of race is a valid one.

ANSWERS & REFERENCES TO FILL-IN OUTLINE

I. HUMAN POPULATIONS
   A. interbreeding
      1. gene pool
      2. species
         a. potentially
         b. genetically closed
   B. 1. breeding isolates
      2. cultural
         a. endogamy
         b. exogamy

II. POPULATION GENETICS
   A. Hardy-Weinberg
   B. evolution
      1. a. large
         b. mutation
         c. gene
         d. not operating
         e. random
      2. no evolution
      3. allele
         a. compared
         b. 1. null
            2. rejected
   C. 1. frequency
      2. recessive
      3. 1

4. genotypic
   a. p^2
   b. heterozygotes
   c. aa

III. EVOLUTION IN ACTION: MODERN HUMAN POPULATIONS
   B. 1. mating
      2. a. 1. more
            2. homozygosity
         b. 1. different
            2. heterozygosity
         c. 1. relatives
            2. variability
            3. incest
            4. encouraged; exogamy

IV. HUMAN POLYMORPHISMS
   A. 1. polymorphic
         a. one
         b. polygenic
      2. populations
         a. evolutionary
         b. frequencies
   B. 1. A, B, and O
      2. red blood cells
      3. a. fixed
         b. B

c. 1. Blackfeet
2. Australia
3. genetic; patterns
C. 1. antigens
2. positive
a. DD, Dd, dd
3. vary
D. 2. MM, MN, and NN
3. polymorphic
E. 1. HLA
a. 30 million
b. supergene
1. immune
2. major histocompatibility complex
2. infectious diseases
F. 1. a. bitter
b. Mendelian
c. distribution
d. taste
2. a. yellow; sticky
b. simple
G. 1. a. DNA
b. shorter
c. 1. less
2. recent
2. a. restriction
b. restriction fragment length polymorphisms

V. HUMAN BIOCULTURAL EVOLUTION
A. culture
B. 1. b. mosquitoes
2. selective
a. biological
b. malarial

3. a. declined (or decreased)
b. malaria
4. balanced polymorphism
a. 1. mutation
2. natural selection
b. heterozygotes
5. thalessemias
C. 1. lactose
b. mammals
c. most
d. lactose intolerance
2. a. pastoralists
b. shift
c. not
3. biocultural

VI. PATTERNS OF HUMAN POPULATION DIVERSITY
A. one
1. clines
2. microevolutionary
3. limitations
B. multivariate
1. b. race
c. diversity
d. 1. highly biased
2. discontinued
2. a. 1. tree
2. relationships
b. 1. maternal
2. African
c. individual

ANSWERS & REFERENCES TO FILL-IN QUESTIONS

1. population, p. 104
2. endogamy, p. 104
3. exogamy, p. 104
4. Hardy-Weinberg, p. 105
5. hypothetical, p. 105
6. we can say that evolution has taken place at that locus. p. 105
7. 1, p. 106
8. genotype, p. 107
9. codominant, p. 107
10. positive assortative, p. 108
11. negative assortative, p. 109
12. incest taboo, p. 109
13. polymorphic, p. 111

14. A, p. 111. The antisera are made by injecting a rabbit with human blood. Antibodies made by the rabbit's immune system become the antiserum. When anti-A comes into contact with type A blood it causes agglutination (a reaction that results in clumping) and this indicates the blood type of the person.
15. Rh, p. 114
16. Rh-, Rh+, p. 114
17. expressed, p. 107. In a codominant system **both** alleles are expressed. Thus, the M allele in the example would also be expressed, making the individual MN.
18. HLA (human lymphocyte antigen), p. 115
19. European, p. 115
20. taster, p. 116
21. tasters, p. 116
22. earwax, p. 117
23. dominant, p. 117
24. mitochondria, p. 118
25. Human Genome Project, p. 118
26. slash-and-burn, p. 119
27. balanced polymorphism, p. 119
28. lactose intolerance, p. 121
29. tawny, p. 122
30. within; individual, p. 124

Answers & References To Multiple Choice Questions

1. C, p. 104
2. D, p. 104
3. B, p. 105
4. A, p. 105
5. C, p. 108, Box 5-1. Because there are 100 people, there are 200 alleles. These can be counted up. Type M individuals carry two M alleles and these 70 people account for 140 M alleles. The 20 MN individuals are heterozygotes and carry one of each allele. Thus, there are 160 M alleles. This number is divided by the total alleles (200) to obtain the M allele frequency, .8. The N allele frequency can also be worked out, but it is easier to simply subtract the M frequency from 1 (always the sum of the allele frequencies) to obtain N, .2. Answer B should have been eliminated immediately because the sum of the allele frequencies did not add up to 1.0.
6. C, p. 108. The first thing to do is to figure out the allele frequencies. The allele frequency for M is .7. Because the sum of the two alleles always adds up to 1.0, subtracting .7 from 1.0 will give you the allele frequency for N, which is .3. You are now ready to work out the Hardy-Weinberg equation, thus $(.7 + .3)^2 = (.49 + .42 + .09)$. See Box 5-1.
7. B, p. 105
8. D, pp. 105-106
9. D, p. 109
10. A, p. 108
11. C, pp. 109-110
12. B, p. 109
13. C, p. 113
14. B, p. 113. Note that answer D refers to a genotype, not an allele.
15. D, p. 113
16. C, p. 113
17. A, p. 114
18. D, p. 114
19. B, p. 115
20. B, p. 117. PTC is analogous to defensive chemicals found in plants of the mustard family. If PTC tasting is an adaptation to tasting these toxins, it would most likely be found among peoples eating large amounts of uncooked plants.
21. D, p. 117
22. A, p. 118
23. C, p. 118. For modern humans to be so similar, they would have to have a recent ancestor, maybe 200,000 years ago.
24. B, p. 118
25. A, p. 119
26. D, p. 121
27. D, p. 121
28. C, p. 122
29. C, p. 123
30. C, p. 124

CHAPTER 6

APPROACHES TO HUMAN VARIATION AND ADAPTATION

LEARNING OBJECTIVES

After reading this chapter you should be able to:
- understand the difference between "race" and "ethnicity" and the problems with using these terms. (pp. 130-133)
- understand the history of how human racial categories were established. (pp. 133-137)
- describe the concept behind biological determinism and associated philosophies. (pp. 136-137)
- describe the reason that different human populations vary. (p. 139)
- list how humans respond to the thermal environment. (pp. 142-145)
- list the ways that humans respond to high altitude stress. (pp. 145-146)
- understand how infectious disease has played a role in human evolution, and vice versa (pp. 146-148)
- discuss the cause of AIDS and the evolutionary scenario of this disease. (pp. 148-150)

FILL-IN OUTLINE

Introduction

The previous chapters focused on the patterns of inheritance from one generation to the next and the physical mechanisms (DNA) for inheritance. You also learned how evolution works and saw how Mendelian traits have been used to study evolutionary factors in human populations.

In this chapter, the focus shifts to polygenic traits, or traits that express *continuous* variation. You will see how these traits have been used as a basis for traditional racial classification and we look at some of the issues that currently surround the topic of race in physical anthropology.

After reviewing the traditional ideas of human biological diversity, more recent explanations of certain polygenic traits are examined; instead of emphasizing their usefulness as "racial" markers, their adaptive value for human populations living in specific environments is emphasized. How populations and individuals differ in their adaptive responses to the environment are also examined. Finally, the role of infectious disease in human evolution and adaptation is considered.

I. THE CONCEPT OF RACE

A. All modern humans belong to the same _____ species, *Homo sapiens*.

    1. A polytypic species consists of local populations that differ from one another in the expression of one or more _____.

    2. Most species are polytypic, thus there is no species "_____" to which all members conform.

B. The traditional concept of race

    1. In the past people were clumped together by various combinations of attributes and placed into categories associated with particular _____ areas.

    2. The term race is often _____ and has developed various definitions.

      a. "Race" has been used synonymously with _____.

      b. Since the 1600s, race has been used to refer to various _____ defined groups.

        1. The perception that there is an _____ between physical traits and many cultural attributes is still widespread.

        2. "Racial traits" are not the only phenotypic expressions that contribute to social identity: _____ and _____ are also critically important.

    3. In the 1950s, the use of the term "race" was challenged and it was proposed that the term "_____" replace it.

    4. The biological use of the word "race"

      a. "Race" refers to geographical _____ of phenotype within a species.

      b. Even within modern biology there are no established _____ by which races of plants and animals are to be assessed. Even for a biologist studying nonhuman life, the classification of an organism into a race is a subjective matter.

5. Prior to World War II, most studies of human variation focused on phenotypic variation between _____ _____ _____ populations.

C. Modern studies of human variation focus on the examination of allele frequencies _____ and _____ populations.

  1. Specifically we want to know the _____ _____ of phenotypic and genotypic variation.

  2. Application of _____ principles to human variation has replaced the older view that was based solely on observed phenotype.

  3. Races are no longer viewed as _____ biological entities, composed of individuals fitting a particular type, which do not change.

  4. While human variability is recognized between geographic areas, the following questions must be asked regarding this phenotypic difference.

    a. What is the _____ significance attached to observed phenotype variation?

    b. What is the _____ of underlying genetic variation that influences the observed variation?

    c. How _____ is the underlying genetic variation?

D. Controversies and debates about human variation

  1. Attempts to reach a _____ regarding "race" in humans have failed.

  2. Some modern anthropologists feel there are at least _____ major human racial groups.

    a. However, no modern scholar subscribes to the pre-modern synthesis concept of races as _____ biological units.

    b. Many who continue to use broad racial categories do not view them as _____.

    c. _____ anthropologists find the phenotypic criteria associated with race to have practical applications.

        1. These anthropologists assist in identification of human _____ remains.

        2. Metrical analysis assists forensic anthropologists in identifying the sex, age, stature and "racial" or "ethnic" background of skeletal remains up to _____ percent accuracy.

    d. Other modern anthropologists see race as a _____ concept when applied to humans.

  3. Objections to racial taxonomies

    a. Such classificatory schemes are _____.

        1. The categories are discrete and based on _____ that comprise a specific set of traits.

        2. Such typologies do not account for individuals who do not _____ to the stereotype for the group.

    b. Many of the characteristics used to define races are _____.

        1. Polygenic traits exhibit a _____ range of variation.

        2. Using polygenic traits to define a group makes it difficult, if not impossible, to draw _____ boundaries between populations.

II. HISTORICAL VIEWS OF HUMAN VARIATION

  A. When humans first came into contact with other human groups they _____ them.

    1. _____ _____ was one of the more noticeable traits that was used to classify people and there were attempts to explain skin color.

    2. During the European "Age of Discovery," there was an increased awareness of human biological _____.

3. _____ schools of thought developed to explain human diversity.

B. Monogeny

   1. Monogenists believed that all humans were descended from a _____

      _____ of humans.

      a. According to monogenists, the reason modern humans exhibited a great deal

         of biological diversity was due to _____ of the human phenotype

         in response to local environmental conditions.

      b. Human races were the result of _____ to the original

         form.

   2. _____ was attractive because it did not contradict Genesis.

C. Polygeny

   1. Polygenists believed that all humans were descended from a number of

      _____ pairs of humans (i.e., different Adams and Eves).

   2. Polygenists believed that, in addition to _____ differences, there

      were differences between humans in intelligence and morality.

   3. Polygenists did not accept the idea that the environment could _____

      a phenotype.

D. Racial classification

   1. Throughout the eighteenth and nineteenth centuries, the primary focus regarding

      human variation was on description and _____.

   2. Linnaeus' classification of life also included _____.

      a. In addition to the physical features used to classify other life forms, Linnaeus

         also used cultural attributes to _____ humans.

      b. Linnaeus ranked humans.

         1. The _____ complimentary traits were assigned to sub-Saharan

            (black) Africans.

2. Europeans were ranked highest and reflected the view that Europeans were _____.

3. J. F. Blumenbach

   a. Blumenbach classified humans into _____ races: Caucasoid, Mongoloid, American, Ethiopian, and Malayan.

   b. Blumenbach emphasized that racial divisions based on skin color were

      _____.

   c. Blumenbach recognized that many traits, including skin color, were not

      _____.

      1. Individuals within a group that expressed traits that were intermediate would be difficult to classify.

      2. Furthermore, many traits showed _____ expression between groups.

4. It was thought that racial taxonomies should be based on characteristics _____ to particular groups and uniformly expressed within them.

   a. Such traits were believed to be stable and not influenced by the environment.

   b. These _____ traits should exhibit only minimal within-group variation.

5. In the end, racial classification wound up ranking human groups with (northern) _____ being at the top of the racial hierarchy.

E. Biological determinism

   1. The idea that there is an association between physical characteristics and behavioral characteristics is called _____ _____; i.e., cultural variations are inherited.

      a. It follows from this logic that there are inherent behavioral and cognitive differences between groups. This is called _____.

b. It also follows from this logic that there are inherent behavioral and cognitive differences between the sexes. This is called _____.

2. When biological determinism is accepted as a reasonable explanation, it is easy to _____ the persecution and enslavement of other peoples.

3. _____ was a scientific discipline which was grounded in biological determinism. Eugenics promoted the idea of "race improvement" and suggested that the government should be involved in this endeavor.

F. By the end of World War I, some scientists began turning away from racial _____ in favor of a more evolutionary approach.

III. RACISM

A. The most detrimental outcome of biological determinism is _____.

1. Racism is based on the false belief that intellect and various cultural factors are _____ along with physical characteristics.

2. According to this view, culturally defined variables _____ all members of particular populations.

3. Such beliefs commonly rest on the assumption that one's own group is _____ to other groups.

B. Racism is a cultural, not a _____, phenomenon, and it is found worldwide.

C. Conclusion

1. What we really observe when we see biological variations between populations are the traces of our _____ past.

a. These variations represent _____ to the different environments that our ancestors moved into while increasing the geographical range of humans.

b. Our variations are a preserved record of how _____ _____ shaped our species to meet different environments.

2. Instead of using our differences as a basis for _____, we should praise them.

IV. INTELLIGENCE

A. Whether there is a(n) _____ between "race" and intelligence has been controversial.

B. Both genetic and environmental factors contribute to _____.

   1. It is not possible to accurately _____ the percentage each factor contributes to intelligence.

   2. IQ scores are often confused with intelligence; IQ scores and intelligence are _____ the same thing.

      a. Many psychologists say that IQ scores measure life _____.

      b. IQ scores can _____ within an individual's lifetime.

   3. Complex cognitive abilities, no matter how measured, are influenced by _____ loci and are strikingly polygenic.

   4. Individual abilities result from complex _____ between genetic and environmental factors.

      a. One product of this interaction is _____.

      b. Elucidating what proportion of the variation in test scores is due to biological factors is probably _____ possible.

C. Innate differences in abilities reflect individual variation within populations, not _____ differences between groups.

D. There is no convincing evidence that populations vary with regard to _____ abilities.

V. THE ADAPTIVE SIGNIFICANCE OF HUMAN VARIATION

A. Physical anthropologists view human variation as the result of adaptations to environmental conditions, both _____ and _____.

B. Physiological response to environmental change is under genetic control and operates at two levels.

   1. _____-_____ (i.e., genetic) _____ changes characterize all individuals within a population or species.

   2. Short-term physiological response to environmental change is called _____; such physiological change is temporary.

C. Solar radiation, vitamin D, and skin color

   1. Before 1500, skin color in populations followed a particular geographical distribution, particularly in the _____ _____.

      a. Populations with the _____ amount of pigmentation are found in the tropics.

      b. Populations with lighter skin color are associated with more _____ latitudes.

   2. Skin color is influenced by _____ substances.

      a. _____, when it is carrying oxygen, gives a reddish tinge to the skin.

      b. _____ is a plant pigment, which the body synthesizes into vitamin A, and it provides a yellowish cast.

      c. _____ is the most important contributor to skin color.

   3. Melanin has the ability to absorb ultraviolet (UV) radiation, preventing damage to _____ to which UV radiation can cause mutations and ultimately skin cancer.

      a. Melanin is produced by specialized cells in the epidermis called _____.

b. All humans appear to have about the same _____ of melanocytes.

c. Exposure to sunlight triggers a protective mechanism which temporally _____ melanin production (i.e., a tan).

4. Natural selection appears to have favored dark skin in areas nearest the _____ where the most intense UV radiation is found.

a. In considering skin color from an evolutionary perspective, three points should be kept in mind:

1. Early hominids lived mostly in the _____.

2. Most earlier hominids spent the majority of time _____.

3. Early hominids did not wear clothing that would have provided some protection against _____ _____.

b. As hominids migrated to the northern latitudes, selective pressures changed.

1. Europe had cloudy skies, a winter with fewer hours of daylight, and with the sun to the south, solar radiation was _____.

2. The use of _____ prevented exposure of the skin to sunlight.

3. Selection favoring dark skin was _____, but there also had to be a selective pressure favoring lighter skin.

c. _____ _____ plays a vital role in mineralization and normal bone growth during infancy and childhood.

1. While vitamin D is available in some foods, the body's primary source comes from its own ability to _____ vitamin D through the interaction of UV light and a cholesterol-like substance found in the subcutaneous layer of the skin.

2. Insufficient amounts of vitamin D during childhood results in _____, which leads to bone deformities.

d. The vitamin D hypothesis

1. Reduced exposure to sunlight would have been detrimental to

    _____ skinned individuals in northern latitudes who would

    have been deficient in vitamin D.

    a. The higher _____ content of their skin would have

        filtered out much of the UV radiation available.

    b. Additionally, if the diet did not provide adequate amounts of vitamin

        D, selective pressures would have shifted over time to favor

        _____ pigmented skin.

2. There is substantial evidence to support this vitamin D _____.

3. At the same time, dark skin can also be partially explained by the vitamin

    D hypothesis.

    a. _____ amounts of vitamin D are toxic.

    b. Deeply pigmented skin in the tropics not only protects against UV

        radiation, but also _____ the overproduction of vitamin D.

5. Perhaps more social importance has been attached to variations in skin color

    than any other single human biological trait.

    a. However, biologically skin color is of no importance except in terms of its

        _____ _____.

D. The thermal environment

1. Mammals and birds have evolved _____, a physiological

    mechanism which enables the organism to maintain a constant body temperature.

2. Humans are found in a wide variety of _____ environments, ranging

    from 120° F to -60° F.

3. Human response to heat

    a. Humans and many other mammalian species have _____

        _____ widely distributed throughout the skin.

1. Sweat on the body surface removes heat through _____ cooling. This is a mechanism that has evolved to a high degree in humans.

2. The capacity to dissipate heat by sweating is a feature found in all human populations almost _____.

    a. However, there is variation in that people not generally exposed to hot conditions need a period of _____ to warmer temperatures.

    b. The downside to heat reduction through sweating is that critical amounts of water and minerals can be _____.

b. Another mechanism for radiating body heat is _____.

    1. Vasodilation refers to a widening (dilation) of the _____.

    2. Vasodilation of the capillaries near the skin's surface permit "hot" blood from the body's core to dissipate heat to the surrounding air.

c. _____ size also plays a role in temperature regulation.

    1. There is a general relationship between _____ and body size and shape in homeothermic species (although, as always in biology, there are exceptions). Two biological rules apply to body size, body proportions, and temperature.

        a. _____ rule states that body size tends to be greater in populations that live in cold environments.

            1. This is because surface area _____ relative to mass as an object increases in size. For example, for every three-fold increase in the mass of a globular animal, there is only a two-fold increase of surface area.

2. Because heat is lost from the surface, increased mass allows for greater heat _____ and reduced heat loss.

b. Allen's rule

1. In colder climates, populations should have shorter _____ (arms, legs, and sometimes noses) to increase mass-to-surface ratios preventing heat loss.

2. In warmer climates, populations should have _____ appendages with increased surface area relative to mass which promotes heat loss.

2. According to both Bergmann's rule and Allen's rule:

a. In _____ environments, body shape should be linear with long arms and legs, such as is found among East African pastoralists.

b. In _____ environments, people should have stocky bodies with shorter arms and legs as is found among the Inuit.

3. There is much human variability regarding body proportions and not all populations conform to Bergmann's and Allen's rules.

4. Human response to cold

a. Humans can respond to cold by increasing heat production or in ways that enhance heat retention; heat retention is _____ efficient because it requires less energy.

b. _____-_____ human responses to cold include:

1. Increased _____ rate uses energy to produces body heat.

a. People living in chronic cold generally have _____ metabolic rates than people living in warmer environments.

      b.   High metabolic rates can be maintained by larger consumptions of animal _____ and _____ such as is seen among the Inuit.

    2.   _____ uses energy to produces body heat.

    3.   _____ is a narrowing of the blood vessels which reduces blood flow to the skin.

        a.   Vasoconstriction _____ heat loss.

        b.   A small amount of energy is used to constrict blood vessels, but more energy is saved by _____ heat and avoiding the use of more energetically expensive responses.

    4.   Behavioral modifications include:

        a.   increased physical activity to produce heat from contracting _____.

        b.   _____ food consumption, which provides more calories from which to produce more energy.

        c.   bringing all body parts into a center, such as a curled-up position, in order to reduce the amount of surface area exposed to the cold.

    c.   Long-term human responses to cold _____ among human groups.

E. High Altitude

    1.   Multiple factors produce stress on the human body at higher altitudes. These include:

      a. _____ intense solar radiation.

      b. cold.

      c. _____ humidity.

d. _____ (which amplifies cold stress, hence the wind chill factor in winter weather reports).

e. Hypoxia

   1. _____ refers to a reduction in the available oxygen.

      a. It can mean reduced oxygen in the _____, due to a lower barometric pressure (i.e. for every cubic meter of air there are actually fewer oxygen molecules at high altitude, than there are in a cubic meter of air at sea level).

      b. It can also refer to decreased oxygen available, or presence, in the body's _____.

   2. Of the factors mentioned, _____ exerts the greatest amount of stress on human physiological systems, especially the heart, lungs, and brain.

2. People who live at higher elevations exhibit a number of manifestations of their hypoxic environment.

  a. Reproduction is affected through

    1. increased rates of infant _____ .

    2. _____ .

    3. _____ .

  b. Low birth weight is more common, probably because of decreased fetal _____ due to impaired maternal-fetal oxygen transport.

3. Adult acclimatization to high altitude

  a. Adult acclimatization occurs when people, born at lower elevations, acclimatize to the higher elevation. These are usually _____-term modifications.

  b. Adult acclimatization to high altitude includes:

1. _____ in respiration rate.

2. _____ in heart rate.

3. increased production of _____ _____ cells.

4. Developmental acclimatization to high altitude

   a. Developmental acclimatization occurs in people born in high altitudes in which they acquire adaptations to high altitude during their _____ and _____.

   b. Development acclimatizations to high altitude include:

      1. greater _____ capacity.

      2. larger _____.

      3. more efficient diffusion of _____ from blood vessels to body tissues.

   c. Developmental acclimatization provides a good example of physiological plasticity by illustrating how, within the limits of genetic factors, development can be influenced by _____.

5. There is evidence that populations can _____ to high attitudes.

   a. Highland Tibetan populations appear to have evolved accommodations to _____ (over the last 25,000 years) and do not have reproductive problems.

   b. Both highland Tibetans and highland Quechua appear to utilize _____ in a way that permits more efficient use of oxygen.

      1. This implies the presence of genetic _____ in the mtDNA.

      2. This also implies that natural selection has acted to increase the _____ mutations in these groups.

F. Infectious Disease

   1. _____ disease refers to those diseases caused by invading organisms such as bacteria, viruses, or fungi.

a. Throughout the course of human evolution, infectious disease has exerted enormous _____ _____ on human populations.

b. Infectious disease influences the frequency of certain alleles that affect the _____ response.

2. There are many diseases that humans have been subjected to.

a. Today, _____ is the disease that more humans suffer from than any other, 300-500 million people worldwide.

   1. Recently some of the malarial parasites have become drug _____, and this disease may become even more of a selective factor.

   2. We have seen in Chapter 5 that malaria has operated in some African and Mediterranean populations to alter allele frequencies at the locus governing hemoglobin formation.

b. _____ accounted for approximately 10-15 percent of all deaths in certain parts of eighteenth century Europe.

c. The best-known epidemic was the _____ plague of the mid-fourteenth century.

   1. Bubonic plague is caused by a _____ that is transmitted from rodents to humans by fleas.

   2. During the initial exposure of bubonic plague, _____-_____ of Europe's population died.

d. Another devastating example was the _____ pandemic that broke out in 1918. Over 21 million people died worldwide.

3. The effects of human infectious disease are due to both _____ and biological factors.

a. Until the advent of agriculture and sedentary living sites, infectious disease was _____ a major problem to human populations.

1. Eventually human settlements became large, crowded, unsanitary cities where the opportunity for _____ was great.

2. Humans also domesticated _____ that carried diseases that affected humans.

b. It was not until the last century that humans became aware of the microbes that cause disease.

c. Humans and pathogens exert selective pressures on _____ other.

1. Disease exerts selective pressures on _____ populations to adapt to that particular organism.

2. Microbes also evolve (very quickly) and adapt to the various _____ _____ exerted upon them by their hosts.

3. From an evolutionary perspective, it is to the advantage of any pathogen to keep its host alive until it can reproduce and infect other hosts.

a. Selection frequently acts

1. to produce _____ in host populations (a benefit to the host),

2. and to reduce the _____ of the disease (also a benefit to host, but this is also a benefit to the disease organisms because it enables them to reproduce more efficiently).

4. Humans are currently speeding up microbe and vector evolution.

a. Antibiotics have exerted selective pressures on bacteria and some species have developed _____-resistant strains.

b. Widespread use of _____ has led to resistant insects that carry many of the diseases that affect humans.

4. AIDS (acquired immune deficiency syndrome) is a _____ infection that was first reported in 1981.

a. The virus that causes AIDS is _____ (human immunodeficiency virus)

b. Viral infection

    1. _____ consist of single strands of DNA or RNA enclosed by a protein jacket.

    2. Once a virus invades a host's body it enters _____ cells.

        a. Viral DNA is inserted into the target cell's _____ .

        b. The end result is that the viral DNA directs the cell to produce _____ particles which go on to infect other cells.

c. HIV is transmitted through the exchange of _____ _____—it is not spread through casual contact.

d. HIV can attack a variety of cell types, but its predilection is for ____ _____ cells, one of the cell types that initiates an immune response. When a person's T cell count drops below minimum levels, "opportunistic" infections, microbes present but not HIV, are able to mount an attack on the body.

e. It is believed that HIV's origins were in Africa.

    1. A very genetically similar retrovirus occurs among African monkeys, _____ (simian immunodeficiency virus).

    2. It is possible that HIV _____ from SIV, perhaps within the last few decades.

f. HIV is the most _____ virus known.

    1. The virus mutates rapidly once it enters a host's body, so that within a single infected person, there are many distinct _____ of HIV.

    2. The mutability of HIV makes developing a _____ for this virus extremely difficult.

KEY TERMS

acclimatization: short-term physiological response by an individual to changes in the environment. The capacity for acclimatization may also typify the entire population or species. This capacity is under genetic influence and is subject to evolutionary factors such as natural selection.

AIDS: acquired immune deficiency syndrome. A condition caused by suppression of the immune system due to the human immunodeficiency virus (HIV). The syndrome includes any number of "opportunistic" infections which are able to attack the body due to an inefficient immune response.

biological determinism: the concept that phenomena, including various aspects of behavior, are governed by genetic factors.

coevolution: evolution of two or more species in which they are exerting reciprocal selective pressures on one another.

endemic: with regard to disease, a population in which there is always some individuals that are infected.

ethnocentrism: viewing other cultures from one's own cultural perspective. This often leads to thinking of other cultures as odd and inferior.

eugenics: a former scientific discipline, now largely discredited, that promoted the improvement of the human species through controlled breedings and sterilizations of "undesirables."

homeostasis: a state of equilibrium in which the body's internal environment remains within a stable range. Homeostasis is maintained through a series of negative feedback loops which act to bring the internal environment back into its stable range.

homeothermy: characteristic of mammals and birds. These animals are able to regulate their body temperatures independent of outside (ambient) temperature fluctuations.

hypoxia: a lack of oxygen, either in the body's tissues or in the atmosphere (at higher altitudes).

intelligence: mental capacity; the ability to learn, reason, or comprehend and interpret information, facts, relationships, meanings, etc.

monogeny: a theory that all living humans are descended from one original pair of humans (Adam and Eve) and that all subsequent human biological variation is due to environment.

pandemic: an extensive outbreak of disease affecting large numbers of people over a wide area; potentially, a worldwide phenomenon.

pathogen: any organism or substance that causes disease.

plasticity: physiological change in response to the environment.

polygeny: the theory that living humans are descended from many different pairs of humans (other Adams and Eves) that has led to different human races.

races: populations of a species that differ from one another in some aspect of the visible phenotype. Biological (AKA geographic) races are taxonomically expressed as subspecies.

stress: in a physiological context, any factor that acts to disrupt homeostasis. In this respect, stress can be microbes or environmental extremes such as climate or altitude, as well as psychological factors.

vasoconstriction: narrowing of blood vessels by decreasing their diameter permitting reduced blood flow to the skin. Vasoconstriction is an involuntary response to cold and reduces heat loss at the skin's surface.

vasodilation: an involuntary expansion of blood vessels by increasing their diameter, permitting increased blood flow to the skin. Vasodilation permits warming of the skin and also facilitates radiation of warmth as a means of cooling.

vector: an agent that serves to transmit disease from one carrier to another.

Now take the Fill-in and Multiple Choice tests. Do not guess. Following completion of the tests, correct them. The correct answers and textbook page references are at the end of this study guide chapter. Note your strong areas and your weak areas to guide you in your continuing study.

FILL-IN QUESTIONS

1. Most species are polytypic. This means that there is no "_____" to which all members conform.

2. When physical anthropologists have tried to define the word "race," they have _____ to reach a consensus.

3. _____ traits exhibit a continuous range of variation.

4. The first step toward understanding natural phenomena is the ordering of variation into _____ that can be named, discussed, and perhaps studied.

5. As early as 1350 B. C., the ancient Egyptians had classified humans on the basis of _____.

6. Judging other cultures by the norms of one's own culture is called _____.

7. A school of thought, popular in the 18th and 19th centuries, that posited that the different varieties of humans were descended from different Adams and Eves was _____.

8. The idea that behavior, including intelligence and morals, is innate due to an individual's (or peoples') genetics is called _____ _____.

9. The scientific discipline founded in the 19th century by Francis Galton that advocated "race improvement," including government intervention to reach this goal, was _____.

10. The most detrimental outcome of _____ _____ is racism.

11. Our biological differences should be viewed as traces of our _____ past which adapted humans to different environments as a species spread throughout the world.

12. Modern physical anthropologists view human variation as the result of adaptation to
_____ conditions.

13. Ultraviolet radiation stimulates the production of _____ _____.

14. Insufficient vitamin D synthesis can cause rickets. The most likely cause of this situation
is lack of exposure to _____ .

15. A hypothesis which attempts to explain why more northern populations have more
lightly pigmented skin is the _____ ___ hypothesis.

16. The vitamin D hypothesis attempts to explain darkly pigmented skin as protection
against overproduction of vitamin D. Why is there a problem with an overproduction of
vitamin D? _____ .

17. The ability to maintain a constant internal body temperature, as found in
_____ and birds, is called homeothermy.

18. In regards to thermal conditions, humans tend to cope better physiologically with
_____ than they do with _____ .

19. Allen's rule involves the length of _____ .

20. Bergmann's rule concerns the relationship between body mass (or volume) to
_____ _____ .

21. Integrated with sweating, reduced amounts of body _____ on humans exposes
more body surface to allow more efficient evaporation to occur.

22. The most serious stress that the human body is exposed to at high altitudes is
_____ .

23. A trait that is genetically determined can be influenced by the environment. This is
called _____ _____ .

24. A tremendous selective factor during the course of human evolution has been
_____ _____ .

25. Disease was probably not a major selective factor on humans prior to _____ years ago.

26. Many _____ factors, such as architectural styles, subsistence techniques, and even religious practices, all affect how infectious disease develops and persists.

27. AIDS is the acronym for _____ _____ _____ _____.

28. The ultimate cause of AIDS is _____ .

29. HIV is the acronym for _____ _____ _____.

MULTIPLE CHOICE QUESTIONS

1. Within *Ammodramus maritimus*, the seaside sparrow, there are four distinct populations that differ from one another in at least one trait. This species is a
   A. monotypic species.
   B. polytypic species.
   C. chronospecies.
   D. syngamic species.

2. The criteria for describing a biological race is
   A. at least 50 percent of the member of one population of a species must be distinguishable from another population.
   B. two populations of the same species are located in two different geographical area.
   C. two populations have different vocalizations or, in humans, languages.
   D. there are no established criteria by which organisms are assessed.

3. Modern studies of human variation emphasize
   A. adaptive significance of variation.
   B. differences between large geographically separated populations.
   C. description of geographically separated populations.
   D. polygenic traits such as skin color.

4. Which of the following statements is true?
   A. Many anthropologists consider groups such as the Japanese to be as race.
   B. Forensic anthropologists can identify the ethnicity of a skeleton to 100 percent accuracy.
   C. Many physical anthropologists see human race as a meaningless concept.
   D. The five races of Blumenbach are still the standard in modern physical anthropology.

5. An objection to the use of racial taxonomies is that they are
   A. typological in nature.
   B. based on polygenic traits.
   C. based on continuous traits.
   D. evolutionary in nature.

6. When a group of people are judged based on the standards and values of another group, it is referred to as
   A. cultural relativity.
   B. ethnocentrism.
   C. humanitarianism.
   D. isolationism.

7. Some polygenists looked for traits that they could use to define races. These traits would not be affected by the environment, would exhibit only minimal in-group variation, and were
   A. non-adaptive traits.
   B. convergencies.
   C. parallelisms.
   D. monogenic traits.

8. Anthropometrists were able to classify European populations into
   A. western and eastern Europeans.
   B. Caucasoids and Mongoloids.
   C. northern and southern Europeans.
   D. brachycephalics and dolichocephalics.

9. A local sheriff believes that the people of a town in his district, who have high arrest and conviction rates, are born thieves because of their genetic constitution. Which of the following would this sheriff's attitudes best fit into?
   A. relativism
   B. ethnocentrism
   C. biological determinism
   D. post-modernism

10. The scientific discipline that provided scientific justification for purging Nazi Germany of its "unfit" was
   A. anthropometry.
   B. eugenics.
   C. genetics.
   D. monogeny.

11. Which of the following is a **true** statement?
   A. Individual abilities are due only to an individual's genetic inheritance.
   B. IQ can change within an individual's lifetime.
   C. IQ scores are essentially the same thing as innate intelligence.
   D. IQ scores are discrete between populations.

12. Black children adopted by advantaged white families score better on IQ tests. This suggests
    A. IQ is correlated with race.
    B. IQ is not correlated with race.
    C. the social environment plays a dominant role in determining the average IQ level of black children.
    D. Both B and C are correct.

13. If an Illinoian leaves the 300-foot elevation of Urbana-Champaign and flies to Quito, Ecuador, elevation 8,000 feet, this person's body will begin to produce more red blood cells to compensate for lower oxygen levels. This type of short-term physiological change is called
    A. acclimation.
    B. homeothermy.
    C. acclimatization.
    D. remodeling.

14. The pigment which helps protect against ultraviolet radiation by absorbing it is
    A. carotene.
    B. melanin.
    C. lactose.
    D. hemoglobin.

15. When insufficient ultraviolet radiation is absorbed during childhood, the condition resulting from a vitamin D deficiency is
    A. cancer.
    B. gastroenteritis.
    C. rickets.
    D. trisomy 21.

16. It has been suggested that Neandertal populations, which inhabited a cloud-covered Europe 100,000 years ago, were the last dark-skin population of Europe. Which of the following would be support for this suggestion?
    A. the use of caves for shelters
    B. deaths that appear to have resulted from cutaneous carcinomas (skin cancer)
    C. Neandertals appear to have been wearing clothing
    D. the prevalence of rickets in these populations

17. Inuits have a large "globular" body, while the body structure of the Kalahari !Kung is thin and linear. This is explained by
    A. Bergmann's rule.
    B. Allen's rule.
    C. Gloger's rule.
    D. Kleiber's rule.

18. The long arms and legs of the East African Masai, and the short arms and legs of the Inuit conform to
    A. Bergmann's rule.
    B. Allen's rule.
    C. Gloger's rule.
    D. Cope's rule.

19. Most human adjustments to cold are
    A. cultural.
    B. biological.
    C. physiological.
    D. metabolic.

20. Which of the following processes is most associated with human acclimatization to cold?
    A. sweating
    B. vasodilation
    C. vasoconstriction
    D. evaporative cooling

21. Which of the following is **not** a short-term response to cold?
    A. increased metabolic rate
    B. shivering
    C. increased food consumption
    D. vasodilation

22. The people with the highest metabolic rates in the world are the
    A. inland Inuit.
    B. Arctic Inuit.
    C. Australian Aboriginals.
    D. Choctaw of Oklahoma.

23. Which of the following is **not** a way that the Inuit adapt to the cold?
    A. clothing
    B. high-fat diet
    C. dark skin
    D. a short "stocky" body build

24. A problem associated with high altitude stress is
    A. kidney failure.
    B. low birth weights.
    C. high red blood cell counts.
    D. high white blood cell counts.

25. There is some evidence that highland Tibetans
    A. do not need to breathe oxygen.
    B. have made genetic adaptations to hypoxia.
    C. have evolved more efficient kidneys.
    D. need to go down to lower elevations in order to reproduce.

26. A disease that currently infects 300-500 million people worldwide and has had tremendous effect on the course of human evolution, as evidence by blood adaptations against it, is
    A. rickets.
    B. malaria.
    C. bubonic plague.
    D. influenza.

27. When two species, which could be a parasite and a host, exert reciprocal selective pressures on one another it is called
    A. infection.
    B. virulence.
    C. coevolution.
    D. opportunism.

28. A serious concern of medical workers is that
    A. disease-causing microbes are evolving resistance against antibiotics.
    B. insect vectors have developed resistance against pesticides.
    C. HIV is going into a dormant stage in which it will be difficult to detect.
    D. Both A and B are correct.

29. Which of the following statements is **true**?
    A. HIV can be transmitted through casual contact.
    B. HIV can be carried by an insect vector.
    C. HIV is transmitted through exchange of body fluids.
    D. HIV is a very stable virus.

30. It is believed that HIV arose from
    A. a similar virus found in African monkeys, SIV.
    B. a CIA laboratory.
    C. a Soviet biological warfare laboratory.
    D. contaminated smallpox vaccine.

Answers To Fill-in Outline

I. THE CONCEPT OF RACE
A. polytypic
   1. traits
   2. type
B. 1. geographical
   2. misused
      a. species
      b. culturally
         1. association
         2. sex, age
   3. ethnicity
   4. a. variation
      b. criteria
   5. large geographically defined
C. within, between
   1. adaptive significance
   2. evolutionary
   3. fixed
   4. a. adaptive
      b. degree
      c. important
D. 1. consensus
   2. three
      a. fixed
      b. important
      c. forensic
         1. skeletal
         2. 80
      d. meaningless
   3. a. typological
         1. stereotypes
         2. conform
      b. polygenic
         1. continuous
         2. discrete

II. HISTORICAL VIEWS OF HUMAN VARIATION
A. categorized
   1. skin color
   2. diversity
   3. two
B. 1. single pair
      a. plasticity
      b. modification
   2. monogeny

C. 1. different
   2. physical
   3. modify
D. 1. classification
   2. humans
      a. classify
      b. 1. least
         2. superior
   3. a. five
      b. arbitrary
      c. discrete
         2. overlapping
   4. unique
      b. nonadaptive
   5. Europeans
E. 1. biological determinism
      a. racism
      b. sexism
   2. justify
   3. eugenics
F. typologies

III. RACISM
A. racism
   1. inherited
   2. typify
   3. superior
B. biological
C. 1. evolutionary
      a. adaptations
      b. natural selection
   2. prejudice

IV. INTELLIGENCE
A. association
B. intelligence
   1. measure
   2. not
      a. experience
      b. change
   3. multiple
   4. interactions
      a. learning
      b. not
C. inherent
D. cognitive

V. THE ADAPTIVE SIGNIFICANCE OF HUMAN VARIATION
A. past, present
B. 1. long-term evolutionary
   2. acclimatization
C. 1. Old World
      a. greatest
      b. northern
   2. three
      a. hemoglobin
      b. carotene
      c. melanin
   3. DNA
      a. melanocytes
      b. number
      c. increases
   4. equator
      a. 1. tropics
         2. outdoors
         3. UV radiation
      b. 1. indirect
         2. clothing
         3. relaxed
      c. vitamin D
         1. synthesize
         2. rickets
      d. 1. darker
            a. melanin
            b. less
         2. hypothesis
         3. a. excessive
            b. prevents
   5. a. adaptive significance
D. 1. homeothermy
   2. thermal
   3. a. sweat glands
         1. evaporative
         2. equally
            a. acclimatization
            b. lost
      b. vasodilation
         1. capillaries
      c. body
         1. climate
            a. Bergmann's
               1. decreases
               2. retention

      b. 1. appendages
         2. longer
   2. a. warmer
      b. cold
   4. a. more
      b. short-term
         1. metabolic
            a. higher
            b. protein, fat
         2. shivering
         3. vasoconstriction
            a. restricts
            b. retaining
         4. a. muscles
            b. increased
      c. vary
E. 1. a. more
      c. low
      d. wind
      e. 1. hypoxia
            a. atmosphere
            b. tissues
         2. hypoxia
   2. a. 1. mortality
         2. miscarriage
         3. prematurity
      b. growth
   3. a. short
      b. 1. increase
         2. increase
         3. red blood
   4. a. growth, development
      b. 1. lung
         2. hearts
         3. oxygen
      c. environment
   5. adapt
      a. hypoxia
      b. glucose
         1. mutations
         2. advantageous
F. 1. infectious
      a. selective pressures
      b. immune
   2. a. malaria
         1. resistant
      b. smallpox

        c. bubonic
            1. bacterium
            2. one-third
        d. influenza
    3. cultural
        a. not
            1. disease
            2. animals
        c. each
            1. host
            2. selective pressures
            3. a. 1. resistance
                    2. virulence
            4. a. antibiotic
                b. pesticides

    4. viral
        a. HIV
        b. 1. viruses
            2. target
                a. DNA
                b. virus
        c. body fluids
        d. T4 helper
        e. 1. SIV
            2. evolved
        f. mutable
            1. variants
            2. vaccine

ANSWERS & REFERENCES TO FILL-IN QUESTIONS

1. type, p. 130
2. failed, p. 132
3. polygenic, p. 132
4. categories, p. 133
5. skin color, p. 133
6. ethnocentrism, p. 134
7. polygeny, p. 134
8. biological determinism, p. 136
9. eugenics, p. 136
10. biological determinism, p. 137
11. evolutionary, p. 137
12. environmental, p. 137
13. vitamin D, p. 141
14. ultraviolet (solar) radiation or, simply, sunlight, p. 141
15. vitamin D, p. 141
16. in large dosages, vitamin D is toxic, p. 141
17. mammals, p. 142
18. heat, cold, p. 142
19. appendages, p. 143
20. surface area, p. 143
21. hair, p. 142
22. hypoxia, p. 145
23. developmental acclimatization, p. 145
24. infectious disease, p. 146
25. 10-12,000, p. 147
26. cultural, p. 147
27. acquired immune deficiency syndrome, p. 148
28. HIV, p. 148
29. human immunodeficiency virus, p. 148

ANSWERS & REFERENCES TO MULTIPLE CHOICE QUESTIONS

1. B, p. 134
2. A, p. 134
3. D, p. 136
4. C, p. 132
5. B, p. 137
6. B, p. 130
7. D, p. 131
8. A, modern studies also emphasize differences in allele frequencies between and within populations. p. 131
9. C, this sheriff believes that the people of this town are <u>biological</u> <u>determined</u> to be thieves because of genetic inheritance. If you answered B, you were assuming more information than we gave—we did not provide enough information to know whether he is judging another ethnic group by his standards. The inhabitants of the town may be from the same ethnic group that the sheriff belongs to. p. 136
10. A, p. 132
11. B, p. 138
12. D, the fact that higher IQs correlate with a change in the social environment should suggest to you that the social environment also plays a role in IQ. p. 138
13. C, p. 139
14. B, p. 140
15. C, p. 141
16. D, modern light-skinned European populations use shelters, fire, and clothing so whether Neandertals were dark-skinned or not would not bear on the use of these things (choices A and C). Dark-skinned populations would be unlikely to die from skin cancers (choice B). Rickets, on the other hand, would suggest that the melanin content of Neandertal skin was heavier than would be optimum for the environment and would result in the lack of vitamin D synthesis. p. 141
17. A, p. 143
18. B, p. 143
19. A, despite the physiological adaptations that we have discussed in this chapter, humans could not survive in cold environments without cultural innovations (technology), p.144
20. C, p. 144
21. D, p. 144
22. A, p. 144
23. C, p. 144
24. B, p. 145
25. B, p. 145
26. B, p. 147
27. C, p. 148
28. D, pp. 147-148
29. C, p. 149
30. A, pp. 149-150

CHAPTER 7

GROWTH AND DEVELOPMENT

LEARNING OBJECTIVES

After reading this chapter you should be able to:
- discuss examples of the interaction of biology and culture in human growth and development. (p. 156)
- define growth and development. (p. 156)
- describe growth in a long bone, both in length and in width. (pp. 157-158)
- discuss human growth in stature. (pp. 158-159)
- list the five basic nutrients and give a function for each. (pp. 161-162)
- explain how evolution has molded our current dietary needs. (pp. 162-165)
- discuss the diet of pre-agricultural humans and how their diet has influence the physiology of modern humans. (pp. 165-167)
- give examples of what happens when humans have some deficiency in their diet (pp. 163-165; 168-169)
- discuss the human life cycle. (pp. 172-180)

FILL-IN OUTLINE

Introduction
As noted throughout the text, modern humans are the result of evolution in which there was a strong interaction between biology and culture. In this chapter, this interaction in human growth and development is discussed. Some genetic characteristics are expressed no matter what the cultural environment is. However, many genetic traits reflect their interaction with the environment. This includes cultural values and such cultural factors as socioeconomic status.

I. FUNDAMENTALS OF GROWTH AND DEVELOPMENT

A. The terms growth and development are often used interchangeably, but they are

   _____ processes.

   1. _____ refers to an increase in mass or number of cells.

      a. An increase in cell number is referred to as _____.

      b. An increase in cell mass is referred to as _____.

   2. _____ refers to differentiation of cells into different types of

   tissues and their maturation.

B. Bone Growth

   1. The skeletal of the human fetus is composed of _____. During

   growth the cartilage cells are gradually replaced by bone cells in a process called

   ossification.

   2. The humerus provides an example of ossification.

      a. The shaft of a long bone is called the _____ .

         1. The two ends of a long bone are called the _____.

         2. Growth is completed when the ephiphyses _____ with the diaphysis.

      b. _____ type of cells are responsible for bone growth.

         1. _____ remove bone or cartilage cells.

         2. _____ deposit new bone cells.

      c. Growth of a bone occurs not only in length, but also in width by

   _____ growth.

         1. Osteoclasts remove bone from the _____ part of the shaft.

         2. Osteoblasts deposit bone on the _____ surface of the bone.

      d. The epiphyses of long bones unite with their shafts in _____

   patterns.

1. This enables anthropologists to estimate the _____ of death of young skeletons.

2. The pattern of fusion occurs at different ages, depending on the bone in question.

C. Stature

  1. Increased stature is a common indicator of _____ status in children.

  2. Growth spurts

    a. There are two ways that height is usually plotted on a graph.

      1. A _____ curve shows the height obtained in a given year.

      2. The other way to plot growth is a _____ curve. Growth spurts stand out on a velocity curve.

    b. Growth spurts can be seen in early _____, encompassing the first six months of fetal growth and the first four years of childhood growth.

    c. At puberty another pronounced increase in growth occurs, the _____ _____ _____. After the adolescent growth spurt, development declines gradually until adult stature is reached.

    d. There are some who argue that the _____ _____ curve is unique to our species.

      1. Others say that _____ show small spurts at puberty making their curves similar to the human growth curve. If so, the adolescent growth spurt may be a characteristic that goes far back into our evolutionary lineage.

      2. Nevertheless, no other mammal shows the growth pattern, to the same degree, of modern _____.

    e. Other parts of the human body also show a similar growth curve as seen for height.

3. Growth curves for boys and girls are significantly _____.

    a. At birth, there is a slight _____ _____ in many body measures, but the major divergence comes at puberty.

    b. The adolescent growth spurt occurs _____ years earlier in girls than in boys.

        1. Males are _____ than females, particularly at age 18.

        2. Females have more _____ _____ than males at all ages.

D. Brain Growth

    1. The head is a relatively _____ part of the body at birth.

        a. The growth rate of the brain after birth is far _____ than any other part of the body.

            1. At birth the brain is about ____ percent of its adult size.

            2. By six months after birth it has reach ____ percent of its adult size.

            3. By age _____ the brain has reached 90 percent of its adult size.

            4. By age _____ the brain is at 95 percent of its adult size.

        b. There is only a very small growth spurt at adolescence making the brain an _____ to the growth curve characteristic of the rest of the body.

    2. The pattern of human brain growth is _____ among primates and other mammals.

        a. The brain of most mammals is _____ percent of the adult size at birth.

        b. The narrow human female pelvis, necessary for bipedal walking, puts a _____ on the size of the fetal head.

II. NUTRITIONAL EFFECTS ON GROWTH AND DEVELOPMENT

A. The primary function of the digestive system is to

    1. take in _____ and break them down into components that provide the basic materials needed for growth and development.

2. The nutrients processed by the digestive system are transported through the circulatory system to provide each cell with the nutrients it needs to perform its functions.

B. There are _____ basic nutrients for growth and development.

1. Proteins are composed of _____ _____.

   a. _____ are important for maintaining cell structure in the body.

   b. Other important body components that are proteins include antibodies, hormones, and enzymes.

   c. After the body has used the protein it needs, the excess amino acids may enter the cell mitochondria where they are _____ into ATP, the molecule that provides energy for the body.

2. Carbohydrates are the main source of _____ for the body.

   a. Carbohydrate digestion

      1. Carbohydrate digestion begins in the mouth where the salivary enzyme amylase begins to break down complex _____ (polysaccharides) into simple sugars called disaccharides (two-sugar units).

      2. In the small intestine pancreatic enzymes further break down disaccharides into _____ (the simplest sugar, one-sugar unit).

      3. In the liver monosaccharides are converted into _____ .

         a. Glucose is the _____ source of energy for the body. This occurs because glucose is converted into ATP by the mitochondria.

         b. Glucose is the _____ source of energy utilized by the brain.

   b. Excess glucose is converted into _____ .

      1. Glycogen may be _____ in the liver or in muscles.

      2. Glycogen may also be stored as _____ .

      3. When glucose levels fall too low, _____ can be reconverted into glucose.

3. Lipids

    a. _____ include fats and oils.

    b. One of the products of lipid breakdown is fatty acids. When they are not used for other purposes fatty acids can enter the _____ and be converted into ATP.

4. Vitamins

    a. Vitamins _____ _____ contribute energy to run our bodies.

    b. Vitamins do function as coenzymes, substances that speed up the chemical reactions necessary for running the body.

    c. There are _____ categories of vitamins.

        1. _____-soluble vitamins are the B vitamins and vitamin C.

            a. These vitamins are _____ in the urine.

            b. Because these vitamins are not _____, they must be consumed almost daily.

        2. Fat-_____ vitamins are vitamins A, D, E, and K.

            a. These vitamins _____ be stored in the liver and a few other organs.

            b. Because they can be stored, deficiencies are _____ to develop.

5. Minerals

    a. Unlike the previous four nutrients, _____ are not organic.

    b. The mineral needed in greatest quality is _____ (important in such actions as nerve conductions and muscle contractions and a major component of the skeleton and teeth).

C. Evolution of nutritional needs

    1. Our nutritional needs have _____ with the types of foods that were available to our evolutionary ancestors.

   a. We have inherited the ability to digest _____ protein from our mammalian forebears.

   b. Early _____ also evolved the ability to digest plant matter.

   c. Our more immediate ape-like ancestors were primarily fruit-eaters and passed on their ability to process _____ to us.

   d. In addition, human needs for specific vitamins and minerals reflect ancestral _____ adaptations.

2. Vitamin C and evolution

   a. _____ ___ is crucial in metabolism and energy production.

   b. Most animals are able to _____ vitamin C.

   c. Early _____ probably were capable of synthesizing vitamin C.

      1. As monkeys evolved, they ate more _____ and _____ and vitamin C was plentiful in their diet.

      2. At some point in primate evolution the ancestors of higher primates _____ the ability to produce vitamin C, probably through a genetic mutation.

         a. There would have been no disadvantage as long as there was sufficient vitamin C in the _____.

         b. Actually, this may have been selectively advantageous because it would _____ the energy require to produce vitamin C.

   d. A deficiency of vitamin C can result in _____ .

      1. This disease was probably rare or absent in _____-_____ populations.

      2. Scurvy became a problem when humans went to sea for long periods and did not have _____ stores of fruits and vegetables.

3. Essential amino acids

   a. There are _____ amino acids that are required for growth and maintenance.

   b. Humans lack the ability to synthesize _____ of the amino acids.

     1. These amino acids must be obtained from the _____.

     2. These eight amino acids are referred to as _____ amino acids.

     3. The amounts of each of the essential amino acids parallel the amounts present in animal _____, suggesting that food from animal sources may have been an important component of ancestral hominid diets.

       a. _____ consumption is expensive, both ecologically and economically.

       b. Most modern populations meet their protein needs by _____ a variety of vegetables.

    4. Despite the fact that humans use cultural responses to adapt to environmental challenges, we still appear to be _____ by our evolved nutritional needs.

      a. Our evolution reflects a food base that includes great _____ .

      b. _____ reduced the amount of variety available to human populations and has resulted in the appearance of nutritional deficiency diseases.

D. Diets of humans before agriculture

   1. The pre-agricultural diet was high in protein, but low in _____.

    a. This is because the fat of non-domesticated _____ animals is primarily

       unsaturated fat.

    b. The diet also was high in complex _____, including

       fiber.

    c. The diet was also low in salt and high in calcium.

2. Many of our biological and behavioral characteristics contributed to our ancestors'

   adaptation, but may be _____ in our modern industrialized

   societies.

    a. An example of this is our ability to store _____.

      1. This was an advantage in the past when food availability alternated

         between abundance and _____.

      2. Today there is a relative _____ of foods in western nations.

         The formerly positive ability to store extra fat has now turned into a

         liability which leads to degenerative diseases.

    b. Geneticist James V. Neel has suggested that the increased incidence of non-

       insulin dependent _____ may be due to our past selection for

       fat-storage ability.

      1. He suggests that genes for fat storage and the genes that predispose

         people to diabetes may be closely associated and combined in a

         "_____ _____."

      2. In the past, the negative consequence of this genotype (diabetes) was

         rarely manifested because of periodic food _____ . More

         recently, high carbohydrate diets and abundant food have resulted in

         dramatic increases of diabetes.

E. Undernutrition and malnutrition

  1. Undernutrition means an _____ quantity of food.

    a. I.e., not enough _____ are consumed to support normal health.

    b. It is estimated that between _____ and _____ percent of the world's population is undernourished.

2. Malnutrition refers to an inadequate amount of some _____ _____ in the diet.

    a. In underdeveloped countries, _____ malnutrition is the most common type of malnutrition.

        1. _____ is one type of protein malnutrition, characterized by a "swollen belly."

        2. _____ combines protein malnutrition with calorie deficiency.

    b. Malnutrition greatly affects reproduction and infant survival.

        1. _____ mothers have more difficulties in producing healthy and surviving children.

        2. Children born of malnourished mothers are smaller and behind in most aspects of _____ _____.

            a. _____ processes often slow down greatly when post-natal environment insults are severe.

            b. Post-natal growth in children of malnourished mothers.

                1. _____-_____ growth can make up some of the deficit in these children.

                2. However, there are _____ periods when certain tissues grow very rapidly.

                3. If a severe interruption occurs during one of these periods, the individual may _____ catch up completely.

    c. Other deficiencies include:

1. _____ deficiencies, such as beriberi (caused by a deficiency of thiamine [vitamin B_1]).

2. _____ deficiencies, such as anemia (caused by a deficiency of iron).

III. OTHER FACTORS INFLUENCING GROWTH AND DEVELOPMENT

A. Genetics

1. Even though environmental factors can influence growth and development, an individual still can not exceed their _____ _____.

   a. _____ sets the underlying limitations and potentials for growth and development.

   b. The _____ determines how the body grows within the genetic parameters.

2. Studies of _____ have yielded information regarding the effects of genes and the environment on growth.

   a. Monozygotic twins

      1. _____ twins come from the union of a single sperm and a single ovum.

      2. They share _____ percent of their genes.

   b. Dizygotic twins

      1. _____ twins are the result of the fertilization of two separate ova by two different sperm.

      2. Dizygotic twins share _____ percent of their genes.

   c. If monozygotic twins are raised apart, yet have, for example, the same stature, we can conclude that genes are the _____ determinant of that trait.

1. Twin studies have revealed that _____ is under strong genetic control.

2. _____, on the other hand, appears to be more strongly influenced by diet and environment than by the genes.

B. Hormones

1. Hormones are substances produced in one cell that have an effect on

_____ _____.

2. Almost all hormones have an effect on _____.

3. The hypothalamus is a region of the brain that is involved with _____ hormonal action.

a. The hypothalamus secretes its own hormones which either _____ or stimulate release of hormones in other cells.

b. A primary target of the hypothalamus' hormones is the _____ gland, sometimes called the "master gland," which is composed of two separate tissues, the anterior pituitary and posterior pituitary.

1. The _____ pituitary produces hormones that regulate reproduction, metabolism, and growth.

2. The _____ pituitary secretes hormones involved with water balance, with inducing labor, and causing milk ejection from the lactating breast.

4. _____ is produced by the thyroid gland.

a. Thyroxine _____ metabolism and is involved with heat production.

b. When thyroxine levels in the blood fall too _____ for normal metabolism a series of events occur.

1. The brain detects this and sends a message to the _____ to release thyrotropin-releasing hormone (TRH).

2. TRH goes to the anterior pituitary where it stimulates the _____ of thyroid-stimulating hormone (TSH).

3. TSH goes to the thyroid and stimulates the release of _____.

4. When the brain detects an increase in the circulating levels of thyroxine, it sends signals to _____ further release of TRH, and by this, TSH.

5. This homeostatic process works by a negative feedback loop in which hormone levels are kept within a constant level and any great change is inhibited.

C. Environmental factors

1. As we have seen in chapter 6, environmental factors such as altitude and climate have effects on _____ and _____.

2. Perhaps the primary influence of such external factors comes from their effects on _____.

   a. Infant birth weight is _____ at high altitude, regardless of such factors as nutrition, smoking, or socioeconomic status.

   b. In general, cold climate populations tend to be _____ and have longer trunks and shorter appendages than populations in tropical areas.

   c. Exposure to _____ also appears to have an affect on growth, probably because of its effects on melatonin and vitamin D synthesis.

IV. THE HUMAN LIFE CYCLE

A. Humans have five phases to their _____ _____.

1. _____ begins with conception and ends with birth.

2. _____ is the period in which the baby nurses.

3. _____ (juvenile phase) is the period from weaning to puberty.

4. _____ is the period from puberty to the end of growth.

5. _____ is marked by the completion of growth.

6. An extra period in females is _____, recognized as one year after the last menstrual cycle.

B. Human life cycles also have the added complexity in that they occur in _____ contexts.

   1. Different developmental _____ mean different things to different cultures.

   2. Collective and individual attitudes toward these life cycle transitions have an effect on _____ and _____.

C. Conception and pregnancy

   1. The biology of conception and pregnancy

      a. A sperm _____ an egg and this union produces a zygote.

      b. The _____ travels through the uterine fallopian tube to become implanted in the wall of the uterus.

      c. The embryo becomes a fetus and it develops until it is _____ enough to survive outside the womb.

      d. Birth occurs

   2. Food restrictions and food aversions

      a. Almost every culture imposes dietary _____ on pregnant women.

      b. Many of these food restrictions appear to keep women from ingesting _____ (that plants contain for defensive purposes) that could harm the fetus.

      c. Women often find certain foods nauseating during pregnancy and will not eat those foods. This is called _____ _____.

      1. Such foods as coffee, alcohol and other bitter substances contain toxins and other substances that may _____ the developing embryo.

      2. Food aversions may also have _____ to protect the embryo and fetus from toxins.

    d. Our biology appears to include adaptations that improve the outcome of pregnancy, but we also reinforce these with _____ _____.

3. It has been suggested that the human _____ period should actually be 15 to 18 months rather than 9 months.

    a. Because the human brain is so large we need to be born at 9 months in order to pass through the narrow birth canal.

    b. An undeveloped brain may also be adaptive for other reasons.

      1. Most of our brain growth takes place in the presence of _____ stimuli.

      2. The language centers of the brain develop during the first _____ years of life.

        a. This is when the brain is undergoing _____ expansion.

        b. This may be particularly important for a species dependent on _____.

D. Birth

    1. Birth is challenging to many primates.

    2. Most primates are born _____ their mothers.

      a. This enables the mother to reach down and _____ the infant out of the birth canal.

      b. The human pelvis is designed for bipedalism.

1. As a result, the head of the human infant fits best against the relatively larger front of the mother's pelvis.

2. Consequently, human infants are born facing the _____ of the mother's birth canal.

3. This neonatal orientation requires that the mother reach _____ her to pull the infant from the birth canal.

c. The difficulty of human birth may explain why humans routinely seek _____ during birth rather than seeking isolation.

1. A survey of world cultures reveals that it is very unusual to give birth _____.

2. Having others present who can help guide the baby out of the birth canal, wipe its face to facilitate breathing, and keep the umbilical cord from choking it, can significantly reduce infant _____.

E. Infancy

1. Infancy is the period during which _____ takes place.

2. Nursing typically lasts _____ years.

a. _____ years is the norm for the great apes.

b. Four years is also the norm for women in _____ societies.

c. This, with other evidence, has led anthropologists to _____ that four years was the norm in the evolutionary past.

3. Nursing and breastmilk

a. Human milk is extremely low in fats and protein. This is _____ for a species in which mothers are seldom separated from their infants.

b. Prolonged and frequent nursing suppresses _____; which helps maintain a four-year birth interval.

c. Breastmilk also provides _____ that contribute to infant survival.

F. Childhood

1. Humans have an unusually _____ childhood.

   a. This reflects the importance of _____ for our species.

   b. During childhood the brain is completing its _____.

   c. Childhood is when the child is also acquiring technical and social _____.

2. Humans may be unique in _____ food for children or juveniles.

3. During childhood, besides the role of the mother, the roles of _____ and older _____ are also significant.

G. Adolescence

1. A number of biological events mark the transition from childhood to adolescence.

   a. _____ body size and _____ in body shape.

   b. Development of _____ and _____ in boys.

   c. Development of _____ in girls.

   d. _____ changes are the driving force behind these physical changes.

   e. _____ is a clear sign of puberty in girls and is usually the marker of the transition from childhood in cultures where this event is ritually celebrated.

2. Females reach sexual maturity _____ males do.

3. For girls, a certain amount of _____ _____ is necessary for menarche and the maintenance of ovulation.

   a. Both diet and activity levels affect the _____ of body fat.

   b. Because pregnancy and nursing require an _____ in calories, body fat may serve as a signal to the body that there is enough caloric reserve to support a pregnancy.

4. Adolescence is the period between puberty and the completion of physical growth. Individuals who have completed biological growth may be _____ _____ as adults from such social events as marriage.

H. Adulthood and aging

1. Pregnancy and child care occupy much of a woman's adult life in most cultures.

   a. When adult women are not pregnant or nursing they have monthly _____, which have two phases.

      1. During the follicular phase the egg is preparing for ovulation, marked by high _____ production.

      2. The luteal phase, during which the uterus is preparing for implantation, is marked by high _____ production.

      3. If a pregnancy does not occur, progesterone production _____ _____ and menstruation, the shedding of the uterine lining, occurs.

         a. A woman who never becomes pregnant may have as many as _____ cycles between menarche and menopause.

         b. This high number of menstrual cycles probably _____ _____ occur before the advent of reliable contraceptives.

         c. During the course of human evolution women may have had as few as _____ menstrual cycles over the course of their lives.

   b. In addition to caring for children, women in the majority of world cultures also participate in economic activities.

2. For women, _____ is a sign of entry into a new phases of the life cycle.

   a. Estrogen and progesterone production begin to _____ until ovulation and menstruation cease altogether.

      b. Throughout the course of human evolution, the majority of humans did not survive to age _____; therefore, few women lived much past menopause.

  3. Why do human females have such a long nonreproductive period? There are several ideas.

      a. Child-rearing theory

          1. It takes children from 12 to 15 years to become _____.

          2. It is suggested that women are biologically "programmed" to live 12 to 15 years beyond the _____ of their last children.

      b. Nonselection theory

          1. Another suggestion is that menopause itself is not the subject of _____ _____.

          2. Menopause is an artifact of the extension of the human _____ _____.

          3. It is further suggested that the maximum life span of the mammalian egg is _____ years (recall that all the ova a woman will ever have are already present at birth).

          4. This theory states that even though the human life span has been increased, the _____ life span has not.

  4. One of the major reasons that people are living longer today is because they are not dying from _____ _____.

  5. The final "phase" of the human life cycle is _____.

KEY TERMS

adolescent growth spurt: the period during adolescence when there is a rapid growth in stature.
anovulatory: menstrual cycle during which ovulation does not occur.
beriberi: disease resulting from a dietary deficiency of thiamine (vitamin B_1).
catch-up period: a period of time during which a child who has experienced delayed growth because of malnutrition, undernutrition, or disease can increase in height to the point of his or her genetic potential.

cretinism: mental and growth retardation in infants resulting from iodine deficiency in the mother during pregnancy.

development: differentiation of cells into different types of tissues and their maturation.

diaphysis: the shaft of a long bone.

distal: towards the end of a structure.

dizygotic twins: twins that are the result of two, almost simultaneously, fertilizations of two different eggs by two different sperm. In lay terms, fraternal twins.

essential amino acids: the eight (nine in infants) amino acids that must be obtained by humans from the diet.

fertility: production of offspring; distinguished from fecundity, which is the ability to produce children.

goiter: enlargement of the thyroid gland resulting from a dietary deficiency of iodine.

growth: increase in the mass or number of cells.

epiphysis (pl., -es): the end of a long bone.

lactation: production of milk in mammals.

malnutrition: a diet insufficient in quality (i. e., lacking some essential component) to support normal health.

monozygotic twins: two individuals that are the result of a cleavage of a single fertilize egg. These two individuals are genetically identical. In lay terms, identical twins.

ossification: process by which cartilage cells are broken down and replaced by bone cells.

proximal: the part of a structure that is closest to the point at which the structure attaches to the body.

scurvy: a disease resulting from a dietary deficiency of vitamin C.

sexual dimorphism: differences in physical characteristics between males and females.

undernutrition: a diet insufficient in quantity (calories) to support normal health.

Now take the Fill-in and Multiple Choice tests. Do not guess. Following completion of the tests, correct them. The correct answers and textbook page references are at the end of this study guide chapter. Note your strong areas and your weak areas to guide you in your continuing study.

FILL-IN QUESTIONS

1. Growth refers to an _____ in the mass or number of cells.

2. The differentiation of cells into different types of tissues, and their maturation, is the

   process of _____.

3. The process in which cartilage cells are replaced by bony tissue is called _____.

4. Cells which deposit new bony tissue are called _____.

5. Bones not only grow in length, but also width. This type of bone growth is called

   _____ growth.

6. The very pronounced increase in growth that occurs in humans at puberty is called the

_____ _____ _____ .

7. Males and females often differ in certain traits. For example, adult males tend to be larger, have beards and deeper voices. Adult females have breasts. These structural differences between the sexes is called _____ _____ .

8. The brain of a newborn human infant is limited in size because of _____ _____

_____ _____ ____ _____ _____ ___ ____ _____ .

9. _____ has an impact on human growth at every stage of the life cycle.

10. A woman's own supply of eggs develop while she is ____ _____ .

11. _____ are composed of amino acids.

12. The nutrient that is the main source of energy for the body is _____ .

13. Glucose provides energy for the body through its conversion into _____ in the mitochondria of the cell.

14. It is rare that a person develops a deficiency of any of the fat-soluble vitamins. This is because these vitamins can be _____ .

15. Higher primates are not able to synthesize vitamin ___ .

16. Most humans can **best** meet their protein needs from _____ products.

17. Insufficient calories, i.e. an inadequate amount of food, is called _____ .

18. Insufficient protein in the diet would fall into the category of _____ .

19. A disease that is caused by a deficiency of the vitamin thiamine, and is the fourth leading cause of death in the Philippines, is _____ .

20. The reason that many of the nutritional deficiency diseases of today were rare in the past was because of the great _____ of foods consumed by our ancestors.

21. The question of whether "nature or nurture" contributes to certain traits is one that scientists have attempted to answer for centuries. One insight to this question, however, is by studying _____ _____ that have been raised in different environments.

22. The structure in the brain, sometimes referred to as a "control center" that is involved with integrating and controlling hormonal action is the _____.

23. The hormone that regulates metabolism is _____.

24. Children tend to grow rapidly in times of _____ sunlight concentration.

25. Monkeys, apes, and humans have an added life cycle phase not found in other mammals, namely the _____ period.

26. The _____ of early pregnancy may function to limit the intake of foods potentially harmful to the embryo at a critical stage of development.

27. It has been suggested that the human gestation period is actually _____ than would be expected considering the infant's development.

28. The time between weaning and puberty in the human life cycle is _____.

29. Humans may be unique in providing food for _____.

30. The end of menstruation in women is called _____.

Multiple Choice Questions

1. An example of a cultural factor that has a strong influence on growth is
    A. an individual's skill as an artisan.
    B. marriage status.
    C. socioeconomic status.
    D. religious beliefs that require an individual to eat a particular species of animal.

2. If a culture values thinness in women, what could we expect to be a behavior among young girls?
    A. purging of food by the girl instigating vomiting
    B. constant dieting, sometimes to the point that it affects health
    C. eating as much food as a girl can manage without getting sick
    D. Both A and B are behaviors that we might expect.

3. An increase in cell mass, such as when a body builder increases the size of individual muscle fibers (cells), is called
    A. neotoma.
    B. sarcoplasm.
    C. hyperplasia.
    D. hypertrophy.

4. Which of the following statements is **not** correct?
    A. The "first" skeleton of the fetus is constructed of small bones which are referred to as models.
    B. The newborn infant has more than 600 centers of bone growth.
    C. By the time growth is complete, there are approximately 206 bones.
    D. Ossification refers to the replacement of cartilage by bone cells.

5. Growth in a long bone, such as the humerus, is complete when
    A. an individual reaches the age of 18.
    B. when an individual produces the first child.
    C. when the epiphyses unite with the diaphysis.
    D. when the osteoclasts have finished depositing new bone on the outer surface of the bone.

6. An archeologist has excavated a site which contains the skeleton of a child. Is there any way to tell how old this child was at the time of death?
    A. It is not possible to tell how old the child was.
    B. The child's age can be determined if any cultural artifacts, such as toys, were found in association with the skeleton.
    C. The growth pattern of the child's skeleton can give us a fairly good idea of the age at death.
    D. Children's skeletons can not be aged well; adult skeleton's have a fairly distinct growth pattern that can accurately tell an adult's age.

7. The shaft of a long bone is called the
    A. epiphysis.
    B. diaphysis.
    C. medullary cavity.
    D. epiphyseal disk.

8. Which of the following is a way that increases in height are typically plotted?
    A. growth spurt
    B. distance curve
    C. velocity curve
    D. Both B and C are correct.

9. Which of the following statements is correct?
    A. No other mammal shows the adolescent growth spurt to the degree that humans do.
    B. Chimpanzees do not show any growth spurt at all at puberty.
    C. Many mammals, such as carnivores and rodents, show an adolescent growth spurt similar to humans.
    D. Both A and B are correct.

10. At all ages, girls generally
    A. are taller than boys.
    B. grow later than boys.
    C. have more body fat than boys.
    D. have more hair than boys.

11. At birth the human brain is only ____ percent of its adult size.
    A. 25
    B. 50
    C. 90
    D. 95

12. Enzymes are
    A. carbohydrates.
    B. proteins.
    C. lipids.
    D. fats.

13. Why are essential amino acids called "essential?"
    A. because these are the only proteins that the human body produces
    B. because they must be produced when we are infants
    C. because they must be obtained from the diet
    D. because they cannot be absorbed in the gut

14. The only source of energy that is utilized by the brain is
    A. sucrose.
    B. sucrase.
    C. fructose.
    D. glucose.

15. ATP is produced in the mitochondria of cells through the citric acid (Krebs) cycle. Which of the following nutrients is **never** converted into ATP?
    A. carbohydrates
    B. lipids
    C. proteins
    D. calcium

16. Scurvy is a disease that is the result of insufficient amounts of
    A. vitamin C.
    B. calcium.
    C. iodine.
    D. vitamin D.

17. Which of the following illustrates how cultural processes interact with biological processes to produce successful adaptations in obtaining the complete complement of proteins?
    A. the habit of consuming black-eyed peas with cornbread in the southern United States
    B. the preference for eating cabbage with potatoes among some Irish populations
    C. consumption of rice among Vietnamese populations
    D. the avoidance of eating pork among Jewish and Muslim populations

18. The disease pellagra, symptoms of which include skin lesions and gastrointestinal disturbances, is caused by a deficiency of niacin. It is common where corn is a major part of the diet. The exception is in the Americas. Why?
    A. Vitamin C in the fruits of the Americas serves as a substitute for niacin.
    B. The habit of adding lime or ashes to cornmeal when cooking it increases the availability of niacin in the corn.
    C. The soil of the Americas is rich in niacin which is taken up through the roots of the corn plants. Soil in the rest of the world is poor in niacin.
    D. The people have adapted genetically to lower amounts of niacin in their diet.

19. Which of the following is **not** correct regarding the pre-agriculture human diet?
    A. high in protein
    B. high in complex carbohydrates
    C. high in fat
    D. high in fiber

20. Diabetes, once rare, is now common among people like the Pima of the American Southwest. The Pima used to live through times of food shortage, but now have a "feast" diet high in fats and sugar. A hypothesis that deals with this topic is the
    A. red queen hypothesis.
    B. thrifty genotype.
    C. broken stick model.
    D. Humpty Dumpty effect.

21. A child born to a malnourished mother is normally smaller and behind in most aspects of their physical development. This can be made up in accelerated growth during
    A. the adolescent growth spurt.
    B. velocity growth curve.
    C. lactation.
    D. the catch-up period.

22. Certain parts of the world have soil poor in iodine, which means that plants and animals in the diets of peoples in those regions are iodine poor. What disease might we expect to find in the adults of these regions?
    A. beriberi
    B. goiter
    C. kwashiorkor
    D. cretinism

23. Which of the following is **not** a hormone secreted by the pituitary gland?
    A. thyroxine
    B. growth hormone (GH)
    C. prolactin
    D. follicle stimulating hormone (FSH)

24. The life cycle phase that ends with birth is
    A. gestation.
    B. infancy.
    C. weaning.
    D. childhood.

25. The language centers of the brain
    A. are difficult to find.
    B. are well developed at birth.
    C. develop in the first three years of life.
    D. do not develop until puberty.

26. Human breastmilk
    A. has the same ratio of fat to protein as in all other mammals.
    B. has a nutrient content similar to that found in mammals that have to be separated from their infants while the mother forages.
    C. is almost identical to cow's milk.
    D. contains some of the mother's antibodies which help to protect the infant from some diseases.

27. There is some evidence that frequent nursing
    A. enables a woman to conceive more quickly after giving birth.
    B. suppresses ovulation.
    C. inhibits gestation.
    D. conserves the mother's energy.

28. A clear sign of puberty in girls is
    A. menarche.
    B. pregnancy.
    C. menopause.
    D. senescence.

29. For menarche to occur normally and for ovulation to be maintained,
    A. females must have high levels of circulating calcium.
    B. high levels of vitamin D must be stored in the liver.
    C. there must be a minimal amount of body fat.
    D. there must be high protein stores available.

30. Which of the following statements is **not** correct?
    A. A woman who never becomes pregnant may have as many as 400 menstrual cycles.
    B. During the course of human evolution, women may have had as few as 60 menstrual cycles during their lives.
    C. One theory regarding menopause is that menopause is simply not the subject of natural selection and is simply an artifact of the increase in human life span.
    D. If, in a particular month, the egg is not fertilized, it is resorbed into the uterine lining and menstruation does not occur.

ANSWERS TO FILL-IN OUTLINE

I. FUNDAMENTALS OF GROWTH AND
   DEVELOPMENT
   A. different
      1. growth
         a. hyperplasia
         b. hypertrophy
      2. development
   B. 1. cartilage
      2. a. diaphysis
            1. epiphyses
            2. unite (or fuse)
         b. two
            1. osteoclasts
            2. osteoblasts
         c. appositional
            1. inner
            2. outer
         d. predictable
            1. age
   C. 1. health
      2. a. 1. distance
            2. velocity
         b. infancy
         c. adolescent growth spurt
         d. human growth
            1. chimpanzees
            2. humans
      3. different
         a. sexual dimorphism
         b. two
            1. larger
            2. body fat
   D. 1. large
         a. greater
            1. 25
            2. 50
            3. five
            4. ten
         b. exception
      2. unusual
         a. 50
         b. limit

II. NUTRITIONAL EFFECTS ON GROWTH AND
    DEVELOPMENT
    A. 1. nutrients
    B. five

1. amino acids
   a. proteins
   c. converted
2. energy
   a. 1. carbohydrates
      2. monosaccharides
      3. glucose
         a. primary
         b. only
   b. glycogen
      1. stored
      2. fat
      3. glycogen
3. a. lipids
   b. mitochondria
4. a. do not
   c. two
      1. water
         a. excreted
         b. stored
      2. soluble
         a. can
         b. slow
5. a. minerals
   b. calcium
C. 1. coevolved
   a. animal
   b. primates
   c. fruit
   d. nutritional
2. a. vitamin C
   b. synthesize (or manufacture or
      produce)
   c. primates
      1. leaves, fruit
      2. lost
         a. diet
         b. conserve
   d. scurvy
      1. pre-agricultural
      2. fresh
3. a. 20
   b. eight
      1. diet
      2. essential
      3. protein
         a. meat
         b. combining

4. constrained
   a. variety
   b. agriculture

D. 1. fats
    a. wild
    b. carbohydrates
  2. maladaptive
    a. fat
      1. scarcity
      2. abundance
    b. diabetes
      1. thrifty genotype
      2. shortage

E. 1. inadequate
    a. calories
    b. 16, 63
  2. key element
    a. protein
      1. kwashiorkor
      2. marasmus
    b. 1. malnourished
      2. physical development
        a. growth
        b. 1. catch-up
          2. critical
          3. never
    c. 1. vitamin
      2. mineral

III. OTHER FACTORS INFLUENCING GROWTH AND DEVELOPMENT
A. 1. genetic potential
    a. genetics
    b. environment
  2. twins
    a. 1. monozygotic
      2. 100
    b. 1. dizygotic
      2. 50
    c. primary
      1. stature
      2. weight

B. 1. another cell
  2. growth
  3. stimulating
    a. inhibit
    b. pituitary
      1. anterior
      2. posterior

4. thyroxine
   a. regulates
   b. low
     1. hypothalamus
     2. release
     3. thyroxine
     4. inhibit

C. 1. growth, development
  2. nutrition
    a. lower
    b. heavier
    c. sunlight

IV. THE HUMAN LIFE CYCLE
A. life cycle
  1. gestation
  2. infancy
  3. childhood
  4. adolescence
  5. adulthood
  6. menopause

B. cultural
  1. phases
  2. growth, development

C. 1. a. fertilizes
    b. zygote
    c. mature
  2. a. restrictions
    b. toxins
    c. food aversion
      1. harm
      2. evolved
    d. cultural restrictions
  3. gestation
    b. 1. environmental
      2. three
        a. rapid
        b. language

D. 2. facing
    a. guide
    b. 2. back
      3. behind
    c. assistance
      1. alone
      2. mortality

E. 1. nursing
  2. four
    a. four
    b. foraging
    c. conclude

3. a. typical
    b. ovulation
    c. antibodies
F. 1. long
    a. learning
    b. growth
    c. skills
    2. providing
    3. fathers, siblings
G. 1. a. increased, change
    b. testes, penes
    c. breasts
    d. hormonal
    e. menarche
    2. before
    3. body fat
    a. accumulation
    b. increase
    4. socially recognized

H. 1. a. menstruations
        1. estrogen
        2. progesterone
        3. drops off
            a. 400
            b. did not
            c. 60
    2. menopause
        a. decline
        b. 50
    3. a. 1. independent
            2. birth
        b. 1. natural selection
            2. life span
        3. 50
        4. reproductive
    4. infectious diseases
    5. death

ANSWERS & REFERENCES TO FILL-IN QUESTIONS

1. increase, p. 156
2. development, p. 156
3. ossification, p. 157
4. osteoblasts, p. 157
5. appositional, p. 158
6. adolescent growth spurt, p. 159
7. sexual dimorphism, p. 159
8. the narrow birth canal of the pelvis of the mother, p. 160
9. diet, p. 160
10. in utero, p. 161
11. proteins, p. 161
12. carbohydrates, p. 161
13. ATP, p. 162
14. stored, p. 162
15. C, p. 163
16. animal, p. 163
17. undernutrition, p. 168
18. malnutrition, p. 168
19. beriberi, p. 168
20. variety, p. 169
21. monozygotic twins, p. 169
22. hypothalamus, pp. 169-170
23. thyroxine, p. 170
24. high, p. 171
25. subadult (or, more commonly for humans, adolescence), p. 172
26. nausea, p. 173
27. shorter, p. 173
28. childhood, p. 176
29. children, p. 177
30. menopause, p. 178

ANSWERS & REFERENCES TO MULTIPLE CHOICE QUESTIONS

1. C, p. 156
2. D, indeed both of these behaviors (bulimia and anorexia nervosa, respectively) are serious problems within our own society which presents very thin women as the ideal, p. 156
3. D, p. 156
4. A, most of the fetal skeleton starts out cartilage, with cartilaginous bones in the shapes, or models, of the bones that they will become, p. 157. Answer C may seem confusing, but there is variation in the number of bones of the normal human skeleton. Some people may have extra skull bones and some people have dermal bones, bones which develop in the skin, usually near joints. These bones are also called sesamoid bones.
5. C, p. 157. If you answered D you mistook osteoclasts for osteoblasts. Osteoclasts resorb bone, they do not deposit it.
6. C, p. 158
7. D, p. 157
8. D, p. 159
9. A, p. 159
10. C, p. 159
11. A, p. 159
12. B, p. 161
13. C, these amino acids are essential because we cannot produce them ourselves. If we do not obtain them from our diets our health suffers, p. 163.
14. D, p. 162
15. D, pp. 161-162
16. A, p. 163
17. A, p. 164
18. B, pp. 164-165
19. C, p. 165
20. B, p. 165
21. D, p. 168
22. B, if you answered D note that cretinism is expressed as mental retardation in infants, p. 168
23. A, p. 170, Table 7-7, p. 171
24. A, p. 173
25. C, p. 173
26. D, p. 176
27. B, p. 176
28. A, p. 177
29. C, p. 177
30. D, p. 178

CHAPTER 8

MACROEVOLUTION:
OVERVIEW AND PRINCIPLES

LEARNING OBJECTIVES

After reading this chapter you should be able to:
- recognize the place of humans in nature. (p. 186)
- understand the ways in which evolutionary biologists deduce relationships between organisms. (pp. 186-188)
- use the classification chart of animal taxonomy. (pp. 187-189)
- recount the major events of vertebrate evolution. (pp. 190-192)
- discuss continental drift and its impact on evolution. (p. 191)
- list the major adaptive complexes of mammals. (pp. 192-195)
- distinguish the three major mammalian groups and be able to discuss their reproductive differences. (pp. 195-198)
- compare and contrast modes of evolutionary change. (pp. 198-200)
- discuss the concept of "deep time." (pp. 202-203)

FILL-IN OUTLINE

Introduction

In the preceding chapters the genetic mechanisms that are the foundation of the evolutionary process were surveyed. Chapters 5 and 6 explained how *microevolutionary* changes are investigated in contemporary human populations. In this chapter the process of macroevolution is studied. A synopsis of the key innovations in vertebrate, and particularly mammalian, evolution is examined over the great depth of time of these major groups. The basics of geological history, principles of classification, and modes of evolution will serve as a basis for topics covered throughout the remainder of the text.

I. THE HUMAN PLACE IN THE ORGANIC WORLD

A. Considering both living and extinct organisms, the amount of biological

_____ is staggering.

   1. In order to understand this diversity biologists have constructed a

_____ system.

   2. The classificatory system that biologists have devised organizes life into convenient

groupings.

     a. This helps to _____ the complexity.

     b. These groupings indicate _____ relationships.

B. All life on earth is part of an organic continuum.

   1. From the beginnings of life, more than 4 billion years ago, all life-forms have

shared in a common _____.

   2. All organisms fall *somewhere* on the continuum.

     a. _____, like all other organisms, are placed on this continuous

framework.

     b. Biologists have judged which organisms are evolutionarily _____

to humans and which ones are more distant.

C. The place of humans in nature

   1. Humans belong to a broad group of organisms that move about and ingest food

which are called _____ .

   2. Humans belong to the group of animals that are multicelled, the _____.

   3. Within the metazoa humans belong to the phylum _____, animals

that possess

     a. A _____ , a stiff supporting rod along the back.

     b. Pharyngeal _____ slits (at some stage of development).

4. Within the chordates, humans belong to the _____.

   a. These animals are characterized by a _____ _____.

   b. Vertebrates have a well-developed _____.

   c. Additionally, vertebrates have _____ sensory structures for sight, smell, and balance.

5. _____ are divided into six classes: bony fishes, cartilaginous fishes, amphibians, reptiles, birds and mammals.

II. TAXONOMY

A. The field that specializes in delineating the rules of classification is _____.

   1. One of the criteria for classifying organisms is _____ similarities.

   2. The crucial criteria for classification, however, is evolutionary _____.

B. Taxonomic concepts

   1. Structures that are shared through descent from a common ancestor are called

      _____.

   2. Structures in organisms that are used for the same function, but are not the result of common descent, are called _____.

   3. Traits that reflect the ancestral condition of the organisms being studied are said to be _____ (or ancestral).

   4. Traits that are shared by all members of a group, but not present before the group's appearance, are said to be shared _____ characteristics.

III. TIME SCALE

A. In addition to the vast array of life, evolutionary biologists must also contend with vast periods of time.

B. Geologists have formulated the geological _____ _____.

   1. This organizes time into hierarchies.

   2. Very large _____ spans are subdivided into eras, periods, and epochs.

IV. VERTEBRATE EVOLUTIONARY HISTORY

A. There are three geological eras: the Paleozoic, Mesozoic, and Cenozoic.

B. The first vertebrates

    1. The earliest vertebrates are present in the _____ record early in the Paleozoic, around 500 m.y.a.

    2. Later in the Paleozoic, several varieties of _____, _____, and _____ appeared.

    3. At the end of the Paleozoic (c. 250 m.y.a.) several types of mammal-like reptiles are present, probably including the ancestor of modern _____ .

C. Continental drift

    1. The evolutionary history of vertebrates was profoundly influenced by _____ events.

    2. The positions of the earth's _____ have dramatically shifted during the last several hundred million years.

       a. This process is called _____ _____ .

       b. Continental drift is explained by the theory of _____ _____ which posits that the earth's crust is a series of gigantic and colliding plates.

    3. In the late Paleozoic, the earth's continents constituted a _____ land mass, the colossal continent Pangea.

       a. In the early Mesozoic, Pangea began to break up forming a southern "super-continent" _____ (consisting of modern South America, Africa, Antarctica, Australia, and India).

       b. The northern continent was called _____, consisting of North America, Europe, and Asia.

       c. By the end of the Mesozoic (c. 65 m.y.a.), the continents were beginning to assume their current positions.

4. The evolutionary ramifications of continent drift were profound. Groups of land animals became geographically _____ from one another.

D. The Mesozoic

1. The reptiles underwent an adaptive radiation, a rapid expansion marked by _____ of many new species.

2. The first mammals are known from fossil traces early in the _____.

3. The _____ mammals do not appear until late in the Mesozoic, around 70 m.y.a.

E. The Cenozoic

1. The Cenozoic is divided into two periods.

   a. The _____ lasted for about 63 million years.

   b. The Quaternary begins 1.8 m.y.a. and continues to the _____.

2. To be more precise, paleontologists usually refer to the seven _____ of the Cenozoic.

V. MAMMALIAN EVOLUTION

A. After the dinosaur extinctions mammals underwent an adaptive _____.

1. The major lineages of all modern _____ arose from this Cenozoic adaptive radiation.

2. Mammals and birds _____ reptiles as the dominant terrestrial vertebrates.

B. Factors contributing to the mammalian success

1. The _____ of the mammalian brain expanded

   a. In particular the _____, which controls higher brain functions, came to comprise the majority of brain volume.

   b. The _____ in brain size led to a greater ability to learn and a general flexibility of behavior in mammals.

2. An efficient mode of prenatal internal _____ is found among the mammals.

   a. This is associated with the need for the longer development of the larger _____.

   b. Mammals are viviparous, i.e. they give birth to _____ young.

3. Mammals have specialized teeth, a condition called heterodonty.

   a. Mammals have four basic type of teeth that are _____ differently to perform different functions.

      1. Incisors are used for _____.

      2. _____ function in grasping and piercing.

      3. Premolars and molars are used for _____ and _____ .

   b. A dental formula is used by mammalogists to identify the type and number of teeth in different mammal species.

   c. Teeth are particularly important in paleontology because there is a disproportionate representation of teeth in the fossil record. (Teeth are the hardest substance in the body.)

4. Mammals are homeothermic; this means that mammals are able to regulate their body _____ and maintain a constant body temperature.

   a. Associated with homeothermy is _____, the ability to generate body heat by muscle action.

   b. Homeothermy and endothermy allows mammals to be active during colder times of the 24-hour day and during the year.

VI. MAJOR MAMMALIAN GROUPS

A. There are _____ major subgroups of living mammals: monotremes, marsupials, and placental mammals.

B. Monotremes are _____ -laying and are extremely primitive; there are only two types existing today.

C. Marsupials

   1. The young are born extremely _____.

   2. The young complete birth in an external _____.

D. Placentals mammals

   1. The placenta is a structure that prevents the mother's immune system from _____ the fetus.

   2. The longer _____ period allows the central nervous system to develop more completely in the fetus

   3. Mammals also have the "bond of _____" between the mother and the offspring.

     a. This period of association between the mother and the offspring provides for a wider range of _____ stimuli.

     b. It is not sufficient that the young mammal has a brain capable of learning; the mammalian _____ systems have provided it with ample learning opportunities.

VII. MODES OF EVOLUTIONARY CHANGE

A. The major evolutionary factor underlying _____ change is speciation.

B. The way new species are produced involves some form of _____

   1. Geographical isolation

     a. Involves some isolating factor such as a geographical _____ or great distance

     b. Members of a single species that become geographical isolated cannot exchange _____

        1. Over time isolation leads to genetic _____ accumulating in populations that have been separated.

        2. Genetic drift will cause _____ frequencies to change in both populations.

        3. Because drift is _____ the effects should not be the same in both populations.

        4. If the populations are inhabiting different environments _____ _____ will cause them to have even more genetic differences.

     c. The end result of geographical isolation will be two populations that can no longer _____.

  2. Behavioral _____ can work in maintaining the genetic differences of two new species even if they come back into contact again.

     a. Behavioral isolation includes differences in behaviors between closely related species.

     b. Behavioral isolation has been well demonstrated in the courtship behavior of birds.

C. The consensus has been that _____ evolution is explained by microevolutionary changes accumulated into macroevolutionary changes. This is now being challenged.

D. Gradualism versus punctuated equilibrium

  1. The traditional view of evolution, as put forth by Darwin, is called _____ _____.

    a. According to gradualism, evolution works by gradual _____ accumulating.

    b. There should be a series of intermediate, or _____, forms in any line.

    c. The reason that such forms are rarely found is attributed to the incompleteness of the _____ record.

2. The concept of punctuated equilibrium challenges the idea of gradualism.

    a. _____ _____ posits that species may persist for long periods with little or no change.

       1. This period of "stasis" comes to an end with a "spurt" of _____.

       2. This uneven, nongradual process of long stasis and quick _____ is called punctuated equilibrium.

    b. Punctuated equilibrium does not challenge that evolution has occurred; it challenges the "_____" and "_____" of gradualist evolution.

       1. Rather than long periods of gradual change, this alternate view postulates long periods of _____ change, punctuated only occasionally by sudden bursts of speciation.

       2. Rather than gradual accumulation of small changes (microevolution) in a single lineage, an additional evolutionary mechanism, _____ speciation, directs macroevolution in a way quite distinct from gradualism.

       3. Speciation events and the longevity of these transitional species are so _____ that they are not preserved in the fossil record.

KEY TERMS

adaptive radiation: the rapid expansion and diversification of an evolving group of organisms adapting to a variety of new niches.

analogies: similarities between organisms based strictly on common function with no assumed descent from a common ancestor; e. g. the wings of an insect and the wings of a bat.

cerebrum: the outer portions of the brain.

Chordata (Chordates): the phylum of the animal kingdom that includes the vertebrates.

cladistics: an approach to taxonomy that groups taxa based on shared derived characteristics.

continental drift: the movement of continents on sliding plates of the earth's surface. This has resulted in dramatic movement of the earth's land masses over time.

convergent evolution: the evolutionary process in which two unrelated, or only distantly related, organisms evolve similar structures in adapting to similar environments.

derived trait: referring to a character that reflects specialization within a lineage and is more informative about the evolutionary relationship between organisms.

ecological niche: the positions of species within their physical and biological environment.

endothermy: production of heat within the animal by means of metabolic processes within the cell (mainly muscle cells). Birds and mammals are the endothermic animals.

geological time scale: the organization of earth history into eras, periods, and epochs.

Gondwanaland: the southern continents that broke off of Pangea. Gondwanaland (AKA Gondwana) included South America, Africa, Antarctica, Australia, and India).

heterodonty: the condition in which there are different kinds of teeth specialized for different functions.

homologies: similarities between organisms based on descent from a common ancestor, e. g., the bones in the wing of a bird and the bones in the arm of a human.

homeothermy: the ability to maintain a constant body temperature. Through physiological feedback mechanisms heat generated through endothermy is either dissipated or retained within the normal range of body temperature for the species.

Laurasia: the northernmost continents that had been part of Pangea. Laurasia included North America, Europe, and Asia.

Metazoa: the multicellular animals, a major division of the animal kingdom. The metazoa are all of the animals except the sponges.

neocortex: the outer layer of brain tissue of the cerebrum, which has expanded during the evolution of the vertebrates, particularly in primates, and most especially in humans. The neocortex is associated with higher mental functions.

parallel evolution: evolution along the same direction in two related lineages that have become separated.

Pangea: the supercontinent that included all of the present-day continents. Pangea began to break up in the early Mesozoic.

phyletic gradualism: the evolutionary concept, first postulated by Charles Darwin, that evolutionary change takes place slowly with slight modifications in each generation.

primitive trait: referring to a character that reflects the ancestral condition within a lineage.

punctuated equilibrium: the evolutionary concept that there are long periods, in the history of a species, in which no change takes place (stasis) followed by a quick spurt of evolutionary change (speciation).

shared derived trait: referring to a character shared in common by two forms and considered the most useful for making evolutionary interpretations.

speciation: the process by which new species are produced from earlier species. The most important mechanism of macroevolutionary change.
subphylum: the subphylum of the chordates characterized by animals with bony backbones. The vertebrates include the fishes, amphibians, reptiles, birds, and mammals.
viviparity: the reproductive process in which the young are born live.

Now take the Fill-in and Multiple Choice tests. Do not guess. Following completion of the tests, correct them. The correct answers and textbook page references are at the end of this study guide chapter. Note your strong areas and your weak areas to guide you in your continuing study.

FILL-IN QUESTIONS

1. From the beginnings of life, more than 4 billion years ago, all life-forms have shared in a

   _____ ancestor.

2. Animals that are characterized by a stiff, flexible rod running along their back and the

   presence of pharyngeal gill slit, at least at some time in their lives, belong to the phylum

   _____.

3. Fishes, amphibians, reptiles, birds, and mammals, animals with backbones, are all

   _____.

4. In order for similarities between organisms to be useful, they must reflect common

   _____ _____.

5. The taxonomic approach that emphasizes shared derived characteristics is called

   _____.

6. Amphibians, reptiles, birds, and mammals all have a very similar upper arm bone called

   the humerus. The humerus bones in these animals are said to be _____.

7. The earliest mammals had five digits per paw. Modern primates also have five digits per

   paw (hand). Five digits per paw is a _____ trait.

8. A useful tool for geologists and paleoanthropologists is the organization of earth history

   into eras, periods, and epochs. This organization is called the _____

   _____ _____.

9. The earliest vertebrates are present in the fossil record early in the _____, about 500 million years ago.

10. During the late Paleozoic, the earth's continents came together to from a "super-continent" called _____.

11. The diversification of many new species from a common stock that expand into new ecological niches is called a(n) _____ _____.

12. The geological era that we are living in today is the _____.

13. The evolution from generalized to specialized characteristics refers to the _____ _____ of a particular trait.

14. The position of a species within its physical and biological environment is that species' _____ _____.

15. Almost all mammals give birth to live young, a characteristic called _____.

16. Mammals have different types of teeth specialized for different functions. This characteristic of mammals is called _____ dentition.

17. The ability to produce internal heat from metabolic processes is referred to as _____.

18. The evolution of two animal lines that diverged from a common ancestor, yet continue to evolve along similar lines, is called _____ _____.

19. The major evolutionary factor underlying macroevolutionary change is _____.

20. The way that new species are first produced involves some form of _____.

21. Darwin described a type of evolution in which there should be a series of forms, many intermediate, between each ancestor and its descendant. This type of evolution is called _____ _____.

22. The mode of evolution which emphasizes a long period of stasis which is interrupted by a quick spurt of speciation is called _____ _____.

23. The way (or the how) that evolution actually works, whether by gradualism or punctuated events, is the _____ of evolution.

24. How quickly, or how slowly, evolution actually works, is the _____ of evolution.

25. The vast expanse of time that has passed on our planet since it first formed and during which evolution of the earth's life-forms has occurred is called _____ _____.

MULTIPLE CHOICE QUESTIONS

1. Humans are
    A. Animals.
    B. Parazoa.
    C. Metazoa.
    D. chordates.
    E. all of the previous except B.

2. The scientific discipline that delineates the rules of classification is
    A. paleontology.
    B. stratigraphy.
    C. homology.
    D. taxonomy.
    E. geology.

3. The primary basis for classifying organisms is similarities in
    A. physical structure.
    B. physiology.
    C. diet.
    D. ecology.
    E. analogies.

4. Bats have wings that allow them to fly. So do birds and insects. Similarities such as wings in different animals that have a common function
    A. does not mean a common ancestry.
    B. are called homologies.
    C. are called analogies.
    D. are derived traits.
    E. Both A and C are correct.

5. Humans and other apes have certain characteristics in common such as a broad sternum, a Y-5 cusp pattern on the molars, and the lack of a tail. These traits are all
    A. analogies.
    B. primitive traits.
    C. shared derived traits.
    D. general traits.
    E. ancestral traits.

6. Continental drift has affected the evolution of organisms by isolating breeding populations through
   A. water barriers.
   B. geographical barriers such as mountains.
   C. different behaviors.
   D. increasing the opportunities for gene flow.
   E. Both A and B are effects of continental drift on organisms.

7. Continental drift is explained by
   A. parallel evolution.
   B. The Big Bang.
   C. the Cenozoic.
   D. plate tectonics.
   E. Pangea.

8. In the early Mesozoic, Pangea broke into two large continents, Gondwana and Laurasia. Laurasia consisted of the present day continents of
   A. South America and Africa.
   B. South America, Africa, and Australia.
   C. South America, Africa, Australia, India, and Antarctica.
   D. North America and Europe.
   E. North America, Europe, and Asia.

9. The dominant terrestrial life forms of the Mesozoic were the
   A. crossopterygians.
   B. amphibians.
   C. reptiles.
   D. birds.
   E. mammals.

10. The reptiles underwent an adaptive radiation that is more properly termed an adaptive explosion. Which of the following was an evolutionary innovation that freed the reptiles from water and led to their adaptive radiation?
    A. a lung
    B. paired appendages
    C. a more efficient hard-shelled (amniotic) egg
    D. more efficient insulation for retaining heat
    E. limbs directly under the body providing for more efficient locomotion

11. The mammalian adaptive radiation occurred at the beginning of the
    A. Pre-Cambrian.
    B. Cambrian.
    C. Paleozoic.
    D. Mesozoic.
    E. Cenozoic.

12. Which of the following is **not** one of the mammalian innovations that has led to their success?
    A. ectothermy
    B. heterodonty
    C. viviparity
    D. homeothermy
    E. endothermy

13. Which of the following is **not** a correct statement?
    A. The surface convolutions of the mammalian brain creates more surface area.
    B. The neocortex controls higher brain functions.
    C. The mammalian brain stem has expanded greatly compared to the reptilian brain stem.
    D. The major lineages of modern mammals rise during the mammalian adaptive radiation of the early Cenozoic.
    E. The larger mammalian brain provides for greater flexibility of behavior.

14. An advantage of heterodont dentition is that it
    A. allows the animal to defend itself more efficiently.
    B. allows for processing a wide variety of foods.
    C. opens up new ways of interacting with potential mates.
    D. allows the animal to grab prey that it could not catch otherwise.
    E. Both A and C are correct.

15. The fossil material that is available for most vertebrates, including primates, are
    A. pelves.
    B. humerus and other arm bones.
    C. dermal ossicles.
    D. teeth.
    E. femurs, which are the largest bones in any vertebrate.

16. The group of mammals that reproduce by laying eggs and generally have more primitive traits than the other mammals are the
    A. monotremes.
    B. metatherians.
    C. marsupials.
    D. placentals.
    E. eutherians.

17. An important aspect of viviparity is a barrier that protects the fetal tissues from the mother's immune system. This barrier is the
    A. placenta.
    B. lymphatic system.
    C. hard-shelled egg.
    D. human lymphatic antigen.
    E. "bond of milk."

18. After birth a young mammal has a period of neural development coupled with learning. Some refer to this period of close association between the young mammal and its mother as the
    A. rehearsal period.
    B. placental connection.
    C. "park."
    D. biosocial perspective.
    E. "bond of milk."

19. The marsupials of Australia resemble, both physically and in lifestyle, the wolf, cat, flying squirrel, anteater, mole, and mouse. The evolutionary process that explains this is
    A. evolutionary constraints.
    B. convergent evolution.
    C. parallel evolution.
    D. contingent evolution.
    E. punctuated evolution.

20. There are two bird species on a midwestern prairie that look very much alike physically and are probably descended from a common ancestor. During courtship, however, the males of one species stand on one leg while looking at the female. The males of the second species use both feet to drum on the prairie floor. The females will only mate with those males who behave appropriately during courtship. This is an example of
    A. parallel evolution.
    B. convergent evolution.
    C. behavioral isolation.
    D. geographical isolation.
    E. Both A and B are correct.

21. The fossil record of many marine invertebrates shows long periods where there is very little change in the species. Then a new species appears without any transitional species. These observations best support the idea of
    A. convergent evolution.
    B. punctuated equilibrium.
    C. phyletic gradualism.
    D. small microevolutionary changes lead to transspecific evolution.
    E. the broken stick model.

22. The primate fossil record does **not** seem to support
    A. slow gradual change from ancestor to descendant.
    B. punctuated equilibrium.
    C. phyletic gradualism.
    D. small microevolutionary changes lead to transspecific evolution.
    E. Either B or D is correct.

23. According to Carl Sagan's "Cosmic Calendar" such events as the European Renaissance, the Ming Dynasty in China, and the development of the scientific method all occur
    A. September 25th.
    B. December 29th.
    C. at noon on December 31st.
    D. on the last second of December 31st.
    E. on the first second of the New Year.

ANSWERS TO FILL-IN OUTLINE

I. THE HUMAN PLACE IN THE ORGANIC WORLD
  A. diversity
    1. classification
    2. a. reduce
       b. evolutionary
  B. 1. ancestry
    2. a. humans
       b. closer
  C. 1. animals
    2. metazoa
    3. chordata
       a. notochord
       b. gill
    4. vertebrates
       a. vertebral column
       b. brain
       c. paired
    5. vertebrates

II. TAXONOMY
  A. taxonomy
    1. physical
    2. descent
  B. 1. homologies
    2. analogies
    3. primitive
    4. derived

III. TIME SCALE
  B. time scale
    2. time

IV. VERTEBRATE EVOLUTIONARY HISTORY
  B. 1. fossil
    2. fishes, amphibians, reptiles
    3. mammals
  C. 1. geographical
    2. continents
       a. continental drift
       b. plate tectonics
    3. single
       a. Gondwanaland
       b. Laurasia
    4. isolated
  D. 1. diversification
    2. Mesozoic
    3. placental

E. 1. a. tertiary
     b. present
   2. epochs

V. MAMMALIAN EVOLUTION
  A. radiation
    1. mammals
    2. replaced
  B. 1. cerebrum
       a. neocortex
       b. increase
    2. development
       a. brain
       b. live
    3. a. shaped
       1. cutting
       2. canines
       3. crushing, grinding
    4. temperature
       a. endothermy

VI. MAJOR MAMMALIAN GROUPS
  A. three
  B. egg
  C. 1. immature
    2. pouch
  D. 1. rejecting
    2. gestation
    3. milk
       a. learning
       b. social

VII. MODES OF EVOLUTIONARY CHANGE
  A. macroevolutionary
  B. isolation
    1. a. barrier
       b. genes
       1. differences
       2. allele
       3. random
       4. natural selection
       c. interbreed
    2. isolation
  C. transspecific
  D. 1. phyletic gradualism
       a. changes
       b. transitional
       c. fossil

2. a. punctuated equilibrium
    1. speciation
    2. spurts
    b. tempo, mode
    1. no
    2. accelerated
    3. short

ANSWERS & REFERENCES TO FILL-IN QUESTIONS

1. common, p. 186
2. Chordata, p. 186
3. vertebrates, p. 186
4. evolutionary descent, p. 187
5. cladistics, p. 188
6. homologies, p. 187, Fig. 8-1
7. primitive, p. 188
8. geological time scale, p. 188
9. Paleozoic, p. 190
10. Pangea, p. 191
11. adaptive radiation, p. 191; also see Box 8-1
12. Cenozoic, p. 191, also see Fig. 8-3, p. 190
13. adaptive potential, p. 193, Box 8-1
14. ecological niche, p. 191
15. viviparity, p. 194
16. heterodont , p. 194
17. endothermy, p. 195
18. parallel evolution, p. 196
19. speciation, p. 198
20. isolation, p. 198
21. phyletic gradualism, p. 199
22. punctuated equilibrium, p. 199
23. mode, p. 199
24. tempo, p. 199
25. deep time, p. 202

ANSWERS & REFERENCES TO MULTIPLE CHOICE QUESTIONS

1. E, the Parazoa are the sponges. This question could be figured out without knowing that, however, if you know that humans are animals, belong to the multicellular animals (Metazoa), and belong to the phylum Chordata, p. 186
2. D, p. 186
3. A, this has been the traditional method for classifying organisms. The recent molecular revolution in biology is already beginning to be applied to taxonomy and in the future organisms will most likely be classified by genetic structure, p. 187
4. E, p. 187
5. C, p. 188
6. E, p. 191
7. D, p. 191
8. E, p. 191, Fig. 8-4, p. 192
9. C, p. 191
10. C, p. 193, Box 8-1
11. E, p. 192
12. A, p. 195
13. C, p. 192
14. B, p. 195
15. D, p. 195
16. A, p. 195
17. A, p. 197
18. E, p. 197
19. B, p. 196, Box 8-2, Fig. 3
20. C, p. 199
21. B, p. 200
22. B, p. 200
23. D, p. 203

CHAPTER 9

AN OVERVIEW OF THE LIVING PRIMATES

LEARNING OBJECTIVES

After reading this chapter you should be able to:
- list and discuss primate evolutionary trends. (pp. 206-209)
- describe the influence of the arboreal environment on primate evolution. (pp. 209-212)
- compare and contrast the "arboreal hypothesis" with the "visual predation hypothesis." (p. 212)
- work out a dental formula. (p. 213, Box 9-2)
- describe the major forms of locomotion found among primates and be able to name one type of primate for each form of locomotion. (pp. 214-216)
- explain how taxonomic classification reflects biological relationships. (pp. 217-219)
- name, compare, and contrast the two major subdivisions of the primates. (pp. 219-222)
- name the major groupings of the anthropoids. (pp. 222-227)
- discuss the differences between New World monkeys and Old World monkeys. (pp. 222-226)
- name the two subdivisions of the Old World monkeys and the features that distinguish these two groups. (p. 225)
- explain why New World monkeys and Old World monkeys appear so similar. (p. 227)
- explain how monkeys and apes differ. (pp. 227-228)
- describe the major characteristics of the various apes that comprise the hominoids. (pp. 228-232)
- explain how new genetic technologies have been used to deduce evolutionary relationships among the hominoids. (pp. 233-234)

FILL-IN OUTLINE

Introduction

The preceding chapters have focused on the basic biological background for understanding human evolution. Now human evolution is dealt with in more detail. In order to understand any organism, it is important to have a frame of reference as to where that organism belongs—how it is similar and how it is different from other closely related organisms. This is done through a comparative approach. Because humans are primates, the organisms that are useful to study are the other 190 species in the Order Primates. This chapter examines the physical characteristics that define the primates, an overview of the living members of the order, and finishes with a discussion of the molecular techniques that are used to deduce evolutionary relationships between primate species.

I. PRIMATE EVOLUTIONARY TRENDS

A. What are evolutionary trends?

1. As mammals, primates _____ a number of traits in common with other

   mammals. These are called primitive, or generalized, traits. These include:

   a. fur, or, as it is referred to in humans, _____ _____.

   b. a relatively long gestation period followed by _____ birth.

   c. different types of specialized teeth, or _____.

   d. _____, the ability to maintain a constant body temperature

      through physiological mechanisms.

   e. _____ brain size.

   f. a great capacity for learning and behavioral _____.

2. As an order, primates have _____ many primitive mammalian traits

   and remain quite generalized.

   a. On the other hand, many other mammals have become increasingly

      _____.

      1. This leads to the modification of anatomical structures for the particular

         function that they become specialized for; e.g., the reduction of digits in

         horses.

2. Some mammals have specialized structures that are not found in any other mammalian group. An example is the four carnassial teeth found only in the order Carnivora.

b. Because primates are generalized mammals they cannot be _____ by one or two common traits.

   1. Primates are defined by _____ trends.

      a. Evolutionary _____ are traits that characterized the entire order to a greater or lesser degree.

      b. It is important to note that primate evolutionary trends are a set of _____ tendencies not equally expressed in all primate species.

   2. The evolutionary trends that have been traditionally used by primatologists are a combination of primitive mammalian traits and common primate specialized traits. These traits define the _____ Primates.

B. Limbs and locomotion

   1. Primates exhibit a tendency towards _____ _____, especially in the upper body, whether sitting, leaping, or standing.

   2. Primates possess a flexible, _____ limb structure which does not lock them into a specialized form of locomotion.

   3. Primate hands and feet possess a high degree of _____ (prehensility). Other features of the hands and feet include:

   a. retention of _____ digits on hand and feet.

   b. an opposable _____ and, in most species, a divergent and partially opposable great toe.

   c. primates possess _____ on at least some digits.

   d. primates have _____ pads enriched with sensory nerve fibers at the ends of digits which appear to enhance the sense of touch.

C. Diet and teeth

    1. Primates lack dietary _____ and tend to eat a wide variety of foods.

    2. Primates possess _____ dentition.

D. The senses and the brain

    1. All primates rely _____ on vision. Primate evolutionary trends in vision include

        a. _____ vision in all diurnal primates. Noctural primates lack color vision.

        b. Depth perception or _____ vision made possible by

            1. eyes positioned forward on the front of the face providing for _____ vision.

            2. Visual information from each eye is transmitted to the _____ centers in both hemispheres of the brain.

            3. Visual information is organized into _____-dimensional images by specialized structures in the brain itself.

    2. Primates have a _____ reliance on the sense of smell (olfaction).

    3. The primate brain has expanded in size and become increasingly _____.

E. Maturation, learning, and behavior

    1. Primates possess the mammalian characteristic of the placenta, which provides for a more efficient means of _____ nourishment. Primates are marked by _____ periods of gestation, _____ numbers of offspring, _____ maturation, and _____ of the entire life span.

    2. Primates exhibit a greater dependence on flexible, learned _____.

    3. Primates tend to live in social groups. Males are _____ members of many primate social groups, a situation unusual among mammals.

    4. Primates tend to be _____.

II. THE ARBOREAL ADAPTATION

A. _____ living was the most important factor in the evolution of the primates.

   1. Arboreal life selected for stereoscopic _____ in a three-dimensional environment.

   2. The primate grasping prehensile hand is adapted to _____ in the trees.

   3. The tropical arboreal environment provided a variety of foods which led to the primate omnivorous _____ and _____ dentition.

   4. Other challenges of the arboreal environment may have led to increased brain size and complexity as well as increased behavioral _____.

   5. This view that the arboreal environment was the major factor influencing primate evolution is called the _____ _____.

B. The visual predation hypothesis

   1. The _____ _____ hypothesis is an alternative to the arboreal hypothesis.

   2. This hypothesis states that primates may have first evolved in the _____ _____ _____.

      a. In this environment _____ - _____ close-set eyes enabled early primates to judge distance when grabbing for insects.

      b. Early primates would have to travel on small vertical limbs which _____ hands would enable them to do.

C. The visual predation and the arboreal hypotheses are not necessarily mutually exclusive explanations.

   1. Many primate features may have begun in _____ settings.

   2. Nevertheless, primates did move into the trees and, if they did have characteristics that evolved in another setting, they were "_____" for life in the trees.

III. THE LIVING PRIMATES

A. Habitats

1. Most living nonhuman primates live in the _____ or semitropical areas of the New and Old Worlds.

2. Most primates are _____, living in forest or woodland habitats.

3. Some Old World monkeys have adapted to life on the _____.

4. Gorillas and chimpanzees spend considerable time on the _____.

5. However, no nonhuman primate is _____ to a fully terrestrial environment—all spend some time in the trees.

B. Teeth

1. Primates are generally _____ and this is reflected in their generalized dentition.

2. The primate generalized _____ enables these animals to process a wide variety of foods.

3. Although the majority of primate species emphasize some food items over others, most eat a combination of _____, _____, and _____.

   a. Some primates (baboons and chimpanzees) occasionally kill and eat small _____.

   b. Some primates, such as the colobine monkeys, are dietary specialists on _____.

C. Locomotion

1. Almost all primates are, to some degree, quadrupedal—using all _____ limbs in their locomotion.

   a. Many primates are able to employ more than one form of locomotion, a product of their generalized _____ structure.

    b. The majority of quadrupedal primates are arboreal, but _____ quadrupedalism is also fairly common.

    c. Limb ratios of quadrupeds differ.

        1. The limbs of terrestestrial quadrupeds are approximately of _____ length, with forelimbs being 90 percent as long as hind limbs.

        2. In arboreal quadrupeds, forelimbs are proportionately _____ and may only be 70-80 percent as long as hind limbs.

    d. Quadrupeds are also characterized by a relatively long and flexible lumbar _____ which positions the hind limbs well forward and enhances their ability to propel the animal forward.

2. Vertical clinging and leaping is found in many _____.

3. Brachiation (arm swinging) employs the forearms and is found among the _____.

    a. Only the small _____ and _____ of Southeast Asia use this form of locomotion exclusively.

    b. Brachiators are characterized by:

        1. arms _____ than legs.

        2. a short stable _____ spine.

        3. long _____ fingers.

        4. reduced _____ .

    c. Brachiator characteristics have been inherited by the great apes from their ancestors who were either brachiators or _____.

    d. Some monkeys that use a combination of leaping with some arm swinging are termed_____.

4. An aid to locomotion is a prehensile tail.

a. Among the primates, prehensile tails are found only among the _____

_____ _____.

b. A _____ tail is capable of wrapping around a branch and

supporting the animal's weight.

IV. PRIMATE CLASSIFICATION

A. Introduction

1. As discussed in previous chapters, organisms have been traditionally categorized

on the basis of _____ _____.

2. Recall that the major objective of modern classification is to show evolutionary

_____.

B. In taxonomic systems organisms are organized into increasingly _____

categories.

1. The highest level for the primates is the _____ .

2. Primates are subdivided into _____ large categories.

a. The _____ includes lemurs, lorises and, traditionally, tarsiers. By

grouping these primates together, an evolutionary statement is made—these

animals are _____ closely related to each other than they are to any of the

anthropoids.

b. The _____ include the monkeys, apes, and humans.

3. At each succeeding level, finer distinctions are made until the _____

level is reached.

4. In this manner, classifications not only organize diversity into categories, but

also illustrate evolutionary and genetic _____ between

species and groups of species.

C. Inherent shortcomings of the traditional method of classification: two cases

1. The place of tarsiers among the primates

    a. Tarsiers are highly derived and display several unique characteristics.

        1. Traditionally they have been classified as _____ because they possess a number of prosimian traits.

        2. However, they also share several traits with the _____.

        3. With regards to chromosomes, they are _____ from both groups.

    b. The problem of where to place tarsiers has resulted in a taxonomic scheme which replaces the traditional _____ with alternative suborders.

        1. Lemurs and lorises are placed in the suborder _____.

        2. The tarsiers and anthropoids are placed in the suborder _____.

2. The great apes

    a. Traditionally all four species of great apes (orangutans, gorillas, chimpanzees and bonobos) have been placed in the family _____.

        1. Genetic data suggests that the _____ relationships exist among the African apes (including humans, whose origins are African) with the orangutan, a very distant relative.

        2. These relationships limit the term pongid in evolutionary meaning because the members of this family represent two evolutionarily _____ groups.

        3. Another problem with the great ape classification is _____ data that shows that humans and chimpanzees have a closer relationship to each other than either does to any other great ape. It would be entirely appropriate to classify humans and chimps in the same family.

V. AN OVERVIEW OF CONTEMPORARY PRIMATES

    A. Prosimians

        1. Prosimians are the _____ primitive of the primates.

        2. Primitive characteristics include:

          a. Greater reliance on _____ compared to the other primates.

            1. This is reflected in the moist _____ at the end of the nose and the relatively long snout.

            2. Prosimians mark their territories with _____.

          b. Prosimians have more _____ placed eyes.

          c. The reproductive physiology, as well as the _____ gestation length and maturation periods, differ from the other primates.

          d. Many prosimians possess a dental specialization called the "dental comb."

            1. This structure is formed by forward-projecting lower _____ and _____.

            2. The dental comb is used in both feeding and _____ .

        3. Lemurs

          a. Lemurs are found only on the island of _____ and several other close by islands off the east coast of Africa.

            1. On Madagascar the lemurs _____ into numerous and varied ecological niches without competition from higher primates.

            2. Lemurs became _____ elsewhere in the world.

          b. Characteristics of lemurs

            1. Body size ranges from the small _____ _____ (5 inches in length, 2 ounces in weight) to the indri (over 2 feet, approximately 22 pounds).

            2. The _____ lemurs are diurnal and exploit a wide variety of vegetable foods ranging from fruit to leaves, buds, bark, and shoots.

3. Smaller lemurs are nocturnal and _____ (insect-feeding).

4. There is great variation in lemur behavior from species to species.

    a. Many forms are arboreal but some, such as the ring-tailed lemur, are more _____.

    b. Some arboreal forms are quadrupedal, while others, such as the sifaka, are _____ _____ and _____.

    c. Some species (e.g. ring-tailed lemurs and sifakas) live in _____ of up to 25 animals, which includes both males and females of all ages.

        1. Others, such as the indrii, live in _____ family units.

        2. Most of the nocturnal species are _____.

4. Lorises

  a. Lorises are very similar in appearance to lemurs.

  b. Lorises were able to survive in continental areas by adopting a nocturnal activity pattern. This enabled the lorises to avoid _____ with the more recently evolved monkeys.

  c. Loris species are found in tropical forests and woodlands of India, Sri Lanka, Southeast Asia, and Africa.

  d. A member of the loris family is the _____, or bushbaby, which is found in forests and woodlands of sub-Saharan Africa.

  e. Characteristics of lorises

    1. Locomotion

      a. _____ employ a slow cautious climbing form of quadrupedalism.

      b. _____ are active vertical clingers and leapers.

    2. Diet

      a. Some lorises are almost completely _____.

      b. Others supplement their diet with _____ of fruit, leaves, gums, and slugs.

      c. These animals frequently forage _____.

   3. Ranges _____ and females frequently form associations for foraging or in sharing the same sleeping nest ("dormitories").

5. Both lemurs and lorises represent the same general primate _____ _____.

      a. Vision is stereoscopic, but not to the extent found in anthropoids. Color vision exists in some diurnal species, but not in the _____ species.

      b. Nails are present, but not on all digits. Most have a "_____ _____" on the second toe.

      c. These animals have longer _____ spans compared to other similar-sized mammals. This is an important primate characteristic associated with longer developmental and learning periods.

B. Tarsiers

   1. Tarsiers are small nocturnal primates found in the islands of _____ _____.

   2. Tarsiers eat insects and small vertebrates which they catch by _____ from branches.

   3. The basic social pattern appears to be a family unit consisting of a _____ pair and their offspring.

   4. Tarsiers exhibit a combination of _____ traits not seen in other primates.

      a. _____ traits include small size, grooming claws, and an unfused mandible (lower jaw bone).

b. Traits shared with _____ include the lack of a rhinarium and orbits completely enclosed by bone. Biochemically tarsiers are also closer to the anthropoids.

C. Anthropoids

1. Anthropoid characteristics that distinguish them from prosimians include:

   a. generally _____ body size.

   b. larger _____ both in absolute size and in relation to body size.

   c. more _____ skull.

   d. complete rotation of the eyes to the front of the face to permit full _____ vision.

   e. _____ plate at the back of the eye orbit.

   f. no _____ (implying reduced reliance on the sense of smell).

   g. _____ parental care.

   h. _____ gestation and maturation periods.

   i. more mutual _____.

2. Monkeys represent about 70 percent of all primate species and are divided into two large groups: _____ _____ monkeys and _____ _____ monkeys.

   a. New World monkeys

      1. A characteristic that distinguishes the New World monkeys from the Old World monkeys is the shape of the _____.

         a. New World monkeys have widely flaring noses with nostrils that face to the _____. New World monkeys are placed in the infra-order Platyrrhini (flat-nosed).

         b. Old World monkeys have narrower noses with _____ facing nostrils. They are placed in the infraorder Catarrhini, which means "downward-facing nose."

2. New World monkeys are almost exclusively _____ .

3. Like Old World monkeys all species, with the exception of the owl monkey,

   are _____ .

4. The New World monkeys are divided into two families: the Callitrichidae

   and the Cebidae.

   a. The _____ are the small marmosets and the tamarins.

      1. The Callitrichids are considered to be the most _____

         monkeys.

         a. They retain _____ instead of nails. The claws assist these

            quadrupedal monkeys in squirrel-like climbing of vertical tree

            trunks.

         b. They give birth to _____ (a prosimian trait among

            primates) instead of single infant.

      2. Socially these monkeys live in family groups composed of either a

         mated pair, or a female and two adult males, plus the offspring.

         Males are heavily involved with _____ care.

   b. There are 30 different cebid species.

      1. _____ are larger than callitrichids.

      2. Diet varies with most eating a combination of fruit and leaves

         supplemented by insects.

      3. The locomotor pattern of most cebids is _____ .

         a. _____ monkeys are semibrachiators.

         b. Some possess _____ tails.

      4. Socially most cebids live in groups of both sexes and all ages, or as

         monogamous pairs with subadult offspring.

b. Old World monkeys

1. Old World monkeys are found from sub-Saharan Africa to the islands of Southeast Asia. Their habitats range from tropical forests to semiarid desert to even seasonally snow-covered areas in Japan and China.

2. General characteristics of Old World monkeys

   a. The locomotor pattern of most Old World monkeys is _____.

   b. They are primarily arboreal. However, some have adapted to life on the ground.

   c. Old World monkeys sit erect and associated with this posture are areas of hardened skin, _____ _____, that serve as sitting pads.

3. All of the Old World monkeys belong to one family, the Cercopithecidae, which is divided into two subfamilies, the cercopithecines and the colobines.

   a. Cercopithecines

      1. Cercopithecines are more _____ than the more specialized colobines.

         a. They have a more omnivorous diet.

         b. A dietary adaptation is the presence of _____ _____ which enables these monkeys to store food while foraging.

      2. Geographical distribution

         a. Most cercopithecines are found in _____.

         b. Several species of _____ are also found in Asia.

   b. Colobines

      1. These animals are dietary specialists on _____.

      2. Geographical distribution

a. The _____ monkeys are exclusively African.

b. Langurs are found in _____ and proboscis monkeys in Borneo.

4. Locomotor behavior is varied.

a. Guenons, macaques, and langurs are _____ quadrupeds.

b. Baboons, patas, and macaques are _____ quadrupeds.

c. _____ monkeys practice semibrachiation and leaping.

5. Many cercopithecine species show a marked difference in size or shape between the sexes. This is called _____ _____ and is particularly pronounced in baboons.

6. Females of several species exhibit pronounced cyclical changes of the external genitalia that advertise to the males that she is sexually receptive. This hormonally initiated period is called _____.

7. Several types of social organization characterize Old World monkeys.

a. Colobines tend to live in small groups that contain only one or two adult _____.

b. Savanna baboons and most macaques live in _____ groups containing adults of both sexes and offspring of all ages.

3. Parallel evolution

a. Despite several differences between New World and Old World monkeys, they nevertheless, are recognizable as monkeys.

b. Depending on the authority, New World and Old World monkeys have been separated from between _____ to _____ million years.

1. One scenario is that both groups evolved from separate _____ ancestors.

2. Current consensus is that both groups evolved from a common _____ ancestor in Africa. New World monkeys would have reached South America, then an island continent, by "rafting."

    a. "_____" is the dispersal of organisms on chunks of land that have broken off from mainland areas and float with currents to another mainland area. These "floating islands," with their biological communities, are still seen today.

    b. At the time that the ancestors of New World monkeys would have rafted to South America, it was in _____ proximity to Africa than it is today. (Recall continental drift from chapter 8).

  c. The evolutionary principle that explains the similarities between New World and Old World monkeys is _____ _____.

    1. Parallel evolution results from geographically distinct populations responding to similar _____ pressures.

    2. Parallel evolution occurs in species that are related, albeit distantly related.

D. Hominoids

  1. The superfamily _____ includes the "lesser" apes (family Hylobatidae, gibbons and siamangs), the great apes (family Pongidae), and the humans (family Hominidae).

  2. Hominoid characteristics that distinguish them from monkeys include:

    a. _____ body size (gibbons and siamangs are exceptions).

    b. absence of a _____.

    c. _____ trunk (lumbar area relatively shorter and more stable).

    d. differences in position and musculature of the _____ joint (adapted for suspensory locomotion).

    e. more _____ behavior.

f. more complex _____ and enhanced _____ abilities.

g. _____ period of infant development and dependency.

3. Gibbons and siamangs

   a. Gibbons and siamangs are found in the _____ areas of southeast Asia.

   b. They are the _____ of the apes—gibbons weigh 13 pounds and siamangs 25 pounds.

   c. Gibbons and siamangs have anatomical features adapted for brachiation. These include:

      1. extremely long _____.

      2. _____ fingers.

      3. _____ thumbs.

      4. powerful _____ muscles.

   d. The highly specialized locomotor adaptations may be related to _____ behavior while hanging beneath branches.

   e. Diet is composed largely of _____ with supplements of leaves, flowers, and insects.

   f. The basic social unit is a _____ pair with their dependent offspring.

      1. _____ are very involved with the rearing of the offspring.

      2. The mated pair are territorial and delineate their territories with elaborate siren-like whoops and "_____."

4. Orangutans (*Pongo pygmaeus*)

   a. Orangutans are found only in heavily forested areas of Borneo and Sumatra.

   b. They are slow, cautious _____.

      1. They are almost completely _____.

      2. They do sometimes travel quadrupedally on the ground.

    c. They are large animals (males = 200 pounds, females = 100 pounds) with

       pronounced _____ _____.

    d. Socially these animals are _____.

    e. They are principally _____ (fruit-eating).

5. Gorillas (*Gorilla gorilla*)

    a. Gorillas are the _____ of the living primates and are confined to

       forested regions of central Africa.

    b. Gorillas exhibit marked sexual dimorphism, males can weigh up to 400 pounds,

       females 200 pounds.

    c. Because of their large size gorillas are primarily terrestrial employing a semi-

       quadrupedal posture called _____ - _____.

    d. Gorillas live in _____ groups.

6. Chimpanzees (*Pan troglodytes*)

    a. Chimpanzees are found in equatorial _____.

    b. Chimpanzees anatomically resemble gorillas in many ways particularly in

       _____ proportions and _____ - _____ shape.

       1. This similarity is due to their mode of terrestrial locomotion, viz.

         _____ - _____.

       2. Due to the similar anatomy many authorities consider chimps and gorillas

         to be members of a single _____.

       3. The _____ adaptations of chimps and gorillas differ with

         chimps spending more time in the trees.

    c. In size chimps are _____ than orangutans and gorillas; although they

       are also sexually dimorphic, it is not to the degree seen in the orangutans and

       gorillas.

d. _____ includes quadrupedal knuckle-walking on the ground and brachiation (especially among younger chimps) in the trees.

e. Chimpanzees are _____.

   1. They eat a large variety of both plant and animal foods.

   2. Chimps _____ and the hunting parties include both males and females.

     a. Chimps kill and eat young monkeys, bushpigs, and antelope.

     b. Prey is _____ among the group members.

f. Chimpanzees live in large, _____ communities of as many as 50 individuals.

   1. The core of the community are bonded _____ who never leave the group they were born into.

   2. Chimp communities are fluid (individuals come and go) and consist of animals who occupy a particular territory, but the individual members are usually dispersed into small foraging parties.

   3. _____ frequently forage alone or in the company of their offspring.

   4. Females may leave the community either permanently or temporarily while in estrus. This latter behavior reduces the risk of mating with _____ relatives (recall that males do not leave their birth group).

7. Bonobos (*Pan paniscus*)

a. _____ are another species of *Pan* and are only found in an area south of the Zaire River in Zaire.

b. Bonobos are the _____ studied of the great apes and their population is believed to number only a few thousand individuals.

c. Bonobos differ from chimpanzees in several features.

   1. A more linear body build with _____ legs relative to arms.

   2. A relatively smaller head, a dark face from birth, and tufts of hair at the side of the face.

d. Behavior

1. Bonobos are more _____ than chimpanzees.

2. Bonobos are less _____ among themselves.

3. Like chimps they live in _____ communities.

4. Bonobos exploit many of the same foods as chimps, including occasional _____ from killed small mammals.

5. Among bobonos it is _____ - _____ bonds that constitute the societal core. This may be due to bonobo sexuality in which copulations are frequent and occur throughout the female's estrous cycle.

8. Humans (*Homo sapiens*)

a. Humans represent the only living species belonging to the family _____.

b. The primate heritage of humans is shown in a number of features including:

1. dependence on _____ for orientation to the world.

2. lack of reliance on _____ cues.

3. flexible limbs and _____ hands.

4. development of the cerebral cortex and reliance on learned behavior, elaborations on long-established primate _____.

c. Several features distinguish humans from other primates, the most distinctive of which is _____ locomotion.

1. Bipedal locomotion has required significant structural _____ of the pelvis and the limbs.

2. We are able to identify a fossil specimen as a hominid when modifications for _____ are present.

VI. PRIMATE CHROMOSOMES, PROTEINS, AND DNA

A. The goal of taxonomy and systematics is to identify biological and evolutionary

relationships between groups of organisms.

1. Recall that traditionally this has been done using _____

   comparisons.

   a. The drawback to using morphology is that similar anatomies may evolve due

      to _____ evolution, confusing relationships between organisms.

   b. To achieve the goal of establishing evolutionary relationships, classificatory

      schemes must be based on _____, the traits that species

      share because they are inherited from a common ancestor.

2. Emerging genetic technologies provide the means to compare DNA and DNA

   products directly.

   a. If two species share similar DNA it must be assumed that this DNA represents

      descent from a _____ ancestor.

   b. DNA analysis provides us with _____ indicators of homologies.

B. Karyotype comparisons

1. One way to make genetic comparisons between species is through _____

   analysis.

   a. This involves identifying similarities and differences in _____

      shape, size, number, and banding patterns.

   b. The more closely two species are related, the more similar their _____

      should be.

2. Hominoid karyotype comparisons

   a. _____ and _____ are the most distinctive among the

      hominoids, indicating that they diverged early from the other hominoids.

b. Among the great apes the _____ karyotype is the most conserva-tive with the human and African ape karyotypes most derived, yet uniform.

c. Comparisons of banding patterns between humans and chimps suggest that human chromosome 2 is a _____ of two smaller chromosomes found in the chimp karyotype.

d. There is some debate regarding the evolutionary relationships between humans and the African apes.

   1. One scenario suggests that humans and chimpanzees share a more _____ ancestry after separating from the gorilla.

   2. Another view posits humans separating from the African ape lineages, which then diverged into the chimp-bonobo lineage and the gorilla lineage.

C. Amino acid sequencing

   1. The _____ of amino acids that comprise specific proteins can be examined for comparative purposes.

   2. Amino acid sequencing of human and Africa ape _____ show remarkable similarities.

D. DNA hybridization

   1. DNA _____ is a technique in which a single strand of DNA from two separate species are combined to form a hybrid DNA molecule.

   2. The genetic similarity of the two species is calculated by measuring the number of _____base pairs along the hybrid DNA sequences.

   3. DNA hybridization, like other genetic techniques, has reaffirmed most of the basic tenets of primate classification.

      a. DNA hybridization shows how _____ genetically humans and the African apes are.

      b. It shows that among the hominoids, the human and _____

lineages were the last to share a common ancestor; i.e., humans and chimps (including bonobos) are more closely related to each other than either is to the gorilla.

KEY TERMS

adaptive niche: the entire way of life of an organism: where it lives, what it eats, how it obtains food, etc.

amino acid sequencing: a molecular technique in which amino acid sequences in proteins are mapped. They can then be compared between species in order to deduce evolutionary relationships.

anthropoid: any of the members of the primate suborder Anthropoidea. This suborder includes the monkeys, apes, and humans.

arboreal: living in the trees.

arboreal hypothesis: the view that primate characteristics, such as stereoscopic vision and grasping hands, are the result of evolutionary adaptation to arboreal habitats.

auditory bulla: a bony structure surrounding the middle-ear cavity that is partially formed from the temporal bone.

binocular vision: vision that results from forward facing eyes, hence overlapping visual fields. Binocular vision is a requirement for stereoscopic vision.

brachiation: a form of suspensory locomotion involving arm swinging. Found mainly among the apes.

Callitrichidae: the family of New World monkeys that consists of the small marmosets and tamarins.

Cebidae: the family of New World monkeys that includes the capuchin, howler, squirrel, and spider monkeys. These monkeys are usually larger than the callitrichids.

Cercopithecidae: the one taxonomic family of the Old World monkeys.

cercopithecinae (cercopithecines): the subfamily of Old World monkeys that includes the baboons, macaques, vervets, and guenons.

colobinae (colobines): the subfamily of Old World monkeys that have evolved anatomical specializations in their teeth and in a large sacculated stomach for consuming a diet of leaves.

cusps: the elevated portions (bumps) on the chewing surfaces of premolar and molar teeth.

derived: refers to specialization found within a particular evolutionary lineage.

diurnal: active during the day.

DNA hybridization: a molecular technique in which two single strands of DNA from two different species are combined to form a hybrid molecule of DNA. Evolutionary relationships can be deduced from the number of mismatched base pairs between the two strands of DNA.

estrus: period of sexual receptivity in female mammals (except humans) correlated, with ovulation. When used as an adjective, the word is spelled "estrous."

evolutionary trends: overall characteristics of an evolving lineage, such as the primates. Such trends are useful in helping to categorize the lineage as compared to other lineages.

frugivory, -ous: a diet that consists mainly of fruit.

ischial callosities: a pad of callused skin over the bone of the ischial tuberosity (a part of the pelvic bone) that serves as a sitting pad in Old World monkeys and gibbons.

morphology: the form (size, shape) of anatomical structures. This can include the entire organism.

nocturnal: an animal that is active during the night.

parallel evolution: the evolution of similar traits in response to similar environmental pressures by two distantly related lineages that have been separated for some time.

postorbital bar: a ring of bone that encloses the eye sockets in the primate skull.

postorbital plate: a plate of bone at the back of the eye orbit in primates.

primates: members of the mammalian order Primates. This includes prosimians, monkeys, apes and humans.

primatologist: a scientist that studies the biology of primates, including primate evolution.

primitive: in evolutionary terms, an organism that is most like the ancestor from which its lineage was derived. A more general member of its group. In primates the prosimians are the most primitive members.

prosimian: any of the members of the primate suborder Prosimii. Traditionally, this suborder includes lemurs, lorises, and tarsiers.

quadrupedal: using all four limbs to support the body during locomotion. This is the basic mammalian (and primate) form of locomotion.

rhinarium: the moist, hairless pad at the end of the nose seen in most mammalian species.

sexual dimorphism: differences in physical features between males and females of the same species. Examples among primates include larger body size of males (baboons and gorillas among others) and larger canine teeth in males (baboons and chimpanzees are representative).

specialized traits: traits that have evolved to perform a particular function. Particular specialized traits are found in a specific lineage and serve to elucidate evolutionary relationships.

stereoscopic vision: a condition, due to binocular vision, in which visual images are super-imposed upon one another. This is interpreted by the brain and results in the perception of depth or three-dimensional vision.

Now take the Fill-in and Multiple Choice tests. Do not guess. Following completion of the tests, correct them. The correct answers and textbook page references are at the end of this study guide chapter. Note your strong areas and your weak areas to guide you in your continuing study.

FILL-IN QUESTIONS

1. The overall characteristics of an evolving lineage, which may include both primitive features and specialized features, that are used to help define the lineage are called

    _____ _____.

2. Primate hands and feet exhibit a high degree of _____.

3. One of the hallmarks of the primates is the possession of a(n) _____ thumb and, in many species, a(n) _____ great toe.

4. In most primate species, mammalian claws have been replaced by _____.

5. _____ primates lack color vision.

6. The situation in which both eyes face forward, resulting in overlapping visual fields, is called _____ vision.

7. The ability to perceive depth, i.e., see objects in three-dimensions, is called _____ vision.

8. Primates have a heavy reliance on vision, while they have a decreased reliance on _____ _____ _____ _____.

9. The single most important factor influencing the evolutionary divergence of the primates was the adaptation for _____ living.

10. Paleontologists consider the _____ _____ and the _____ _____ as the two best diagnostic skeletal traits of the primate order.

11. The idea that many primate characteristics are due to adaptations to life in the trees is called the _____ _____.

12. An alternative hypothesis to many primate features being selected by the arboreal environment is the _____ _____ hypothesis. This hypothesis posits that early primates evolved in the bush layer of the forest where they traveled on thin vertical supports and fed on insects.

13. Locomotion which involves walking on all four legs is termed _____.

14. A form of locomotion, found principally among prosimians, which involves pushing off of tree trunks, rotating in mid-air so that the feet land on the tree trunk that the animal is moving towards, is called _____ _____ and _____.

15. A primate with arms longer than legs, a short stable lumbar spine, long curved fingers, and reduced thumbs would have _____ as its primary mode of locomotion.

16. The traditional classification of primates divides the order into two suborders, the

_____ and the _____.

17. Based on DNA, chimpanzees are most closely related to _____.

18. The _____ are the most primitive group of primates.

19. A dental adaptation that assists lemurs in both grooming and feeding is the _____

_____.

20. Lorises survived on continental areas, such as Africa and Asia, by adopting a

_____ activity pattern.

21. Most lemurs and lorises retain a claw on the second toe. This is the _____

claw.

22. Tarsiers are more similar biochemically to _____ than they are to

prosimians.

23. _____ represent approximately 70 percent of all primates species.

24. _____ _____ _____ are the most widely geographically distributed

of all living nonhuman primates.

25. Callused skin over the ischial tuberosities of Old World monkeys, which are used as

sitting pads, are called _____ _____.

26. The subfamily of the Cercopithedae that specializes on eating leaves is the _____.

27. Some terrestrial cercopithecines have a marked difference in body size between the

males and the females. The males are sometimes twice the size of the females. This

difference between the sexes is called _____ _____.

28. Female baboons (as well as some other cercopithecine species) have a pronounced

swelling and color change in their external genitalia. These changes are associated with a

type of reproductive cycling called _____.

29. Apes and humans belong to the superfamily _____.

30. The most distinctive feature of gibbons and siamangs relate to their functional adaptation for _____.

31. The largest living primate is the _____.

32. An adult male gorilla that has a saddle of white fur across its back is referred to as a _____ male.

33. The genus *Pan* consists of two species. The common names for these two species are chimpanzees and _____.

34. The most distinctive characteristic of humans that has affected a number of anatomical traits and makes us unique among the primates is habitual _____.

35. _____ _____ is a technique in which strands of DNA from two separate species are combined to form a "hybrid" molecule. This molecule can be examined for mismatched pairs to deduce genetic relatedness.

MULTIPLE CHOICE QUESTIONS

1. Which of the following is **not** an evolutionary trend of primates?
   A. a tendency for males to be permanent members of primate social groups
   B. a tendency for most species to be active at night, i.e. nocturnal
   C. the lack of any dietary specialization
   D. binocular vision
   E. Both A and B are not primate evolutionary trends.

2. Which of the following is **not** a primate trend?
   A. stereoscopic vision
   B. highly developed sense of smell
   C. orthograde or upright posture
   D. opposable thumbs and great toes
   E. retention of the clavicle

3. Binocular vision in primates results in
   A. color vision.
   B. dichromatic vision.
   C. panoramic vision.
   D. stereoscopic vision.
   E. lateral vision.

4. Primates are characterized by pentadactyly. This is the presence of
    A. generalized dentition.
    B. an upright posture.
    C. five digits on the hands and feet.
    D. a postorbital bar.
    E. tactile pads.

5. The hypothesis that primates evolved as a result of selective pressures for "life in the trees" is known as the
    A. pollinator hypothesis.
    B. arboreal hypothesis.
    C. visual-predation hypothesis.
    D. bug-snatching hypothesis.
    E. fine branch support hypothesis.

6. The formula 2-1-2-3 corresponds to what order of teeth?
    A. molar, pre-molars, canines, incisors
    B. premolars, incisors, molars, canines
    C. canines, premolars, incisors, molars
    D. incisors, premolars, canines, molars
    E. incisors, canines, premolars, molars

7. The dental formula in all Old World monkeys, apes, and humans is
    A. 3-1-4-4.
    B. 2-1-3-4.
    C. 2-1-3-3.
    D. 2-1-2-3.
    E. 2-1-3-2.

8. The tarsier has a dental formula of 2-1-3-3/1-1-3-3. How many incisors does a tarsier have?
    A. 2
    B. 3
    C. 4
    D. 6
    E. 8

9. Referring to the question above, how many teeth do tarsiers have?
    A. 17
    B. 18
    C. 34
    D. 36
    E. 38

10. Which of the following statements is correct?
    A. Arboreal quadrupeds have slightly shorter forelimbs.
    B. Terrestrial quadrupeds have nearly equal length forelimbs and hindlimbs.
    C. Brachiators have longer hindlimbs than forelimbs.
    D. Prehensile tails are only found in monkeys.
    E. Both A and B are correct.

11. A form of locomotion found among some of the smaller lemurs and tarsiers is
    A. vertical clinging and leaping.
    B. quadrupedalism.
    C. scampering.
    D. bipedalism.
    E. brachiation.

12. In what part of the world would you find the monkey that is illustrated below?
    A. South America
    B. Africa
    C. Madagascar
    D. eastern Asia
    E. the islands of Southeast Asia

13. Taxonomically tarsiers are classified with
    A. prosimians.
    B. anthropoids.
    C. strepsirhines.
    D. haplorhines.
    E. Both A and D, depending on the taxonomic scheme.

14. Prosimians are considered to be the most primitive of the primates. What does "primitive" mean in evolutionary biology?
    A. least derived
    B. most like the ancestor
    C. poorly adapted
    D. inferior
    E. Both A and B are correct.

15. In which type of primate would a "dental comb" be found
    A. lemur.
    B. New World Monkey.
    C. Old World Monkey.
    D. gibbon.
    E. orangutan.

16. Lemurs are found exclusively in
    A. Madagascar.
    B. India.
    C. Borneo.
    D. Sri Lanka.
    E. the Malay peninsula.

17. Lemurs seem to have survived on Madagascar because
    A. it was the center of their adaptive radiation.
    B. they were isolated from competition with higher primates.
    C. there were no birds for competition for arboreal resources.
    D. they lived on the ground.
    E. both B and C are correct.

18. Which of the following traits is characteristic of the ring-tailed lemur?
    A. terrestrial
    B. completely enclosed bony orbits
    C. solitary
    D. prehensile tail
    E. brachiation

19. Which of the following is **not** true of tarsiers?
    A. nocturnal
    B. insectivorous
    C. lack a rhinarium
    D. can rotate their heads almost 180°
    E. well-developed color vision

20. Which of the following is **not** generally a characteristic of anthropoids?
    A. a bony plate that encloses the orbit
    B. decreased gestation period
    C. a relatively larger brain
    D. an absolutely larger brain
    E. increased parental care

21. The only nocturnal monkey is the
    A. baboon.
    B. chimpanzee.
    C. tamarin.
    D. howler.
    E. owl monkey.

22. Which of the following is **not** true regarding New World monkeys?
    A. some have prehensile tails
    B. nostrils face downward
    C. almost all are arboreal
    D. one group retains claws
    E. Both B and C are true.

23. Which of the following structures are found in cercopithecines?
    A. dental comb
    B. prehensile tail
    C. claws
    D. sacculated stomach
    E. cheek pouch

24. The term "sexual dimorphism" refers to
    A. differences in size and structure between males and females.
    B. differences in behavior between males and females.
    C. differences in reproductive physiology between males and females.
    D. females being biologically more important than males.
    E. parallel evolution between males and females of different species.

25. The reproductive cycle in nonhuman female primates is called
    A. estrus.
    B. menarche.
    C. menstruation.
    D. ischial callosities.
    E. hylobates.

26. New World monkeys and Old World monkeys have been geographically separated for a
    minimum of 30 million years, yet they are clearly recognizable as monkeys. This is an
    example of the evolutionary principle of
    A. reciprocal evolution.
    B. convergent evolution.
    C. parallel evolution.
    D. evolutionary reversal.
    E. Dollo's Law.

27. Brachiation is
    A. the presence of four cusps on a molar tooth.
    B. two structures which function similarly in two completely unrelated animals.
    C. a social group consisting only of a mother and her offspring.
    D. a form of locomotion employed by gibbons.
    E. a diet consisting only of gums and saps.

28. Which of the following hominoids delineate their territories by sound?
    A. siamangs
    B. orangutans
    C. gibbons
    D. gorillas
    E. Both A and C are correct.

29. A frugivore is standing in front of a vending machine. Which item will the frugivore select?
    A. Koala Brother's Eucalyptus Cough Drops
    B. Rainbow Fruit Bar
    C. Rigney's Chewing Gum
    D. Sunnyview Farms Sunflower Seeds
    E. Rip Tyle's Chocolate-Covered Ants

30. Which of the following applies to chimpanzees?
    A. insectivorous
    B. live in monogamous family units
    C. usually bipedal
    D. occasionally hunt and eat young monkeys
    E. smallest of the great apes

31. In what way do bonobos differ from chimpanzees?
     A. more terrestrial than chimps
     B. larger head relative to body size
     C. longer legs relative to arms
     D. larger body size
     E. dietary specialists

32. Which of the following statements is **not** true?
     A. Genetic data has been in conflict with taxonomies based on morphology.
     B. A problem with morphologically based taxonomy is similarities in species resulting from parallel evolution.
     C. Humans have 46 chromosomes; chimpanzees have 48 chromosomes.
     D. DNA hybridization studies suggest that humans and chimpanzees are more closely related to each other than either is to the gorilla.
     E. Humans and chimpanzees differ in only one amino acid in the hemoglobin beta chain.

ANSWERS TO FILL-IN OUTLINE

I. PRIMATE EVOLUTIONARY TRENDS
    A. 1. share
            a. body hair
            b. live
            c. heterodontism
            d. endothermy
            e. increased
            f. flexibility
        2. retained
            a. specialized
            b. defined
                1. evolutionary
                    a. trends
                    b. general
                2. order
    B. 1. erect posture
        2. generalized
        3. flexibility
            a. five
            b. thumb
            c. nails
            d. tactile
    C. 1. specialization
        2. generalized
    D. 1. heavily
            a. color
            b. stereoscopic
                1. binocular

            2. visual
            3. three
        2. decreased
        3. complex
    E. 1. fetal, longer, reduced, delayed, extension
        2. behavior
        3. permanent
        4. diurnal

II. THE ARBOREAL ADAPTATION
     A. arboreal
         1. vision
         2. climbing
         3. diet, generalized
         4. flexibility
         5. arboreal hypothesis
     B. 1. visual predation
         2. bushy forest undergrowth
             a. forward-facing
             b. grasping
     C. 1. nonarboreal
         2. preadapted

III. THE LIVING PRIMATES
      A. 1. tropical
          2. arboreal
          3. ground
          4. ground
          5. adapted

B. 1. omnivorous
   2. dentition
   3. fruit, leaves, insects
      a. mammals
      b. leaves
C. 1. four
      a. limb
      b. terrestrial
      c. 1. equal
         2. shorter
      d. spine
   2. prosimians
   3. apes
      a. gibbons, siamangs
      b. 1. longer
         2. lumbar
         3. curved
         4. thumbs
      c. climbers
      d. semibrachiators
   4. a. New World monkeys
      b. prehensile
IV. PRIMATE CLASSIFICATION
A. 1. morphological similarities
   2. relationships
B. narrow
   1. order
   2. two
      a. Prosimii, more
      b. Anthropoidea
   3. species
   4. relationships
C. 1. a. 1. prosimians
         2. anthropoids
         3. distinct
      b. suborders
         1. Strepsirhini
         2. Haplorhini
   2. a. Pongidae
         1. closest
         2. distinct
         3. DNA
V. AN OVERVIEW OF CONTEMPORARY
   PRIMATES
A. 1. most

2. a. olfaction
      1. rhinarium
      2. scent
   b. laterally
   c. shorter
   d. dental comb
      1. incisors, canines
      2. grooming
3. a. Madagascar
      1. diversified
      2. extinct
   b. 1. mouse lemur
      2. larger
      3. insectivorous
      4. a. terrestrial
         b. vertical clingers and
            leapers
         c. groups
            1. monogamous
            2. solitary
   4. b. competition
      d. galago
      e. 1. a. lorises
            b. galagos
         2. a. insectivorous
            b. combinations
            c. alone
         3. overlap
   5. adaptive level
      a. nocturnal
      b. grooming claw
      c. life
B. 1. Southeast Asia
   2. leaping
   3. mated
   4. anatomical
      a. prosimian
      b. anthropoids
C. 1. a. larger
      b. brain
      c. rounded
      d. binocular
      e. bony
      f. rhinarium
      g. increased
      h. increased
      i. grooming

2. New World, Old World
   a. 1. nose
        a. outside
        b. downward
     2. arboreal
     3. diurnal
     4. a. callitrichids
          1. primitive
            a. claws
            b. twins
          2. infant
        b. 1. cebids
          3. quadrupedalism
            a. spider
            b. prehensile
   b. 2. a. quadrupedalism
        c. ischial callosities
     3. a. 1. generalized
            b. cheek pouches
          2. a. Africa
            b. macaques
        b. 1. leaves
          2. a. colobus
            b. Asia
     4. a. arboreal
        b. terrestrial
        c. colobus
     5. sexual dimorphism
     6. estrus
     7. a. males
        b. large
3. b. 50-, 30
     1. prosimian
     2. monkey
        a. rafting
        b. closer
        c. parallel evolution
          1. selective
D. 1. Hominoidea
   2. a. larger
     b. tail
     c. shortened
     d. shoulder
     e. complex
     f. brain, cognitive
     g. lengthened
   3. a. tropical
     b. smallest

     c. 1. arms
        2. curved
        3. short
        4. shoulder
     d. feeding
     e. fruit
     f. monogamous
        1. males
        2. songs
4. b. climbers
        1. arboreal
   c. sexual dimorphism
   d. solitary
   e. frugivorous
5. a. largest
   c. knuckle-walking
   d. family
6. a. Africa
   b. limb, upper-body
     1. knuckle-walking
     2. genus
     3. ecological
   c. smaller
   d. locomotion
   e. omnivorous
     2. hunt
        b. shared
   f. fluid
     1. males
     3. females
     4. close
7. a. bonobos
   b. least
   c. 1. longer
   d. 1. arboreal
     2. aggressive
     3. fluid
     4. meat
     5. male-female
8. a. Hominidae
   b. 1. vision
     2. olfactory
     3. grasping
     4. trends
   c. bipedal
     1. modifications
     2. bipedalism

VI. PRIMATE CHROMOSOMES, PROTEINS, AND
     DNA
     A. 1. morphological
           a. parallel
           b. homologies
        2. a. common
           b. direct
     B. 1. karyotype
           a. chromosome
           b. karyotypes

     2. a. gibbons, siamangs
        b. orangutan
        c. fusion
        d. 1. recent
     C. 1. sequence
        2. proteins
     D. 1. hybridization
        2. mismatched
        3. a. close
           b. chimpanzee

ANSWERS & REFERENCES TO FILL-IN QUESTIONS

1. evolutionary trends, p. 207
2. prehensility, p. 207
3. opposable, opposable, p. 207
4. nails, p. 208
5. nocturnal, p. 208
6. binocular, p. 208
7. stereoscopic, p. 208
8. the sense of smell or olfaction, p. 208
9. arboreal, p. 209
10. postorbital bar, auditory bulla, Box 9-1, p. 210
11. arboreal hypothesis, p. 212
12. visual predation, p. 212
13. quadrupedalism, p. 214
14. vertical clinging and leaping, p. 215
15. brachiation, p. 216
16. Prosimii, Anthropoidea, p. 217
17. humans, p. 219
18. prosimians, p. 219
19. dental comb, p. 219

20. nocturnal, p. 220
21. grooming, p. 220
22. anthropoids, p. 222
23. monkeys, p. 222
24. Old World monkeys, p. 224
25. ischial callosities, p. 225
26. colobines, p. 226. Do not get the subfamily colobinae confused with the African colobus monkey. The colobus is one of the species that belongs to the colobines.
27. sexual dimorphism, p. 225
28. estrus, p. 226
29. Hominoidea, p. 227
30. brachiation, p. 228
31. gorilla, p. 229
32. silverback, p. 229
33. bonobos, p. 231
34. bipedalism, p. 232
35. DNA hybridization, p. 234

ANSWERS & REFERENCES TO MULTIPLE CHOICE QUESTIONS

1. B, p. 209
2. B, p. 208
3. D, p. 208
4. C, p. 211
5. B, p. 212
6. E, p. 213, Box 9-2
7. D, p. 213, Box 9-2
8. D, this question is asking for the number of only one type of tooth. The dental formula indicates that tarsiers have two upper and one lower canine on each side of the mouth. Multiplied by two this gives us a total of six incisors for tarsiers, p. 213, Box 9-2.
9. C, p. 213, Box 9-2.

10. E, p. 214
11. A, p. 215
12. A, the key to figuring out this question is the prehensile tail of the spider monkey. Only New World monkeys, primates found in Central and South America, have prehensile tails. It is interesting to note that almost all mammals with prehensile tails are found, or had their evolutionary origins, in South America, p. 216 and p. 223.
13. E. This may seem like a trick question, but it is really a critical thinking question. Traditionally, tarsiers have been classified as prosimians and many primatologists still adhere to this classification. In recent years, many primatologists have classified tarsiers as haplorhines, which enables them to be in the same group as monkeys, apes, and humans. Thus, both A and D are correct answers, p. 217.
14. E, p. 219
15. A, p. 219
16. A, p. 220
17. B, p. 220
18. A, p. 220
19. E, p. 222
20. B, p. 222
21. E, p. 222
22. B, p. 222-223
23. E, p. 225
24. A, p. 225
25. A, p. 226
26. C, p. 227. B is an answer that many of you may have selected. Parallel evolution and convergent evolution both are the result of organisms that are separated responding to similar selective pressures. The difference, however, is that parallel evolution occurs in species that are considered to be somewhat closely related, as is the case with New World and Old World monkeys. What is meant by "closely related" is subjective in many cases. Convergent evolution occurs among species not closely related such as the thylacine (marsupial wolf) and the wolf, which have not had a common ancestor for a minimum of 120 million years, and probably much longer.
27. D, p. 228
28. E, p. 228
29. B, p. 229
30. D, p. 231
31. C, p. 231
32. A, p. 233

CHAPTER 10

FUNDAMENTALS OF PRIMATE BEHAVIOR

LEARNING OBJECTIVES

After reading this chapter you should be able to:
- describe characteristics that set humans apart from other primates. (p. 240)
- understand why anthropologists study nonhuman primate behavior. (p. 241)
- describe a variety of characteristics common to most nonhuman primates. (pp. 241-243)
- describe different types of nonhuman primate social groups. (p. 242)
- understand the complexity of socioecology. (pp. 244-248)
- discuss the types of food that primates eat, the variations they exhibit in obtaining it, and possible explanations for these variations. (pp. 244-248)
- discuss aspects of social behavior found among all nonhuman primates, i.e., dominance hierarchies, grooming, mother-infant relationship, alloparenting and reproductive strategies. (pp. 248-254)
- have a general understanding of sociobiological concepts and terms. (pp. 255-258)
- understand the problems in applying sociobiology to primate behavior. (pp. 258-260)

FILL-IN OUTLINE

Introduction

In the last chapter the student was introduced to the primate order and some of the biological characteristics that distinguish different groups of primates. This chapter looks at behavioral characteristics found among primates including dominance, grooming, reproductive strategies and mother-infant relationships. Field methods in primatology and the complexity of interpreting data from a socioecological perspective are discussed. An overview of sociobiology is presented along with the problems in applying it to primate behaviors.

I. BEHAVIOR AND HUMAN ORIGINS

A. Human uniqueness

1. When compared with other primates humans are not really _____ unique.

2. _____ attributes set humans apart from other primates.

3. _____ is the human mode of locomotion.

4. Humans live in permanent _____ social groups.

5. _____ is the central hominid adaptive strategy.

II. NONHUMAN PRIMATES

A. Modern African apes and humans last shared a common ancestor between _____ and _____ million years ago.

B. Primates solve their major adaptive problems within the context of _____ _____.

C. Typically, primate social groups include _____ _____ and _____ ages.

D. _____ refers to members of one sex leaving the natal group.

E. _____ refers to remaining in one's natal group.

F. In primate social groups, individuals must be able to evaluate a situation before acting. This would have placed selective pressures on _____ _____.

G. A brain that can assess social situations and store the information would have to be proportionately _____ and more _____.

III. PRIMATE FIELD STUDIES

A. Animals living in their natural habitat are referred to as _____-_____.

B. To understand the _____ and _____ of nonhuman primates, it is necessary to study them in their natural habitat.

C. It is difficult to study _____ primates.

D. Most systematic information on primates comes from free-ranging animals that spend considerable time ____ _____ _____.

E. _____ _____ _____ off the coast of Puerto Rico is an example of a large provisioned colony of primates.

IV THE ECOLOGY OF NONHUMAN PRIMATES

A. Socioecology refers to studying free-ranging primates by focusing on the relationship between _____ and the _____.

B. Primatologists view ecology, behavior and biology as complexly _____.

C. The relationships among ecological variables, social organization and behavior _____ _____ been worked out.

D. Certain _____ factors exert strong influence on group size and structure.

E. Environment and Social Behavior

1. Five monkey species have been studied in detail in the _____ Forest of western _____.

2. _____ refers to different species living in the same area.

3. Black and white colobus monkeys are found in _____-_____ groups.

4. Red colobus monkeys are found in _____/_____ groups.

5. Many primate species are exceedingly _____ regarding group composition.

6. _____ move about more than folivores.

7. The _____ the body size, the larger the groups tends to be.

8. The area exploited by an animal or social group is called the _____ _____.

V. SOCIAL BEHAVIOR

A. Dominance

    1. Dominance hierarchies are frequently referred to as _____ _____.

    2. Dominant animals have priority access to _____ and _____.

    3. Rank is not _____.

    4. Many factors influence one's status including _____, _____,

    _____, _____, _____, perhaps _____

    and sometimes _____.

    5. Position in the hierarchy is _____.

    6. _____ and _____ are indications of dominance and

    subordination.

B. Grooming

    1. _____ grooming is mostly a primate activity.

    2. Serves _____ functions.

    3. Occurs in a _____ of contexts.

    4. Has been called the "_____ _____ of primates."

C. Reproduction

    1. Females are sexually receptive when they are in _____.

    2. Visual cues to a female's sexual readiness include _____ and

    changes in color of the skin around the _____ _____.

    3. The temporary relationship between male and female savanna baboons for

    mating purposes is called _____.

D. Mother-infant relationships

    1. Except in those species in which _____ or _____

    occurs, males do not participate in rearing offspring.

2. For a nonhuman primate mother to properly care for her offspring she should have had a _____ _____ with her own mother.

3. The close mother-infant relationship does not always end with _____.

4. _____ _____ reinforces early primate attachment to mother.

5. _____ _____ early in life can have devastating effects on the behavioral development of primate species.

6. _____ is a term used for individuals other than the mother holding and interacting with an infant.

VI. SOCIOBIOLOGY

A. Looks at _____ from an evolutionary context.

B. _____ code for certain behaviors.

C. Problems arise when trying to apply the mechanics of behavioral evolution in complex _____ animals with _____ neurological responses.

D. Sarah Blaffer Hrdy's explanation of _____ among Hanuman langurs of India is cited as an example among primates.

E. Individuals act to maximize _____ _____ reproductive success.

F. Male and female reproductive strategies

1. The _____ is to produce and successfully rear to adulthood as many offspring as possible.

2. _____-_____ refers to producing few offspring with increased parental investment.

3. Female primates are under _____ stress due to carrying and caring for offspring.

4. If an individual female is able to enhance not only her own ability to survive but also her close relatives this increases her _____ _____.

5. Marmosets and tamarins are _____ with two adult males regularly

mating with one female.

VII. PRIMATE SOCIOBIOLOGY — LIMITATIONS AND CRITIQUES

A. The six central problems with primate sociobiological research include:

_____,

_____,

_____,

_____,

_____,

_____.

B. Evidence suggests that natural selection often works simply "___ _____ ____."

KEY TERMS

alloparenting: a common behavior in many primate species whereby individuals other than the parent(s) hold, carry, and in general interact with infants.

consortships: temporary relationship between one adult male and an estrous female.

dispersal: members of one sex leave the natal group at puberty.

dominance hierarchies: systems of social organization wherein individuals are ranked relative to one another based on priority access to food and sex.

ecological: relationship between organisms and all aspects of their environment.

estrus: period of sexual receptivity in female mammals (except humans) correlated with ovulation.

free-ranging: noncaptive animals living in their natural habitat.

grooming: picking through fur to remove dirt, parasites or any other material that may be present.

home-range: the area exploited by an animal or social group for food, water and sleeping areas

inclusive fitness: the total contribution of an individual's genes to the next generation, including those genes shared by close relatives.

infanticide: the killing of infants.

K-selected: a reproductive strategy wherein the individuals produce fewer offspring but increase parental investment of care, time and energy.

monogamous pair: a mated pair and its young.

natal group: the group in which an individual is born.

philopatric: remaining in one's natal group or home range as an adult.

polyandry: one female with multiple males.
reproductive strategies: behavioral patterns that contribute to an individual's reproductive success, i.e., producing and successfully rearing to adulthood as many offspring as possible.
social grooming: grooming done for pleasure. Common among primates and reinforces social relationships.
social structure: the composition, size, and sex ratio of a group of animals.
sociobiology: a theoretical framework which looks at behavior within an evolutionary context. If a behavior has a genetic basis it will be subject to natural selection.
socioecology: attempts to find patterns of relationship between environment, biological needs and social behaviors when studying animals.
sympatric: two or more species who live in the same area.

Now take the Fill-in and Multiple Choice tests. Do not guess. Following completion of the tests, correct them. The correct answers and textbook page references are at the end of this study guide chapter. Note your strong areas and your weak areas to guide you in your continuing study.

FILL-IN QUESTIONS

1. It is the behavioral attributes of humans that set us apart from other primates. Our central

   adaptive strategy has been _____.

2. Humans are behaviorally unique compared with other primates in a variety of ways.

   Seven features are mentioned that set humans apart. Of these behavioral characteristics,

   other primates may exhibit some of them but only humans exhibit them all. These

   characteristics include _____, _____, _____,

   _____, _____, _____,

   _____.

3. Primate social groupings take numerous forms. Those mentioned in the text include:

   _____, _____,

   _____, _____, and

   _____.

4. Dispersal, members of one sex leaving the natal group at puberty, seems to be related to

   two factors. These factors are _____ and _____.

5. Evolutionarily speaking, primates have been selected for social intelligence. One ability they have developed is to _____ a situation before acting.

6. Studying nonhuman primates in their natural habitats has been a focus of anthropology since before World War II. By the early _____ field research was in full swing.

7. Noncaptive animals living in their natural habitat, largely free from human influence describes _____-_____ animals.

8. Methodological problems are inherent in studying certain primate groups. Arboreal primates are difficult to observe because _____.

9. Much primate research has focused on langurs, gorillas, chimps, macaques, baboons, vervets and patas monkeys because they _____.

10. At present, we have field data on more than _____ nonhuman primate species.

11. Primatologists are attempting to analyze the relationship between social behavior and the natural environment. This approach is called _____.

12. Primate social structure is integrated. To understand the function of any single aspect of primate social structure one must look at its relationship with numerous other aspects of the environment including _____, _____,
    _____, _____, _____,
    _____, _____, _____.

13. Solitary foraging may be related to _____ and distribution of _____.

14. The five Old World monkey species that have been studied in the Kibale Forest of western Uganda include _____, _____, _____,
    _____ and _____.

15. The five species of monkey to be studied in Kibale Forest live in the same area. These species are therefore termed _____.

16. The results of the long-term studies at Kibale Forest reveal that the social organization of these primate species are _____.

17. Among the primates studied in Kibale Forest, female sexual swelling is obvious only in those species living in _____ groups.

18. The average life span of most Old World monkeys is approximately _____-_____ years.

19. Dominance hierarchies are learned, change throughout life and are determined by priority access to food and sex. These factors help to _____ physical violence within primate social groups.

20. Grooming is found among most primate species. Its functions are numerous including _____, _____ or _____.

21. Estrus is the period of female sexual receptivity associated with ovulation in female non-human primates. A male nonhuman primate would know that a female was in estrus by certain physical cues, namely, _____ and _____ _____.

22. The mother-infant relationship among primates is critical. However, for a female to be a good mother and for a male to know how to copulate studies have shown that they must have had _____.

23. Most infant primates are cared for by the mother. However, among the _____ and _____ the males are the primary care givers only returning the infant to the mother for nursing.

24. The assumption of sociobiology is that if a behavior has a genetic basis, it will be subject to natural selection. The problem of applying this approach to primate behavior is

_____

_____.

25. Due to pregnancy, lactating and child care female primates are under great physiological stress. The skeletons of older female chimpanzees from Gombe show evidence of

_____.

MULTIPLE CHOICE QUESTIONS

1. Behavioral characteristics that distinguish humans from other primate groups include all but which of the following?
   A. bipedalism
   B. reproductive strategy
   C. culture
   D. bisexual social groups

2. Modern African apes and humans last shared a common ancestor
   A. 20 m.y.a.
   B. 15 m.y.a
   C. 8 to 5 m.y.a.
   D. 11 m.y.a.

3. Among nonhuman primates a polyandrous social group would include
   A. one female with two males.
   B. one male with one female.
   C. one male with two females.
   D. None of the above.

4. An example of a monogamous pair of primates would include
   A. gibbons.
   B. gorillas.
   C. indris.
   D. All of the above are correct.
   E. Both A and C are correct.

5. If one is the philopatric sex, this means she/he
   A. do not reproduce.
   B. protects the group from predators.
   C. stays in the natal group.
   D. transfers out of the natal group.

6. The nonhuman primate brain
   A. is proportionately large and complex.
   B. has been selected for social intelligence.
   C. functions mostly on instinct.
   D. All of the above
   E. Both A and B are correct.

7. To understand the adaptations and behaviors of nonhuman primates,
   A. they can be studied in any setting, but they must be in groups.
   B. they are best studied in a controlled setting.
   C. they are best studied in a free-ranging environment.
   D. they are best studied in the trees.

8. To understand how one component of primate social behavior functions,
    A. it is best to determine its relationship with other environmental factors.
    B. it is best to narrow the field of study to that particular behavior.
    C. it is best to study one individual.
    D. it is best to study one group.

9. Primatologists view ecology, behavior, and biology as
    A. distinct areas that one should observe separately.
    B. complexly interdependent.
    C. areas that occasionally influence each other.
    D. unimportant when studying group dynamics.

10. The detailed study of monkeys in the Kibale Forest of Uganda reveals that
    A. old World monkeys follow a similar pattern in exploiting the environment.
    B. monkeys enjoy the same foods.
    C. male and female reproductive strategies are similar.
    D. there is little correlation between social organization and feeding strategies.

11. Dominance hierarchies
    A. increase aggression and fighting within a group.
    B. have no apparent function in social groups.
    C. provide a degree of order.
    D. are limited to adult males.

12. Alloparenting
    A. is not as common in primates as it is in other mammals.
    B. may help a young female learn proper techniques of infant care.
    C. is interacting with the infant of another individual.
    D. All of the above are correct.
    E. Both B and C are correct.

13. Mothering among primates appears to be
    A. instinctive.
    B. learned.
    C. dependent on a normal experience with one's own mother.
    D. Both B and C are correct.

14. Sociobiology holds that
    A. behavior is learned.
    B. behavior has a genetic basis.
    C. a primatologist should consider the environmental influences affecting primate behavior.
    D. All of the above are correct.

15. Which of the following is not true of chimpanzees?
    A. Males participate in child care.
    B. Females transfer out.
    C. Males are tightly bonded.
    D. Males organize to defend against other males.

ANSWERS TO FILL-IN OUTLINE

I. BEHAVIOR AND HUMAN ORIGINS
   A. 1. structurally/physically
       2. behavioral
       3. bipedalism
       4. bisexual
       5. culture

II. NONHUMAN PRIMATES
   A. 8, 5
   B. social groups
   C. both sexes, all
   D. dispersal
   E. philopatric
   F. social intelligence
   G. larger, complex

III. PRIMATE FIELD STUDIES
   A. free-ranging
   B. adaptations, behaviors
   C. arboreal
   D. on the ground
   E. Cayo Santiago Island

IV. THE ECOLOGY OF NONHUMAN PRIMATES
   A. social behavior, environment
   B. interdependent
   C. have not yet
   D. environmental
   E. 1. Kibale, Uganda
       2. sympatric
       3. one-male
       4. multimale/multifemale
       5. flexible
       6. omnivores
       7. smaller
       8. home range

V. SOCIAL BEHAVIOR
   A. 1. pecking order
       2. food, sex
       3. permanent
       4. sex, age, level of aggression, time spent in group, intelligence, motivation, mother's social position
       5. learned
       6. gestures, behaviors

   B. 1. social
       2. hygenic
       3. variety
       4. social cement
   C. 1. estrus
       2. swelling, genital area
       3. Consortships
   D. 1. monogamy, polyandry
       2. normal experience
       3. weaning
       4. physical contact
       5. social isolation
       6. alloparenting

VI. SOCIOBIOLOGY
   A. behavior
   B. genes
   C. social, flexible
   D. infanticide
   E. their own
   F. 1. goal
       2. K-selected
       3. physiological
       4. inclusive fitness
       5. polyandrous

VII. PRIMATE SOCIOBIOLOGY — LIMITATIONS AND CRITIQUES
   A. Lack of long-term data on demographics and social behavior of large groups of individually known animals, lack of long-term data on distribution of resources in time and space, lack of information on genetic relatedness through the male line, difficulty in assigning reproductive and other costs and benefits to particular behaviors, ignorance of the genetics of primate social behavior and many sociobiological models are untestable.
   B. To get by

ANSWERS & REFERENCES TO FILL-IN QUESTIONS

1. culture, p. 240
2. Bipedal, permanent bisexual social groups with males often bonded to females, large brains relative to body weight and capable of complex learning, highly advanced use of symbolic language, culture as the central hominid adaptive strategy, obtain food through male/female sexual division of labor, transport food back to base camp (home) and share, and concealed ovulation with females sexually receptive throughout the year. p. 240
3. one male, multimale/multifemale, monogamous pair, polyandry and solitary. p. 242
4. reduced competition for mates, to decrease close breeding. p. 242
5. evaluate, p. 243
6. 1960s, p. 243
7. free-ranging, p. 243
8. They move quickly through dense vegetation, p. 244
9. are on the ground and/or travel and feed in open country, p. 244
10. 100, p. 244
11. socioecology, p. 244
12. quantity and quality of foods, distribution of food, water, predators, sleeping sites, activity patterns, relationships with other nonpredator species, and impact of human activities. p. 245
13. diet, resources, pp. 245-46
14. black and white colobus, red colobus, mangabey, blue monkey and redtail monkey, p. 246
15. sympatric p. 247
16. varied, p. 247
17. multimale, p. 248
18. 12-14, p. 248
19. reduce, p. 249
20. social, hygenic, pleasure, p. 249
21. swelling, changes in skin color around the genital area, p. 251
22. a normal experience with their own mother, p. 252
23. marmosets, tamarins, p. 254
24. among primates learned behavior is increased and genetically influenced behavior is therefore reduced, p. 255
25. loss of bone and bone minerals, p. 257

ANSWERS AND REFERENCES TO MULTIPLE CHOICE QUESTIONS

1. B, p. 240	6. E, p. 243	11. C, p. 248
2. C, p. 241	7. C, p. 243	12. E, p. 254
3. A, p. 242	8. A, p. 244	13. D, p. 252
4. E, p. 242	9. B, p. 245	14. B, p. 255
5. C, p. 242	10. D, p. 247	15. A, p. 258

CHAPTER 11

·PRIMATE MODELS FOR HUMAN EVOLUTION

LEARNING OBJECTIVES

After reading this chapter you should be able to:
· • understand the relationship between primate body size and diet. (pp. 267-268)
  • discuss the index of encephalization and its importance in hominid evolution. (pp. 268-269)
  • identify various modes of nonhuman primate communication including autonomic, displays and ritualized behaviors. (pp. 269-273)
  • understand the importance of communication in social groups. (pp. 269-273)
  • give a brief overview of language studies done with nonhuman primates. (pp. 273-275)
  • distinguish affiliative behaviors among nonhuman primates. (p. 277)
  • analyze and debate the motivation and advantages of aggressive interactions among nonhuman primates and their possible implications for human evolution. (pp. 277-280)
  • discuss what makes chimpanzees good models for early hominid cultural evolution. (pp. 280-284)
  • help educate people on the dangers of primate extinction and the value of preserving their habitat and saving our close relatives. (pp. 284-287)

FILL-IN OUTLINE

Introduction
   The last chapter looked at behavioral patterns among primates, methodologies of primatology, socioecology and sociobiology. This chapter concerns patterns of primate behavior including communication, affiliative behaviors, aggressive interactions and nonhuman primate cultural behaviors. The adaptive significance of these behaviors is explored with an emphasis on implications for human evolution. We end the chapter with a look at current dangers to primates and the destruction of their habitat.

I. INTRODUCTION

A. A biological perspective in primatology

1. Attempts to explain _____ certain patterns of primate behavior have evolved.

2. Looks at the _____ _____ _____ since behaviors are grounded physiologically.

3. Examines the components of an animal's development and physiology termed _____ _____.

II. ASPECTS OF LIFE HISTORY AND BODY SIZE

A. Body size includes body mass and _____.

B. Primate body weight ranges from _____ to _____.

C. Smaller bodied species primarily eat _____.

D. Larger bodied species primarily eat _____.

E. Almost all species eat some _____.

F. Small animals have _____ energy needs because their _____ is higher.

G. Larger animals expend less _____.

H. _____ _____ is correlated with locomotion.

I. Suspensory behavior is found among _____ arboreal primates.

III. BODY SIZE AND BRAIN SIZE

A. Brain size and body size are closely _____.

B. _____ brain size is more important than actual brain size.

C. The index of encephalization is the predictable relationship between _____ and _____ size in a species.

D. The encephalization of early *Homo* and *australopithecus* is _____ _____ modern humans.

E. In both humans and nonhuman primates, the brain grows rapidly _____ birth.

F. In humans rapid brain growth also occurs for at least _____ _____ after birth.

G. Early hominids _____ from *Homo sapiens* in body size.

H. _____ refers to the relative growth of one anatomical part in relation to the entire organism.

IV. COMMUNICATION

A. Raised body hair or enhanced body odor are examples of _____ responses.

B. Vocalizations, intense staring and branch shaking are examples of _____ modes of communication.

C. _____ gestures might include a quick yawn to expose canines or bobbing back and forth in a crouched position.

D. Reassurance can take the form of _____, _____, _____ or _____ _____.

E. To appropriately use body language to communicate, a primate must be reared in a _____ social context.

F. Communicatory actions are _____.

G. _____ serve to communicate emotional states.

H. Mounting among baboons is a good example of _____ _____.

I. Vervet monkeys have three different vocalizations to indicate _____.

J. Human language, as a mode of communication, is _____.

K. Humans have the ability to think _____.

L. Humans and apes have differences in the anatomy of the _____ _____ and the _____-_____ structures in the brain.

M. Washoe learned _____.

N. Sara learned to recognize _____ _____ as symbols for objects.

O. Koko, a female _____, uses more than _____ signs of _____.

P. Chimps have also shown that they can _____ unfamiliar objects.

Q. Kanzi _____ acquired language and used symbols by age 2 1/2 yrs.

R. Humans _____ _____ the only species capable of symbolic thought.

S. For human evolution _____ became very important.

T. For most humans the language center of the brain is located in the _____ hemisphere.

U. _____ area is involved with perception of speech.

V Broca's area is involved with _____ of speech.

W. The _____ of neurological structures enabled humans to develop language.

V. AFFILIATIVE BEHAVIORS

A. _____ group cohesion

B. are _____ behaviors

C. Most affiliative behaviors involve _____ _____

D. Hugging, kissing and grooming are all examples of _____ behaviors.

E. Bonobos use _____ as an affiliative behavior.

VI. AGGRESSIVE INTERACTIONS

A. Members of the same species are referred to as _____.

B. _____ _____ is the area where a primate lives permanently.

C. _____ is the area that a primate might defend.

D. Nonaggressive arboreal primates use _____ to avoid other groups in the canopy.

E. Before entering a peripheral area, chimpanzees will _____ and _____ to see if any other animals are around.

F. Chimps are tense and quiet when they _____ _____.

G. Chimpanzees have been observed and documented brutally _____ _____ _____ _____ lone individuals.

H. Chimpanzee males have strong affiliative _____ between adult males of the same group.

I. Chimpanzee males are _____ and _____ toward individuals from other groups.

J. Humans and chimpanzees are the only known mammalian species where _____ and unprovoked _____ occurs between conspecific groups.

K. In chimpanzees and most traditional human cultures males are _____.

L. In most conflicts involving _____ the attacks are not fatal.

M. The apparent benefit to lethal aggressive behavior seems to be acquisition of _____and _____.

N. Shared patterns of strife between populations may be a _____ that chimpanzees and early hominids inherited from a common ancestor.

VII. PRIMATE CULTURAL BEHAVIOR

A. Cultural behavior is _____ and passed on from one generation to the next.

B. By _____ young primates learn appropriate behaviors.

C. Imo was a Japanese macaque who began _____ her sweet potatoes before eating them.

D. Imo also invented an efficient way to clean sand out of _____.

E. Dietary habits and _____ preferences are learned.

F. Examples of chimpanzee tools include _____, _____, _____ and _____.

G. Chimpanzees exhibit regional _____ in their tool use.

H. Kanzi learned to strike two stones together and make _____-_____ _____.

I. Kanzi resolved his difficulties in making flakes by throwing the stone _____ __ _____ _____ _____ ___ ___ _____.

J. Evolution is not _____-_____.

K. Nonhuman primate behaviors that have been recently documented by humans are not _____ _____ in our nonhuman primate relatives.

VIII. PRIMATE CONSERVATION

A. Over _____ of all living non-human primates are in jeopardy.

B. The three basic reasons for the danger to primates are: _____ _____, _____ and _____ _____.

C. Tropical forests are disappearing at a rate of one acre per _____.

D. The economic motivations for destruction of habitat include _____, _____ and _____.

E. It is estimated that 1.5 billion people in the Third World are short of _____.

F. Malnutrition and undernutrition contribute to the increasing problem of hunting primates as a source of _____.

G. Primates are also killed for their _____, _____ and other body parts.

H. Live primates are used for _____, _____ _____ and _____ _____ _____.

KEY TERMS

affiliative: friendly relations between individuals.
agonistic: aggressive or defensive social interactions.
allometry: the relative growth of a part of an organism in relation to the entire organism.
autonomic: involuntary physiological responses.
Broca's area: an area of the brain responsible for the production of speech.
Central Nervous System (CNS): The brain and spinal cord.
conspecifics: members of the same species.
core areas: a portion of a home range where reliable resources are found such as food, water and sleeping trees.
displays: physical movements that convey an emotional state.
encephalization: a predictable relationship between brain size and body size.
home range: a geographic area where a primate group remains permanently.
inter: between (i.e., intergroup).
intra: within (i.e., intragroup).
lexigrams: computer board containing keys with symbols representing a "language."
life history: components of an animal's development and physiology including body size, proportional brain size, metabolism, maturation, lifestyles and reproduction.
motor cortex: the outer layer of the brain. In humans movement of the mouth, larynx and tongue for language production are located in this area of the brain.
philopatric: remaining in one's natal group.
physiology: the physical and chemical phenomena involved with the functions and activities of an organism or any of its various parts.
presenting: a subordinate animal presents his/her rear to a dominant animal.
territory: the part of the home range that animals will defend.
Wernicke's area: an area of the brain responsible for perception of speech.

Now take the Fill-in and Multiple Choice tests. Do not guess. Following completion of the tests, correct them. The correct answers and textbook page references are at the end of this study guide chapter. Note your strong areas and your weak areas to guide you in your continuing study.

FILL-IN QUESTIONS

1. The components of an animal's development and physiology including body size, proportional brain size, metabolism, maturation, lifestyle, maturation and reproduction are termed _____ _____.

2. A _____ _____ is concerned with the adaptive significance of certain behavioral patterns.

3. Growth, development, body size and metabolism are correlated with the _____ organization of primate neurology.

4. The overall measure of body mass, such as stature, refers to _____ _____.

5. Among extant primates we see a wide range in body size. Insectivores tend to be _____, while folivores tend to be _____.

6. Fruit is eaten by virtually all primates but since it lacks protein it must be _____ by eating other foods.

7. Primates eat a variety of foods to obtain protein including _____, _____, _____ or _____.

8. _____ are an efficient source of proteins and calories.

9. Body size and metabolic rate are correlated. Mature leaves require more time and a specialized _____ to metabolize. Generally folivores are _____ than insectivores.

10. Logic would dictate that body size, locomotion, and habitat are related. Generally, arboreal primates are _____. If an arboreal primate is larger it will exhibit more _____ behaviors than the smaller animals.

11. Monkeys (or apes) that weigh over 22 pounds are usually primarily _____.

12. The proportional relationship between brain size and body size is an important variable to consider when attempting to interpret the fossil record. When looking at the remains of early *Homo* or the *australopithecines* one can see that they are not nearly as _____ as modern humans.

13. The difference between nonhuman primate and human brain growth is that the nonhuman primate brain develops rapidly before and _____ _____ birth while the human brain develops rapidly before and for at least _____ _____ after birth.

14. Over 50% of human infant metabolic output goes toward _____ _____.

15. The relative size of different anatomical parts of an organism is referred to as _____ or "scaling."

16. Communication is a critical aspect of primate social structure. It can be unintentional or deliberate. Unintentional communication that conveys an emotional state is called _____ and _____ _____ _____ would be an example of it.

17. An example of deliberate nonhuman primate communication could include _____ _____ _____ or _____.

18. Certain nonhuman primate behaviors are meant to convey friendly, submissive or reassuring messages. Baboons may convey submission by _____ _____ _____ _____.

19. If a chimpanzee bends at the waist and bobs the upper body up and down, it is attempting to convey _____.

20. Grooming has hygenic and social functions. In a social context grooming may convey _____ or _____.

21. The chimpanzee and bonobo fear grin indicates _____ or _____ (much like the human grin/smile indicates "I am friendly—no threat to you.").

22. Since gestures, behaviors and expressions are not solely the result of genetics, nonhuman primates must _____ how to appropriately use them as a mode of communication. In order to accomplish this task, they should be reared in a relatively _____ social context or environment.

23. Displays can be combinations of gestures, facial expressions, vocalizations and movements that communicate emotional states. They are usually associated with _____ or _____ behaviors.

24. A type of display that can incorporate "intention movements" and/or threats ("If you don't back off, I'll do this for real") would include _____ or _____ in gorillas and _____, _____ or _____ in chimpanzees.

25. Primates are social creatures that live in groups. In order to maintain harmony, they must maintain a balance between competitive and cooperative behaviors. They achieve this through _____.

26. Humans are said to have an open system of communication because we can think symbolically. To think symbolically means to _____ _____.

27. One of the main reasons that apes cannot speak is due to _____ _____.

28. In attempting to teach apes language, humans have taught them ASL which stands for _____ _____ _____.

29. When Loulis was an infant he was put with Washoe, a chimp who had been raised speaking ASL. Washoe _____ _____ Loulis some signs.

30. Bonobos Kanzi and his sister were exposed to lexigrams while _____ _____ was being trained.

31. Kanzi and his sister had never received any lexigram training yet began _____ using the symbols at _____ _____ of age.

32. Broca's area and Wernicke's area are the areas of the brain responsible (at least in part) for speech perception and production. They are located on the _____ hemisphere and in the outer layer of the brain called the _____ _____.

33. Comparative brain anatomy is a very new science. However, it is currently believed that rather than brain size, it was the reorganization, elaboration and/or reduction of _____ _____ that allowed language to emerge in humans.

34. Affiliative behaviors can be used in reconciliation, reassurance or just to be friendly. Examples of affiliative behaviors might include _____, _____ or _____.

35. _____ are unique in their use of sex as an affiliative behavior.

36. Aggressive interactions can be used for _____ _____ or to acquire _____ or _____.

37. Vocalizations are used by _____ tree dwellers to space themselves throughout the forest canopy.

38. Jane Goodall and her team observed warlike (meaning organized and cooperative attacks using strategy) behavior among chimpanzees. These attacks took place over _____ years and were the result of an apparent dispute over the _____ _____.

39. Chagnon states that the Yanomamo Indians of Brazil are warlike due to competition among males for _____.

40. Culture is learned, shared and passed from one generation to the next. Chimpanzees and other nonhuman primates exhibit these characteristics particularly in their use of tools. To open nuts chimps use _____, to make a sponge to absorb water; for drinking or cleaning they use _____-_____; and to clean between their teeth, they may use a _____ as a toothpick.

41. Kanzi (the very bright bonobo) showed brilliant problem-solving ability in attempting to learn how to make cutting implements out of stone. He realized that if he _____ _____ the stone would shatter and produce plenty of cutting tools. He would then use these tools to cut open a bag containing food.

42. Free-ranging primates are in grave and immediate danger. Many species number in the hundreds in the wild while many others are in the low thousands. The three primary reasons for the threat to primate species are _____ _____, _____ and _____ _____.

43. Deforestation is occurring at the rate of 1 acre per second. This devastation is motivated by short-term _____ gains such as farmland or ranchland, trees for lumber and large scale _____ operations.

44. At least 70% of the habitat destruction has occurred since _____.

Multiple Choice Questions

1. Primates as a group
    A. have neurological complexity comparable with other mammals.
    B. have increased neurological complexity compared with other mammals.
    C. exhibit primarily instinctive behaviors.
    D. None of the above are correct.

2. Human behavior is
    A. no more complex than that of other primates.
    B. predominantly learned.
    C. predominantly genetic.
    D. similar to that of early hominids.

3. Small bodied species of primates
    A. have high energy needs.
    B. have higher metabolism.
    C. eat insects as a quick source of protein and energy.
    D. All of the above are correct.
    E. Both A and C are correct.

4. Folivorous primates
    A. are usually larger bodied.
    B. have a specialized gut for digestion.
    C. are usually smaller bodied.
    D. are usually arboreal.
    E. Both A and B are correct.

5. Suspensory behavior is exhibited more in
    A. small, arboreal primates.
    B. large, arboreal primates.
    C. terrestrial primates.
    D. vertical clingers.

6. When looking at brain size, it is important to also consider
    A. body size.
    B. the allometry of the species.
    C. whether the species engages in ritualized behaviors.
    D. All of the above are correct.
    E. Both A and B are correct.

7. Unintentional modes of communication among nonhuman primates might include
    A. body posture.
    B. raised body hair.
    C. a quick yawn to show canines.
    D. All of the above are correct.
    E. Both A and B are correct.

8. Touching, patting, hugging and holding hands are examples of
   A. reassurance.
   B. mating behaviors.
   C. submission.
   D. All of the above are correct.

9. Displays
   A. communicate an emotional state.
   B. reassure others in the group.
   C. console others.
   D. All of the above are correct.

10. An example of ritualized behaviors might include
    A. hugging and holding hands.
    B. social grooming.
    C. chest slapping among gorillas.
    D. vocalizations.

11. Mounting behavior among baboons
    A. is done by both sexes to both sexes and all ages.
    B. is the normal position used during copulation.
    C. indicates dominant/subordinate status.
    D. Both B and C are correct.

12. Group living among primates
    A. has virtually no disadvantages.
    B. is crucial for survival.
    C. provides better protection.
    D. All of the above are correct.
    E. Both B and C are correct.

13. Vervet monkey communication
    A. dispelled the previously held belief that primate vocalizations could not include external events or objects.
    B. is limited to scent marking and an occasional bark.
    C. includes specific sounds for different categories of predators (air, tree or ground).
    D. Both A and C are correct.

14. Apes cannot speak because
    A. they lack the intelligence.
    B they lack the anatomical structures necessary.
    C. they don't have anything they want to say.
    D. All of the above are correct.

15. Sara is a chimpanzee who
    A. learned ASL from her mother.
    B. learned to recognize plastic chips as symbols for various objects.
    C. spontaneously began signing after observing others.
    D. taught an infant ASL.

16. Koko
    A. is a female lowland gorilla.
    B. has learned over 500 signs of ASL.
    C. communicates with a male gorilla named Michael using ASL.
    D. All of the above are correct.
    E. Both A and B are correct.

17. Kanzi
    A. is an orangutan.
    B. has learned to make stone tools.
    C. spontaneously learned language through observation.
    D All of the above are correct.
    E. Both B and C are correct.

18. Ape language experiments
    A. show that apes are not capable of symbolic thought.
    B. may suggest clues to the origins of human language.
    C. show that all signing apes have the same understanding of the relationship
       between symbols and the objects they represent.
    D. have no value in assessing the evolutionary relationship between humans and apes.

19. In most humans, the language centers of the brain
    A. include Broca's area.
    B. are located on the left hemisphere.
    C. include the temporal lobe.
    D. All of the above are correct.
    E. Both A and B are correct.

20. The study of comparative brain structure
    A. is quite sophisticated.
    B indicates that brain size is the most important factor in the development of
       language.
    C indicates that it is the reorganization of neurological structures that is most important
       in the development of language.
    D. All of the above are correct.
    E. Both A and B are correct.

21. Affiliative behaviors
    A. arise when there is competition for resources.
    B. enhance group cohesiveness.
    C. are rare among primates.
    D. may include displays.

22. Conspecifics refers to
    A. cooperative hunters.
    B. a mating pair.
    C. members of the same species.
    D. those who remain in their natal community.

23. Territory refers to
    A. a portion of the home range that is actively protected.
    B. the area where an animal permanently lives.
    C. a geographic region that contains food, water and sleeping sites.
    D. All of the above are correct.

24. Chimpanzee border patrollers
    A. are tense and silent.
    B. are loud and physical.
    C. will attack a lone animal they encounter.
    D. are looking for other groups to play with.
    E. Both A and C are correct.

25. When female macaques and baboons band together in an aggressive encounter with other female groups,
    A. they do not usually result in fatalities.
    B. they mirror male attacks in motivation and results.
    C. they are usually the result of competition for resources.
    D. Both A and C are correct.

26. Nonhuman primate culture
    A. appears to be taught from one generation to the next.
    B. appears to be uniform among members of the same species.
    C. although learned is usually done by observation.
    D. includes regional variation in tool use.

27. Primates are endangered primarily because of
    A. habitat destruction.
    B. hunting.
    C. live capture.
    D. All of the above are correct.

28. Primates are killed
    A. to be eaten.
    B. to sell their skins.
    C. to sell their skulls.
    D. All of the above are correct

ANSWERS TO FILL-IN OUTLINE

I. INTRODUCTION
   A. 1. how
      2. central nervous system
      3. life history

II. ASPECTS OF LIFE HISTORY AND BODY SIZE
   A. weight
   B. 66 g or 2.4 ounces, 117 kg. or 258 pounds
   C. insects
   D. leaves
   E. fruit
   F. high, metabolism
   G. energy
   H. body size
   I. larger

III. BODY SIZE AND BRAIN SIZE
   A. correlated
   B. proportional
   C. body, brain
   D. less than
   E. before
   F. one year
   G. varied
   H. allometry

IV. COMMUNICATION
   A. autonomic
   B. deliberate
   C. threat
   D. touching, patting, hugging, holding hands
   E. normal
   F. learned
   G. displays
   H. ritualized behaviors
   I. predators
   J. arbitrary
   K. symbolically
   L. vocal tract, language-related
   M. ASL
   N. plastic chips
   O. gorilla, 500, ASL
   P. categorize
   Q. spontaneously
   R. are not

   S. communication
   T. left
   U. Wernicke's
   V. production
   W. reorganization

V. AFFILIATIVE BEHAVIORS
   A. promote
   B. friendly
   C. physical contact
   D. reconciliation
   E. Sex

VI. AGGRESSIVE INTERACTIONS
   A. conspecifics
   B. home range
   C. territory
   D. vocalizations
   E. hoot, display
   F. patrol borders
   G. attacking and sometimes killing
   H. bonds
   I. hostile, violent
   J. lethal, aggression
   K. philopatric
   L. females
   M. sex, food
   N. predisposition

VII. PRIMATE CULTURAL BEHAVIOR
   A. learned
   B. observation
   C. washing
   D. grain
   E. food
   F. termite sticks, leaf sponges, toothpicks, hammers and anvils
   G. variation
   H. sharp-edged flakes
   I. onto a hard floor causing it to shatter
   J. goal-directed
   K. newly developed

VIII. PRIMATE CONSERVATION
   A. half
   B. habitat destruction, hunting, live capture

C. second
D. farmland/ranchland, lumber, mining
E. fuelwood

F. food
G. skins, skulls
H. zoos, biomedical research, exotic pet trade

ANSWERS & REFERENCES TO FILL-IN QUESTIONS

1. life history, pp. 266-267
2. biological perspective, p. 266
3. physiological, p. 266
4. body size, p. 267
5. small, large, p. 267
6. supplemented, p. 267
7. insects, young buds, leaves, shoots, p. 267
8. insects, p. 267
9. gut, larger, p. 267
10. smaller, suspensory, p. 268
11. terrestrial, p. 268
12. encephalized, p. 268
13. immediately after, at least one year, p. 268
14. neurological growth, p. 268
15. allometry, p. 268
16. autonomic, raised body hair or enhanced body odor, p. 269
17. gestures, facial expressions, vocalizations, p. 269
18. presenting their hind quarters, pp. 269-271
19. submission, p. 269
20. submission, reassurance, p. 269
21. fear, submission, p. 269
22. learn, normal, pp. 269-270
23. reproductive, agonistic, p. 270
24. chest slapping, tearing of vegetation, screaming, waving arms, sticks/branches, p. 270
25. communication, p. 272
26. Have arbitrary symbols with no relationship to what they stand for, p. 273
27. differences in the anatomy of the vocal tract and language-related structures in the brain, p. 273
28. American Sign Language (for the deaf)
29. deliberately taught, p. 273
30. their mother, p. 274
31. spontaneously, 11 months, p. 274
32. left, motor cortex, p. 275
33. neurological structures, p. 276
34. physical contact such as hugging, kissing, grooming, p. 277
35. bonobos, p. 277
36. Defense of territories, sex, food, pp. 277 & 279
37. nonterritorial, p. 278
38. 3-4, home range, p. 278
39. mates (females), p. 280
40. Hammerstones, leaf-sponges, twig, p. 282
41. threw the stone onto the hard floor, p. 283
42. habitat destruction, hunting, live capture, p. 284
43. economic, mining, p. 284
44. World War II, p. 284

Answers & References to Multiple Choice Questions

1. B, p. 266	8. A, p. 269	15. B, p. 273	22. C, p. 277
2. B, p. 266	9. A, p. 270	16. D, p. 274	23. A, p. 277
3. D, p. 267	10. C, p. 270	17. E, p. 274	24. E, p. 278
4. E, p. 267	11. D, p. 271	18. B, p. 275	25. D, p. 279
5. B, p. 268	12. E, p. 271	19. D, pp. 275-276	26. C, p. 280
6. E, p. 268	13. D, p. 272	20. C, p. 276	27. D, p. 284
7. E, p. 269	14. B, p. 273	21. B, p. 277	28. D, p. 286

CHAPTER 12

PRIMATE EVOLUTION

LEARNING OBJECTIVES

After reading this chapter you should be able to:
- discuss the difficulties of distinguishing the primates of Paleocene from other placental mammals of that time. (p. 295)
- state during which epoch, and in what geographical locations, the earliest undoubted primates appear; what type of modern primate do the earliest primates most resemble? (pp. 296-297)
- comment on some of the characteristics that are important in identifying an early anthropoid from a fossil prosimian. Where are the earliest anthropoids found? (pp. 297-299)
- discuss the current ideas for the origins of New World monkeys. (pp. 299-301)
- explain what rafting is and why this concept is important in primate evolution. (pp. 297, 300)
- list the types of primates found at the Fayum in the Oligocene. (pp. 301-305).
- discuss the groupings of Miocene hominoids and what these groupings mean evolutionarily. (pp. 305-306)
- discuss the role of geological events of the mid-Miocene on hominoid evolution. (pp. 307-308)
- compare and contrast the Miocene hominoids of Africa, Europe, and Asia. (309-315)
- discuss the problems of classifying fossil forms at both the species and genus levels. (pp. 315-321)

FILL-IN OUTLINE

Introduction

Chapter 12 turns to the fossil history of the primates over the last 60 million years and, by so doing, it looks at our own evolutionary history as well. With what you have learned about primate anatomy, ecology, and social behavior, you will be able to "flesh out" the bones and teeth that make up the evolutionary record of primate origins.

I. TIMESCALE

A. Review the geological timescale on p. 294.

B. Text organization and evolution

1. Evolution is **NOT** a _____ - directed process, nor is there anything in evolution analogous to _____.

2. This text focuses on human evolution, but it should not be interpreted as implying that humans are the end product of evolution or that more recent organisms are "_____" than ancient ones.

II. EARLY PRIMATE EVOLUTION

A. Primate origins begin in the _____ _____ radiation at the start of the Cenozoic.

1. Primates diverged very _____ from the primitive placental mammals.

2. Discerning early primates from these very early generalized mammals is quite difficult.

B. Plesiadapiforms

1. Until recently plesiadapiforms were considered to be the earliest

   _____.

   a. Only fragmentary evidence of _____ and _____ were known.

   b. Subsequent fossil material, including elements of the hand and wrist (where primate characteristics would be obvious), suggest these mammals are more closely related to colugos.

2. This group has been removed from the order Primates.

3. Nevertheless, plesiadapiforms are probably closely linked to the early roots of the primates, but the primates had already _____ by the appearance of this group.

C. The bottom line: we are left with extremely scarce traces of the beginnings of the primate radiation.

III. ANCIENT LANDSCAPES AND EARLY PRIMATE EVOLUTION

A. The world land masses were positioned quite differently during the early stages of primate evolution than they are today (see p. 191). In the northern hemisphere, North America and Europe were connected via _____.

   1. This provided a _____ for terrestrial animals to migrate and disperse over.

   2. This accounts for why "primate-like" mammals were found in both North America and Europe.

B. As the continents drifted, _____ conditions changed dramatically affecting local ecosystems.

   1. Climates _____.

   2. These climatic changes affected _____ communities.

     a. The Cenozoic became a time of rapid _____ of new varieties of plants.

     b. Many of these plants were pollinated by _____.

     c. As insects became more abundant, so did animals that fed on them, including early _____.

IV. EOCENE PRIMATES (55-34 M.Y.A.)

A. Prosimian radiation

   1. The first fossil forms that are clearly primates are "_____" and come from the Eocene.

   2. The best known of the Eocene prosimians are the Adapidae, a _____ -like family of primates.

a. The _____ are found in both North America and Europe

b. Primate tendencies in the adapids include

   1. complete _____ bar.

   2. larger, rounded braincase.

   3. _____ instead of claws.

   4. eyes rotated forward indicating _____ vision.

   5. indications of prehensility in the limbs as well as a(n) _____ large toe.

c. While the adapids resemble lemurs in overall appearance, they do not show the same _____ found in modern lorises and lemurs, such as a dental comb.

   1. Malagasy lemurs appear to have separated from the other prosimians by _____ Eocene times.

   2. The Malagasy lemurs probably reached _____ by rafting.

3. The other major group of Eocene prosimians were the family Omomyidae.

a. _____ were the most widely distributed of the Eocene prosimians; fossil localities include North America, Europe, and a few specimens from Asia.

b. The early generalized members of the omomyids may provide a base from which the _____ could have arisen.

   1. It has been suggested that some of the omomyids are closely related to the tarsier.

   2. One omomyid feature, the position of the olfactory portion of the brain, links the omomyids with later _____.

4. There is no consensus as to which Eocene primate gave rise to the anthropoids. The only agreement is that the anthropoids did evolve from some

_____.

B. Early anthropoids

   1. The major paleontological site for late Eocene and Oligocene primates is the

      _____ .

     a. Today the Fayum is desert, 60 miles southwest of Cairo, but in the Oligocene

        it bordered the Mediterranean and was _____ _____ forest.

     b. Altogether thousands of specimens from the period _____-_____ m.y.a. have

        been recovered from the Fayum.

     c. It appears that the early Fayum anthropoids were _____-bodied and may

        have eaten a mixed diet of fruits and insects.

   2. *Catopithecus* is the best known of the early _____ found at

    the Fayum.

     a. This genus has several shared _____ characteristics with anthropoids,

        viz.,

        1. closure of the back of the _____.

        2. _____ of the midline of the frontal bone into a single bone.

        3. anchoring of the _____ by a bone hoop to the wall of the ear.

        4. rounded _____ on the lower molar teeth.

     b. *Catopithecus* also has a mixture of retained primitive features reminiscent of

        _____ including a long snout and small brain.

   3. The question of anthropoid origins has in no way been settled. *Eosimias* from

        _____ is only one of a number of other candidates vying for the title of

    "earliest anthropoid." See Table 12-1 for a list of other potential Eocene

    anthropoids.

V. NEW WORLD MONKEYS

A. New World monkey evolution requires an understanding of geological events.

1. In the late Eocene and early Oligocene, _____ _____ was an island continent separate from North America and Africa.

2. The distance between South America and Africa was much less than it is today. Monkeys from Africa could have _____ this distance to the New World.

B. It is unlikely that Old and New World primates share any evolutionary history after the early _____.

C. New World monkey fossil record

1. Eocene prosimian fossils abound in North America. However, note that North and South America were not connected at this time.

2. The fossil record for New World anthropoids in South America is extremely _____. This makes tracing the evolutionary heritage of New World monkeys very difficult.

VI. OLIGOCENE (34-22.5 M.Y.A.)

A. By the end of the Oligocene, cercopithecoid and hominoid lineages have diverged from their last _____ ancestor.

B. Oligocene primate paleontology

1. Presumably, _____ species of anthropoids were adapting to varied ecological niches in Africa, Asia, and Europe.

2. Unfortunately, the **only** paleontological site for Oligocene primates is the _____. Over a thousand specimens have been recovered, but all we know about Oligocene primate evolution comes from this site.

C. *Apidium* (two species)

1. The genus _____ is the most abundant fossil primate recovered from the Fayum.

2. *Apidium* was _____ size and had several anthropoid features.

3. This anthropoid's dental formula was 2-1-3-3, retaining a _____

_____ which is unlike any modern Old World monkey.

    a. Some have suggested that *Apidium*, and its close relatives, may even predate

      the _____ of Old and New World anthropoids.

    b. On the whole, the teeth suggest a diet of fruit and probably seeds.

4. Limb material suggests that *Apidium* was a small arboreal _____

proficient at leaping and springing.

D. *Propliopithecus* (four species)

    1. This genus is a very _____ Old World anthropoid without

      derived tendencies towards any direction.

    2. Significant is the presence of a ___ - ___ - ___ - ___ dental formula, the same

      formula as contemporary Old World anthropoids.

    3. This was a small to medium anthropoid that most likely consumed fruits.

E. *Aegyptopithecus* (one species)

    1. _____ is one of the most completely represented and

      significant fossil genera from the Fayum.

    2. This is the _____ of the Fayum anthropoids (13-18 pounds, about the

      size of a howler money).

    3. *Aegyptopithecus* bridges the gap between Eocene prosimians and the Miocene

      _____.

    4. Teeth

      a. The dental formula is ___ - ___ - ___ -___.

      b. The teeth are primitive for an Old World anthropoid; they do not have shared

         _____ characteristics of either the hominoids or the Old World

      monkeys.

   c. Dental interpretations

      1. Until recently it was believed that the dental pattern of the Old World

         monkeys was more _____ and the Y-5 molar cusp pattern

         of the hominoids was more _____.

      2. Reevaluation of fossil materials now suggests that the Old World monkey

         pattern is more derived and the hominoid _____ arrangement is the

         more primitive.

   d. Y-5 pattern

      1. The Y-5 pattern refers to a Y-shaped "valley" formed by the distribution of

         five cusps on hominoid molars. See Fig. 12-3.

      2. The Y-5 pattern is considered a derived trait found only among the hominoids.

5. Skull

   a. The skull is small and resembles a _____ skull in some details.

   b. The organization of the brain is somewhat _____

      between prosimians and anthropoids.

      1. The _____ cortex is large compared to prosimians.

      2. There is a reduction of the _____ bulbs, approaching the

         anthropoid condition.

      3. However, a prosimian-like trait is that the _____ lobes are not

         especially expanded.

      4. Overall, the brain size is _____ (30-40 cm ^{3}).

6. Reconstruction of the appendages indicate that *Aegyptopithecus* was a short-limbed,

   heavily muscled, slow-moving _____ quadruped.

7. There was great variation between individuals in _____ size in

   Aegyptopithecus.

a. This implies that male-female _____ _____ was

marked.

b. Using _____ primates as models, great canine sexual dimorphism is

found among primates with polygynous mating patterns.

1. In such primate species, there is fierce _____ among

males for mates.

2. Based on these modern primate species, it can be inferred that these

behaviors were typical of _____.

8. Overall, *Aegyptopithecus* is a paleontological _____.

a. In most respects it is a very primitive Old World anthropoid.

b. This animal could have been the _____ to both Old World

monkeys and hominoids.

c. There is a hint in the teeth, however, that has led some to place

Aegyptopithecus on the _____ line; others are not as convinced.

VII. EARLY FOSSIL ANTHROPOIDS: SUMMARY

A. The diverse array of fossils from the Fayum between 36 and 33 m.y.a. demonstrates

that the anthropoids _____ along several different evolutionary lines.

B. The fragmentary nature of the fossil record makes precise _____

risky.

C. New World monkey origins

1. It appears that _____ and its close relatives may be near or even

before the Old World-New World monkey split.

2. The above inference would fit the scenario of an _____ origin for the

New World monkeys, who then reach South America during the Oligocene.

D. Old World anthropoid origins

1. *Aegyptopithecus* and its relatives are seen as _____ the major split in catarrhine (Old World anthropoid) evolution.

2. It would appear that the split between the Old World monkeys and the hominoids occurred late in the _____ or very early in the _____.

VIII. HOMINOIDS: LARGE AND SMALL; AFRICAN AND ASIAN; FOSSIL AND MODERN

A. Evolutionary relationships among the living hominoids

1. The living hominoids serve as a _____ for most of the major radiations that occurred in the past.

2. Based on _____ there are two major subgroupings.

a. The _____-bodied hominoids are the gibbon and siamang and all of their ancestors and related side branches back to the time of their split with the other hominoids.

b. There are four genera of large-bodied hominoids: *Pongo, Gorilla, Pan*, and *Homo*. These four genera can then be divided into _____ large-bodied (orangutans) and _____ large-bodied hominoids (gorillas, chimpanzees, bonobos, and humans).

3. These _____ designations can be used to denote their respective lineages back to the time when they split from one another.

B. Understanding the fossil record

1. One way we can attempt to understand the diversity of the fossil record is by _____ the fragments and by projecting our conclusions forward to later forms.

2. Another way is to use living forms and infer _____ (working backwards), highlighting the major adaptive radiations that have occurred.

a. A problem with referential models is that only a small proportion of all the primates that have ever lived are _____ today.

b. Thus, living primates cannot give us insight into species that have no living relatives.

c. Care must be taken not to limit interpretations to simple models derived from living primates only.

3. By _____ fossil interpretations (from functional anatomy and ecology) with referential models (especially biochemical data) most primate evolutionists would agree that there have been four major "events" or evolutionary splits in anthropoid evolution prior to the emergence of the hominids, viz., the splits between

a. the _____ _____ and _____ _____ anthropoids.

b. Old World monkeys and _____.

c. _____ -bodied and _____ -bodied hominoids.

d. _____ and _____ lines of large-bodied hominoids.

IX. MIOCENE (22.5-5 M.Y.A.)—HOMINOIDS APLENTY

A. The _____ was the "heyday" of the hominoids, marked by a spectacular radiation.

1. Hominoids ranged from western _____ to eastern _____ as well as Africa.

2. There is a great amount of hominoid fossil material from the period _____ - ___ m.y.a.

3. The large amount of fossil material actually caused great taxonomic confusion with a vast number of genera and species proposed.

a. Part of the problem was that the fossil material was accumulated over a period of _____ years and from three different _____.

b. In the 1960s, the material was reevaluated by several researchers and

"_____" into two genera.

   1. One genus was presumed more "_____ -like."

   2. The other genus was presumed more "_____ -like."

c. Recently a tremendous amount of new data has come to light which questions

the validity of the earlier "lumping."

B. The hominoid evolutionary radiation of the Miocene produced a whole array of

_____ organisms.

1. Many of the Miocene hominoids have no _____ descendants.

2. Today about 30 genera of Miocene hominoids are recognized. Unlike earlier

taxonomy, the more recent classifications are firmly based on biological principles

and _____ methods.

C. Paleogeography and Miocene hominoid evolution

1. We have seen that there was a proliferation of Old World anthropoid forms from

the Fayum of North Africa during the Oligocene.

a. In the early Miocene, the evidence is also restricted to eastern _____.

b. It appears that hominoids originated in Africa and underwent a successful

_____ _____ there.

   1. The earliest hominoids appeared before _____ m.y.a.

   2. These early hominoids were exclusively African, and East Africa was

believed to be a heavily _____ area.

2. African fauna were _____ on an island continent until 16 m.y.a.

a. Around 16 m.y.a. the movement of tectonic plates caused Africa to "_____"

with Eurasia through the Arabian Peninsula.

b. The collision of Africa with Asia provided a bridge for African faunas, including

the hominoids, to _____ out of Africa and into Eurasia.

3. The earliest hominoids were undoubtedly arboreal.

   a. However, ecological changes were occurring in Africa. By 16 m.y.a. much of the tropical rain forest in East Africa was being replaced by open _____ (a mosaic environment of trees, like oak, separated from one another by open grassy areas) and _____ (grasslands).

   b. Some African hominoids were radiating into niches in these more open areas at around _____ - _____ m.y.a.

      1. Part of this adaptation probably involved exploitation of different foods and more _____ living.

      2. These hominoids, partly terrestrial and mosaic environment-adapted, were capable of migrating into _____.

D. Miocene hominoids—changing views and terminology

   1. Once the hominoids migrated into Eurasia, they dispersed rapidly and diversified into a variety of _____.

   2. An enormous amount of fossil material for the mid-Miocene has been recovered recently. This has sparked a _____ of previous theories of early hominoid evolution, as is normal in such a situation for any scientific discipline.

E. African forms (23-14 m.y.a.)

   1. A wealth of hominoid fossils come from East Africa.

   2. These diverse forms are classified in two families with arguments made for a third family.

   3. The best known of these fossils is _____ (family Proconsulidae) and this genus exhibits considerable variation.

      a. Body size estimates for the species that belong to this genus range from _____ pounds (the size of a small monkey) to between _____ and _____ pounds (the size of a female gorilla).

    b. Environmental niches were also quite varied: some species were confined to dense rain forests while others may have exploited open _____.

    c. It has been suggested that there was also great variation in locomotor behaviors, including some that were at least partly _____.

    d. Despite the other anatomical variation, dentition was quite _____ among *Proconsul*.

        1. All showed the typical Old World anthropoid pattern, ___ - ___ - ___ - ___.

        2. *Proconsul* had broad upper incisors and large sexually dimorphic _____.

        3. Molars had thick _____, but the soft dentin of the tooth penetrated into the cusps so that the enamel was worn through fairly quickly.

        4. The characteristic __ - __ molar pattern of hominoids was present.

        5. This type of dentition suggests that *Proconsul* consumed fruit.

    e. Brain

        1. The brain size estimates indicate a brain the size of modern _____ _____ _____, but not as large as living hominoids.

        2. The surface features of the brain are _____.

  4. The taxonomy for the proconsulids is confusing and in a state of flux.

  5. It appears that the proconsulids are primitive hominoids. Many primate evolutionary biologists place these forms before the _____ of the small- and large-bodied hominoids.

F. European forms (13-11 m.y.a.)

  1. The European Miocene hominoid fossil record consists mainly of jaws and teeth.

  2. These forms are assigned to the genus *Dryopithecus*.

    a. The main characteristic of *Dryopithecus* is thinly _____ molars.

    b. It is unlikely that *Dryopithecus* is related to any _____ hominoid.

G. South/Southwest Asian forms (16-7 m.y.a.)

   1. _____ is an Asian form that ranges from Turkey to India and Pakistan.

   2. Characteristics of *Sivapithecus*

      a. _____-bodied, ranging from 70-150 pounds.

      b. It probably was arboreal.

      c. The concave facial profile and projecting incisors bear a remarkable resemblance to the modern _____.

         1. Thus, there is fossil evidence suggesting some ancient traces of the orangutan lineage. In this case the views of _____ and _____ agree more closely.

         2. It should be noted, however, that except for the face and jaw, *Sivapithecus* does _____ resemble an orangutan.

      d. In the _____, *Sivapithecus* is not like any other known hominoid.

         1. The forelimb suggests a mixture of traits indicating some mode of arboreal _____.

         2. The forelimb gives no hint of a _____ capability, a very unorangutan-like trait.

      e. All in all, *Sivapithecus* could best be described as highly _____.

H. Other Miocene hominoids

   1. *Pliopithecus* (c. 16-11 m.y.a.).

      a. This is a small hominoid originally suggested as a gibbon ancestor; however, upon more detailed examination the similarities with gibbons are only _____.

      b. For the most relevant anatomical details *Pliopithecus* is a remarkably _____ hominoid.

c. This ape lived in Eurasia.

2. *Ouranopithecus* (10-9 m.y.a.).

a. This Miocene ape was recovered from Greece.

b. *Ouranopithecus* has a mixture of traits making its precise evolutionary relation-ships _____.

3. Lufeng, Yunnan Province, China

a. An enormous amount of fossil hominoid material has been recovered at this site.

b. It is uncertain how many genera are present.

c. The evolutionary relationships of these Chinese specimens are unclear. Because of the Asian location it might be expected that they would show affinities with the *Sivapithecus* - _____ lineage, but this is not the case.

X. THE MEANING OF GENUS AND SPECIES

A. Our study of fossil primates has introduced us to a number a taxonomic names for extinct primates.

1. What do these names mean in evolutionary terms?

2. Our goal is to make meaningful _____ statements when we assign taxonomic names.

B. Definition of species

1. The most precise taxonomic level that we would like to assign fossil primates to is the _____.

a. Recall from Chapter 2 that a living biological species is a group of interbreeding, or potentially interbreeding, organisms that are reproductively isolated and produce viable and fertile offspring.

b. Do fossil species meet these criteria? We cannot _____ them so we cannot know for certain.

2. A question that must be answered in dealing with the species concept is, What is the biological significance of the _____ that is present? There are two possible answers.

   a. Variation is accounted for by individual, age, and sex differences, i.e.,

      _____ variation.

   b. Or, variation represents differences between reproductively isolated groups, i.e., _____ variation.

   c. Making the choice

      1. In order to make a choice between the two possibilities we must use

         _____ species as models and observe their reproductive behavior.

      2. If the amount of morphological variation observed in fossil samples is consistent with the variation of modern species of closely related forms, then we should not "_____" our sample into more than one species.

3. Our evolutionary interpretations of the vast array of variable Miocene hominoids should adhere to the following relevant biological criteria.

   a. _____ the relevant material must be examined. Splitting fossil groups into several is not justified on the basis of only presumed differences in the sample.

   b. The variation observed in the sample must be statistically extrapolated to realistic dimensions of _____ biological populations.

   c. _____ dimensions of variation in closely related groups of living primates are then referred to, keeping in mind the expected effects of age, sexual dimorphism, and individual variation.

   d. The results are then extrapolated to the _____ sample and the judgment is made: How many species are represented?

    e. Because fossil forms are scattered through time, we must also place the different species within a firm _____ (time-frame).

    f. Finally, we want to make interpretations of which forms are evolutionarily _____ to other forms. To do this we must pay careful attention to primitive traits versus derived traits.

4. The above procedure helps to reduce confusion; however, the biological interpretation of fossils into taxonomic categories is not simple nor is it unambiguous.

    a. One serious problem with fossil species is the _____ _____ involved.

       1. _____ variation is possible in fossil species because individual specimens may be separated by thousands, perhaps millions, of years.

       2. Standard Linnaean taxonomy is designed to account for the variation present at a particular time (in living species) and, basically, describes a _____ situation (no change, or evolution, occurring).

       3. *Homo erectus* is a good example of a hominid paleospecies.

          a. Until recently it was generally accepted that *Homo erectus* spanned more than one _____ years.

          b. There are some _____ differences between the earliest representatives of *Homo erectus* and later representatives.

    b. Where can meaningful species boundaries be established in such a temporally dynamic situation?

       1. The task is made easier if there is an _____ fossil record.

          a. Fossil samples may be separated by great gaps of _____.

          b. _____ differences may be great in samples separated by time gaps.

       2. Classification is more difficult when fossil populations are _____ in both time and morphology.

a. Such a lineage, with slow gradual evolution of form, is said to be

_____ (straight-line evolution).

b. Such a lineage can be viewed as a single _____.

3. Most populations do _____ appear to be anagenetic; anagenesis seems to be the exception rather than the rule.

a. _____ (i.e., speciation) is much more typical of evolutionary change, consistent with punctuated equilibrium (see p. 199).

b. It is imperative in evolutionary interpretation to understand ancestor-_____ relationships.

1. Traditionally, anatomical comparisons were made of fossil samples which were then constructed into _____ (evolutionary trees).

2. A more recent approach is the construction of _____ (a set of relationships shown as a hypothesis).

a. In this approach a detailed interpretation of primitive versus derived character states is stated.

b. Several cladograms can usually be constructed from the _____ set of data.

c. The cladograms that are most _____ (i.e., require the fewest steps to get from species A to species B) at explaining the patterns of derived characteristics are provisionally accepted, while the less adequate cladograms are rejected.

d. A basic assumption of cladistic analysis is that trait patterns are developed as the result of ancestor-descendant relationships and that _____ are not so common to be overly confusing.

C. Definition of genus

    1. The next higher level of taxonomy from the species is the _____. The classification of fossils at the genus level presents its own problem.

        a. One definition of a genus is a group of _____ composed of members more closely related to each other than they are to species from another genus. This often becomes very subjective.

        b. In order to have more than one genus there must be at least _____ species.

    2. Another definition of a genus is a number of species that share the same broad adaptive zone, or an "_____ _____."

        a. This represents a general _____ lifestyle more basic than the particular ecological niches characteristic of species. This ecological definition is more useful for applying to fossil genera.

        b. _____ are the most often preserved parts and they are excellent ecological indicators.

        c. If some of the Miocene hominoids appear to _____ different adaptive/ecological zones, we are justified in postulating more than one genus present.

        d. Thus, operationally, categorization at the _____ level becomes the most practical biological interpretation of fragmentary extinct forms.

KEY TERMS

Adapidae: the Eocene primate family that most closely resembles the lemurs among the extant primates.

Aegyptopithecus: the largest of the Fayum anthropoids. This primate was primitive enough to have been the ancestor to both the Old World monkeys and the hominoids. Based on the teeth some think it gave rise to the hominoids.

anagenesis: straight-line evolution in which there is continual evolution and change occurs at a gradual pace. Anagenetic evolution is not characterized by speciation events and a phylogenetic tree that reflects anagenetic evolution resembles a "ladder."

Apidium : the fossil primate genus from the Fayum that has three premolars. It may be ancestral, or related to whatever was, to the New World monkeys.

Cenozoic: the geological era during which primate evolution occurred. It encompasses the last 65 million years.

cladogenesis: branching evolution characterized by speciation events. Cladogenetic evolution produces a phylogenetic tree that resembles a bush, rather than a ladder

Dryopithecus : the Miocene hominoid genus that inhabited Europe. This hominoid was characterized by thin molar enamel.

Fayum: a rich paleontological site in Egypt that yields late Eocene primates and is the only site for Oligocene primates.

interspecific: refers to between two or more species.

intraspecific: refers to within one species.

Omomyidae: the most widely distributed Eocene primate family. The earliest generalized members may form the ancestral basis for all later anthropoids.

-pithecus: the Greek suffix meaning "ape."

plesiadapiforms: a family of primate-like mammals of the Paleocene. Long thought to be the earliest primates they have now been removed from the primate order.

paleospecies: groups of fossil organisms that are assigned to the same species. Paleospecies exhibit more variation than in living species. This is because of the time span involved; in humans *Homo erectus* covers more than one million years.

Proconsul : the genus of Miocene hominoid from Africa. *Proconsul* was the most primitive of the Miocene hominoids.

Sivapithecus : the Miocene hominoid found in Asia that has several derived characteristics that link it to the orangutan.

Y-5 molar pattern: a pattern on hominoid molars in which the five cusps surround a pattern of crevice that forms a Y. See illustration on p. 303.

Now take the Fill-in and Multiple Choice Tests. Do not guess. Following completion of the tests correct them. The correct answers and textbook page references are at the end of this study guide chapter. Note your strong areas and your weak areas to guide you in your continuing study.

FILL-IN QUESTIONS

1. Evolution is not _____ - _____. Nor is there anything in evolution analogous to progress.

2. The ancestor of the modern _____ is sometimes confused as an one of the earliest primates. Despite their close relationship these two groups had already diverged by Paleocene times.

3. The first fossil forms that are clearly identifiable as primates appear during the _____.

4. The adapids, although they do not have some of the derived characteristics seen in modern prosimians, appear to be the ancestors of the _____.

5. The most important Oligocene fossil primate locality in the Old World is the _____.

6. The Oligocene primate that best bridges the gap between the Eocene prosimians and the Miocene hominoids is _____.

7. The hominoid molar cusp pattern, now believed to be the primitive anthropoid condition, is called the _____ pattern.

8. Based on canine sexual dimorphism, it has been speculated that *Aegyptopithecus* had a _____ mating pattern with competition between males for mates.

9. The gibbons and siamangs represent the living _____ - _____ hominoids.

10. Gorillas, chimpanzees, bonobos, and humans represent the living _____ large-bodied hominoids.

11. A living species that is used to infer conclusions about a fossil species is called a _____ model.

12. The great hominoid radiation, the epoch of apes, occurred during the _____.

13. When a large number of genera are condensed into a much smaller number of genera, it is referred to as _____.

14. The earliest hominoids, Miocene apes, come from _____ _____.

15. The most primitive of the Miocene hominoid families was the _____.

16. The best known Miocene ape from Europe belongs to the genus _____.

17. Variation within a species is known as _____ variation.

18. Variation between different species is called _____ variation.

19. A group of fossil organisms placed within the same species, that encompasses a considerable period of time, is referred to as a _____.

20. A lineage that evolves continuously over time without marked speciation events is referred to as _____.

21. _____ is the approach in which relationships can be examined by comparing primitive versus derived traits and testing a set of relationships shown as a hypothesis.

22. The illustration below is referred to as a _____ .

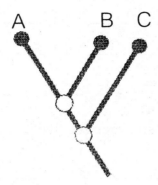

23. Fill in the phylogenetic tree that illustrates the major branches of anthropoid evolution.

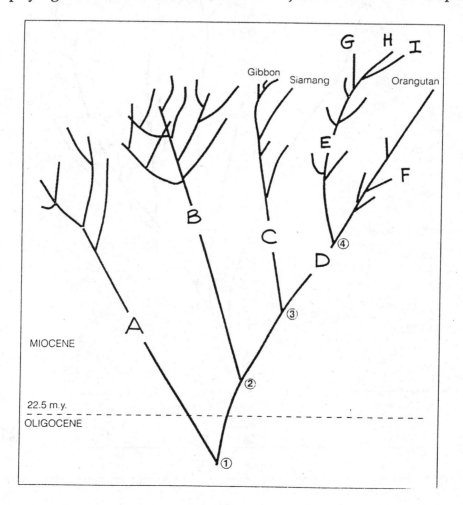

A. _____   F. _____

B. _____   G. _____

C. _____   H. _____

D. _____   I. _____

E. _____

24. Fill in the phylogenetic tree that summarizes the evolutionary relationships of Miocene hominoids.

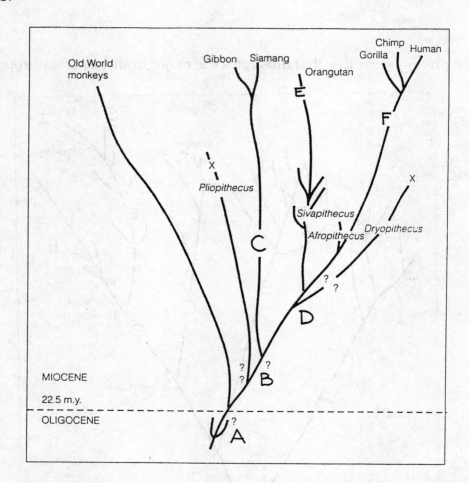

A. _____   D. _____

B. _____   E. _____

C. _____   F. _____

MULTIPLE CHOICE QUESTIONS

1. Which of the following is **not** a correct statement?
    A. As we trace the chronological sequence of fossil forms, we find that evolution culminates with humans as the final goal.
    B. More recent organisms are not evolutionarily superior to more ancient organisms.
    C. Evolution is not a goal-directed process.
    D. Evolution does not occur through progress.

2. The early primate evolution of the Paleocene
    A. is well represented by the genus *Plesiadapis*.
    B. is quite fragmentary and no indisputable primate can be identified.
    C. is represented mainly by limb bones with few skull parts preserved.
    D. Both B and C are correct.

3. Which of the following is **not** correct regarding the early Cenozoic?
    A. It was a time of rapid diversification of new varieties of plants.
    B. Primates were mainly confined to North America and Europe up until about 40 m.y.a.
    C. The world looked very much like it is today.
    D. Temperatures increased from what they had been in the Mesozoic.

4. The time of greatest prosimian radiation was during the
    A. Paleocene.
    B. Eocene.
    C. Oligocene.
    D. Miocene.

5. The Adapidae were
    A. lemur-like.
    B. tarsier-like.
    C. anthropoid-like.
    D. hominoid-like.

6. The most widely distributed of the Eocene prosimians were the
    A. plesiadapids.
    B. adapids.
    C. omomyids.
    D. tarsiers.

7. Which of the following characteristics is an anthropoid characteristic, not found in any non-anthropoids, present in *Catopithecus*?
    A. eyes rotated forward
    B. opposable great toe
    C. nails
    D. closure of the back of the orbit

8. Which of the following statements about New World monkey evolution is **not** correct?
    A. It is very unlikely that the Old and New World primates have shared any evolutionary history since the early Oligocene.
    B. The fossil history of the New World monkeys is rich in South America.
    C. In the early Oligocene, South America was an island continent, much closer to Africa than it is today.
    D. *Apidium* may be related to whatever was the ancestor of the New World monkeys.

9. According to most primate evolutionary biologists, *Aegyptopithecus*
    A. is the ancestor of the hominoids.
    B. is near, or even before, the split of Old and New World anthropoids.
    C. is the direct ancestor of the New World anthropoids.
    D. precedes the major split in catarrhine evolution.

10. Which of the following is **not** as closely related as the other three?
    A. orangutan
    B. gorilla
    C. chimpanzee
    D. human

11. The living hominoids today are
    A. the most diverse group of primates that has ever existed.
    B. the most diverse group of hominoids that has ever existed.
    C. a small remnant of a very successful Miocene radiation.
    D. the most successful hominoids that have ever lived.

12. Miocene hominoid fossil taxonomy has been equivocal and confusing. A major reason for this is that
    A. there such a small collection of individual fossils.
    B. discoveries took place on three continents.
    C. discoveries spanned more than a century.
    D. Both B and C are major reasons.

13. The event which resulted in an exchange of fauna between Africa and Eurasia was
    A. a land bridge that was formed when Africa collided with Arabia.
    B. extensive mountain building.
    C. the replacement of desert by tropical rain forests.
    D. an ice age.

14. A major ecological change that occurred in Africa around 16 m.y.a. was
    A. an extensive ice age.
    B. increased aridity and replacement of tropical rain forest with open woodlands and savannas.
    C. an increase in temperature and humidity resulting in an extension of tropical rain forest.
    D. a major extinction of hominoids.

15. Which of the following is a Miocene African hominoid?
    A. *Dryopithecus*
    B. *Sivapithecus*
    C. *Proconsul*
    D. *Pliopithecus*

16. An African Miocene hominoid that shares some characteristics, such as large central incisors and thick molar enamel, yet shares other important anatomical features with the African large-bodied apes is
    A. *Proconsul.*
    B. *Sivapithecus.*
    C. *Dryopithecus.*
    D. *Afropithecus.*

17. A characteristic of the Miocene hominoids of Europe was
    A. short canines.
    B. thick molar enamel.
    C. thin molar enamel.
    D. longer hindlimbs than forelimbs.

18. The Miocene ape that bears a striking resemblance to the modern orangutan in the face, but not in the postcranium, is
    A. Dryopithecus.
    B. Sivapithecus.
    C. Proconsul.
    D. Pliopithecus.

19. *Sivapithecus* was
    A. unlike any known hominoid.
    B. probably was a suspensory ape that spent most of its time in the trees.
    C. was a very primitive hominoid.
    D. was a terrestrial seed-eater.

20. For a number of years "*Ramapithecus*" was declared a possible human ancestor. What has since happened to this genus of Miocene hominoid?
    A. it was discovered to be a modern human that had become mixed into a Miocene deposit.
    B. further finds of postcrania show this to be an Old World monkey.
    C. it has been reassigned ("lumped") to *Sivapithecus*.
    D. it was a complete hoax, but the perpetuator is unknown.

21. Which of the following statements is **not** correct?
    A. Some of the Miocene hominoids, such as *Dryopithecus,* are derived in directions unlike any living ape.
    B. The Chinese hominoids from Lufeng do not show shared derived features of the *Sivapithecus*-orangutan lineage.
    C. *Sivapithecus* has several derived features of the face that link it with the Asian large-bodied hominoid line.
    D. *Pliopithecus* is a highly derived hominoid that appears to be the direct ancestor of the gibbon.

22. Researchers have been attempting to time the hominid-pongid split through the use of
    A. a "molecular clock."
    B. Carbon 14.
    C. bio-stratigraphy.
    D. the amounts of fluorine-uranium-nitrogen found in fossils.

23. A major difference between paleospecies and biological species is that a paleospecies
    A. is more variable.
    B. adds a temporal component.
    C. does not interbreed among itself.
    D. Both A and B are correct.

24. Branching evolution is consistent with
    A. anagenesis.
    B. phyletic gradualism.
    C. punctuated equilibrium.
    D. Cole's paradox.

25. Closely related species are grouped together in a
    A. species.
    B. subspecies
    C. genus.
    D. subfamily.

26. Species that share the same broad adaptive zone is another definition for a
    A. species.
    B. genus.
    C. family.
    D. infraorder.

27. When working with the fragmentary fossil remains of extinct forms, the most practical taxonomic level to work with is the
    A. species.
    B. genus.
    C. family.
    D. infraorder.

ANSWERS TO FILL-IN OUTLINE

I. TIMESCALE
   B. 1. goal, progress
      2. better

II. EARLY PRIMATE EVOLUTION
   A. placental mammalian
     1. early
   B. 1. primates
      a. jaws, teeth
     3. diverged

III. ANCIENT LANDSCAPES AND EARLY PRIMATE EVOLUTION
   A. Greenland
     1. landbridge
   B. climatic
     1. cooled
     2. plant
      a. radiation
      b. insects
      c. primates

IV. EOCENE PRIMATES (55-34 M.Y.A.)
   A. 1. prosimian
     2. lemur
      a. adapids
      b. 1. postorbital
       3. nails
       4. binocular (This, of course would imply stereoscopic vision.)
       5. opposable
      c. specializations
       1. late
       2. Madagascar
     3. a. Omomyidae or omomyids
      b. anthropoids
      2. haplorhines
     4. prosimian
   B. 1. Fayum
      a. tropical rain
      b. 36-33
      c. small
     2. anthropoids
      a. derived
       1. orbit
       2. fusion
       3. eardrum
       4. cusps
      b. prosimians
     3. China

V. NEW WORLD MONKEYS
   A. 1. South America
     2. rafted
   B. Oligocene
   C. 2. sparse

VI. OLIGOCENE (34-22.5 M.Y.A.)
   A. common
   B. 1. diverse
     2. Fayum
   C. 1. *Apidium*
     2. squirrel
     3. third premolar
      a. divergence
     4. quadruped
   D. 1. generalized
     2. 2-1-2-3
   E. 1. *Aegyptopithecus*
     2. largest
     3. hominoids
     4. a. 2-1-2-3
      b. derived
      c. 1. primitive, derived
       2. cusp
     5. a. monkey
      b. intermediate
       1. visual
       2. olfactory
       3. frontal
       4. small
     6. arboreal
     7. canine
      a. sexual dimorphism
      b. modern
       1. competition
       2. *Aegyptopithecus*
     8. mosaic
      b. ancestor
      c. hominoid

VII. EARLY FOSSIL ANTHROPOIDS: SUMMARY
   A. radiate
   B. conclusions
   C. 1. *Apidium*
     2. African
   D. 1. preceding
     2. Oligocene, Miocene

VIII. HOMINOIDS: LARGE AND SMALL; AFRICAN AND ASIAN; FOSSIL AND MODERN
  A. 1. model
     2. size
        a. small
        b. Asian, African
     3. subgroup
  B. 1. reconstructing
     2. referentially
        a. living
     3. combining
        a. Old World, New World
        b. hominoids
        c. small, large
        d. Asian, African

IX. MIOCENE (22.5-5 M.Y.A.)—HOMINOIDS APLENTY
  A. Miocene
     1. Europe, Asia
     2. 22-7
        a. 100, continents
        b. lumped
           1. pongid
           2. hominid
  B. diverse
     1. living
     2. cladistic
  C. 1. a. Africa
        b. adaptive radiation
           1. 20
           2. forested
     2. isolated
        a. dock
        b. migrate
     3. a. woodland, savanna
        b. 16-17
           1. ground
           2. Eurasia
  D. 1. species
     2. reevaluation
  E. 3. *Proconsul*
        a. 10, 150 and 200
        b. woodlands
        c. terrestrial
        d. uniform
           1. 2-1-2-3
           2. canines
           3. enamel
           4. Y-5
        e. 1. Old World monkeys
           2. primitive (i.e., not derived)

     5. split
  F. 2. a. enameled
        b. living
  G. 1. *Sivapithecus*
     2. a. large
        c. orangutan
           1. biochemists, paleo-anthropologists
           2. not
        d. postcranium
           1. quadrupedalism
           2. suspensory
        e. derived
  H. 1. a. superficial
        b. primitive
     2. b. uncertain
     3. c. orangutan

X. THE MEANING OF GENUS AND SPECIES
  A. 2. biological
  B. 1. species
        b. observe
     2. variation
        a. intraspecific
        b. interspecific
        c. 1. modern (or contemporary)
           2. split
     3. a. all
        b. actual
        c. known
        d. fossil
        e. chronology
        f. related
     4. a. time span
           1. more
           2. static
        3. a. million
           b. physical
              1. incomplete
                 a. time
                 b. morphological
              2. intermediate
                 a. anagenetic
                 b. paleospecies
           3. not
              a. branching
              b. descendant
                 1. phylogenies
                 2. cladograms
              b. same
              c. economical
              d. parallelisms

C. 1. genus
    a. species
    b. two
  2. adaptive plateau
    a. ecological
    b. teeth
    c. inhabit
    d. genus

ANSWERS & REFERENCES TO FILL-IN QUESTIONS

1. goal-directed, p. 294
2. colugo (AKA "flying lemur"), p. 295
3. Eocene, p. 296
4. lemurs, p. 297
5. Fayum, p. 301
6. *Aegyptopithecus*, p. 302
7. Y-5, p. 303
8. polygynous, p. 303
9. small-bodied, p. 305
10. African, p. 306
11. referential, p. 306
12. Miocene, p. 306
13. lumping, p. 307
14. East Africa (Kenya and Uganda), p. 309
15. proconsulids, p. 310
16. *Dryopithecus*, p. 311
17. intraspecific, p. 316
18. interspecific, p. 316
19. paleospecies, p. 319
20. anagenetic, p. 320
21. cladistics, p. 320
22. cladogram, p. 320
23. Fig. 12-6, p. 305
  A. New World monkeys
  B. Old World monkeys
  C. small-bodied hominoids
  D. large-bodied hominoids
  E. African (large-bodied hominoids)
  F. Asian (large-bodied hominoids)
  G. gorilla
  H. human
  I. chimpanzee
24. Fig. 12-14, p. 318
  A. *Aegyptopithecus*
  B. proconsulids
  C. small-bodied hominoids
  D. large-bodied hominoids
  E. Asian forms
  F. African forms

ANSWERS & REFERENCES TO MULTIPLE CHOICE QUESTIONS

1. A, p. 294
2. B, p. 295
3. C, p. 296
4. B, p. 296
5. A, pp. 296-297
6. C, p. 297
7. D, p. 298
8. B, pp. 300-301
9. D, p. 304
10. A, p. 306
11. C, p. 306
12. D, p. 307
13. A, p. 308
14. B, p. 308
15. C, p. 309
16. D, p. 310
17. C, p. 311
18. B, p. 312
19. A, p. 312
20. C, p. 313
21. D, p. 313
22. A, p. 316, Box 12-1
23. D, p. 319
24. C, p. 320
25. C, p. 320
26. B, p. 321
27. B, p. 321

CHAPTER 13

PALEOANTHROPOLOGY

LEARNING OBJECTIVES

After reading this chapter you should be able to:
- list the important distinguishing characteristics of a hominid. (p. 326-327)
- discuss what mosaic evolution is and the mosaic nature of human evolution. (p. 326, pp. 328-329)
- explain how and why paleoanthropology is a multidisciplinary science. (pp. 330-332)
- outline the steps and the types of individuals involved in finding an early hominid site through the interpretation of the site. (pp. 330-332)
- discuss the significance of Olduvai Gorge to paleoanthropology. (pp. 332-337)
- compare relative dating techniques to chronometric techniques. (p. 337)
- describe the various dating techniques in terms of how they are used and for what time periods (if applicable) they can be used for. (pp. 337-341)
- discuss the application of dating methods at Olduvai Gorge. (pp. 341-344)
- list and describe the types of early hominid sites found at Olduvai. (pp. 345-346)
- discuss how paleoanthropologists attempt to reconstruct early hominid diet. (pp. 346-347).

FILL-IN OUTLINE

Introduction

   We have seen in previous chapters that humans are primates and we share our evolution, and even much of our behavior, with other primates. At some point, however, our ancestors took their primate heritage and went off in another direction to become the unique primate we are today. Some primitive hominoid may have begun this process before 10 m.y.a., but after 5 m.y.a. there is certainly definite hominid fossil evidence in East Africa. One of the factors influencing hominid evolution was their particular type of behavior, once again emphasizing the biocultural nature of human evolution. This chapter looks at how scientists deduce early human behavior and the methods used by paleoanthropologists.

I. DEFINITION OF HOMINID

   A. Modern humans and our hominid ancestors are distinguished from our closest relatives in a number of characteristics. Various researchers have pointed to certain hominid characteristics as being significant (at some stage) in defining what a hominid is.

      1. large _____ size

      2. _____ behavior

      3. _____ locomotion

   B. Mosaic evolution

      1. All of the above mentioned characteristics did not evolve _____.

      2. The evolutionary pattern in which different features evolve at different _____ is called mosaic evolution.

      3. The major defining characteristic for all hominid evolution is _____ _____.

         a. Bipedal locomotion predates other specialized traits that makes hominids unique.

         b. Thus, skeletal evidence for bipedal locomotion is the only truly reliable _____ of hominid status.

      4. In later stages of hominid evolution, other features, particularly those relating to neurology and behavior, do become significant. Precisely the pattern of _____ evolution.

   C. Biocultural evolution: the human capacity for culture

      1. The most distinctive behavioral feature of modern humans is our extraordinary elaboration and dependence on _____.

      2. Culture encompasses much more than just toolmaking capacity.

a. Culture integrates an entire _____ _____ involving cognitive, political, social, and economic components.

b. The material _____, tools, and other items, is but a small portion of this complex.

3. The record of earlier hominids is almost exclusively remains of _____ culture, especially residues of stone tool manufacture.

a. Thus, it is difficult to learn anything about the _____ stages of hominid cultural development before the regular manufacture of stone tools, circa 2.5 m.y.a.

b. Without "_____" evidence, we cannot know exactly what the earliest hominids were doing.

1. Before they began making stone tools, hominids were probably using other types of _____ (such as sticks) made of "soft" perishable materials.

2. We also cannot know anything about the cultural behavior of these earliest humans.

4. The fundamental basis for human cultural elaboration relates directly to _____ abilities.

a. When did the unique combination of cognitive, social, and material cultural adaptations become prominent in human evolution?

1. Care must be taken to recognize the manifold nature of culture and to not expect it always to contain the same elements across species or through _____.

2. We know that the earliest hominids did _____ regularly manufacture stone tools.

    a. The earliest members of the hominids, _____,

        date back to approximately 7-5 m.y.a.

    b. The protohominids may have carried objects such as naturally sharp

        stones or stone flakes, parts of carcasses, and pieces of wood. At the

        least, we would expect them to have displayed these behaviors to the

        same degree as is found in living _____.

b. Over periods of _____ million years numerous components

    interacted, but they did not all develop simultaneously.

    1. As cognitive abilities _____, more efficient means of

        communications and learning resulted.

    2. As a result of _____ reorganization, more elaborate tools and

        social relationships also emerged.

    3. More elaborate tools and social relationships selected for greater

        _____, which in turn selected for further neural

        elaboration in a positive feedback loop.

    4. These mutual dynamics are at the very heart of hominid _____

        evolution.

II. THE STRATEGY OF PALEOANTHROPOLOGY

A. The task of recovering and interpreting the remains of early _____ is

    the province of paleoanthropology.

    1. _____ is the study of ancient humans.

    2. Paleoanthropology is a diverse _____ field that

        seeks to reconstruct the dating, anatomy, behavior, and ecology of our ancestors.

B. Site survey

    1. _____ do the initial survey work to locate potential early hominid

    sites.

2. They can generally give quick estimates of the geological age of a site. In this way fossil beds of a particular geological _____, in which we might find humans, can be isolated.

C. Site excavation

1. The actual excavation is conducted by either an _____ or a human paleontologist.

2. Hominid sites do not need to contain actual fossilized skeletal material for us to know that they _____ the site.

   a. _____ provide behavioral clues of early hominid activities.

   b. There is no solid evidence of the earliest stages of hominid _____ modifications.

   c. At some point hominids began modifying _____ and this indestructible material leaves us a preserved record of human activity.

      1. Stones are _____ from one place to another.

      2. Stones are used for a number of things such as throwing projectiles, cutting tools, or simply for use in windbreaks.

      3. The oldest artifact site now documented is from the _____ region of Ethiopia, c. 2.4 m.y.a.

D. Site interpretation

1. In the laboratory materials recovered must be cleaned, sorted, and labeled.

2. Animal and plant remains can help _____ the local paleo-ecological setting.

3. _____ analysis can help in reconstructing early hominid diet.

4. In the final stages of interpretation, the paleoanthropologist pulls together the

   a. dating, which includes

1. _____ dating (based on geological stratigraphy).

2. _____ dating (based on such things as the known time periods for certain plants or animals recovered at the site).

3. _____ dating (based on dating techniques that measure radioactive decay).

b. Paleoecology, based on

   1. _____ (the recovery and study of fossil organisms).

   2. _____ (the study of fossil spores, pollen, and other microscopic plant parts)

   3. _____ (changes in the earth's land which, of course, affects climate)

   4. _____ (the study of the deposition of bones and other materials)

c. archeological traces of _____

d. _____ evidence from hominid remains

5. The paleoanthropologist attempts to tie all this information together to "flesh out" the kind of animal that may have been our direct _____.

a. _____ may contribute information comparing humans and contemporary nonhuman primates.

b. _____ anthropologists may contribute ethnographic information on the behavior of more recent humans, particularly the ecological adaptations of contemporary hunter-gatherer groups exploiting roughly similar environmental settings as reconstructed for a hominid site.

III. PALEOANTHROPOLOGY IN ACTION—OLDUVAI GORGE

A. The greatest abundance of paleoanthropological information concerning the behavior of early hominids comes from _____ _____, Tanzania.

1. continuous excavations were done by Louis and Mary Leakey between 1935 and 1984; others continue their work.

2. Olduvai is a steep-sided valley with a deep ravine that exposes 70 miles of potential _____ sites (see Fig. 13-4).

   a. The semi-arid pattern of modern Olduvai is believed to be similar to most of the past environments preserved there over the last ____ million years.

   b. Olduvai is part of the Serengeti Plains and the surrounding countryside is a grassland _____ that supports vast numbers of mammals, representing an enormous supply of "meat on the hoof."

3. Olduvai is located on the eastern branch of the Great Rift Valley of East Africa.

   a. The geological processes associated with the formation of the _____ Valley makes Olduvai extremely important to paleoanthropological investigation.

   b. Three results of geological rifting are most significant:

      1. _____ (earth movement) exposes geological beds near the surface that are normally hidden by hundreds of feet of accumulated overburden.

      2. active volcanic processes cause rapid sedimentation, which often yields excellent _____ of bone and artifacts.

      3. volcanic activity provides a wealth of radiometrically _____ material.

B. The greatest contribution of Olduvai to paleoanthropological research is the estab-lishment of an extremely well documented and correlated sequence of geological, paleontological, archeological, and hominid remains over the last ____ million years.

   1. At the very foundation of all paleoanthropological research is a well-established _____ _____. Another hominid site can be accurately dated relative to other sites in the Olduvai Gorge by cross-correlating known marker beds.

2. Paleontological evidence includes more than 150 species of _____ .

   a. This evidence provides clues to the _____ conditions that the earliest humans lived in.

   b. Species present for known periods of time and dated at Olduvai can be used to estimate dates for sites that do not contain radiometrically datable materials. These species are known as index fossils.

   c. Analysis of bones associated with artifacts yield information about hominid diets and _____ - _____ techniques.

3. The archeological sequence is well documented for the last 2 million years.

   a. The earliest hominid site is from around _____ million years ago.

      1. There is already a well-developed stone _____ tool kit, which includes choppers and some flake tools.

      2. The Oldowan tradition continues into later beds, being somewhat modified into what is called _____ Oldowan.

   b. At around 1.6 m. y. a., the Acheulian industry appears as a new _____ tradition.

      1. This tool industry is characterized by large _____ tools (i.e., flaked on both sides) known as hand-axes and cleavers.

      2. For several hundred thousand years, _____ and Developed Oldowan are both found at Olduvai.

4. Partial remains of several fossilized _____ have been recovered at Olduvai. These range from the earliest occupation levels to recent *Homo sapiens*.

IV. DATING METHODS

   A. One of the essentials of paleoanthropology is putting sites and fossils into a _____ framework (i.e., how old are they?).

B. The two types of dating methods used by paleoanthropologists are _____ dating and _____ (absolute) dating.

C. Relative dating

   1. Relative dating tells you which object is older or younger than another object, but not in actual _____.

   2. One type of relative dating is _____, the study of the sequential layering of deposits.

      a. Stratigraphy is based on the law of _____ , i.e., that the oldest stratum (layer) is the lowest stratum and higher strata are more recent.

      b. Problems associated with stratigraphy

         1. Earth _____ such as volcanic activity, river activity, mountain building, or even modern construction companies, can shift strata making it difficult to reconstruct the chronology.

         2. The _____ period of a particular stratum is not possible to determine with much accuracy.

   3. Fluorine analysis

      a. This relative dating technique can only be used on _____.

      b. When a bone is buried it is exposed to fluorine in the groundwater which seeps into the bone and deposits _____ during the fossilization process.

         1. The _____ a bone is in the ground, the more fluorine it will contain.

         2. Bones with the most fluorine are _____ than bones with less fluorine.

      c. Fluorine analysis can only be done with bones found at the same _____, i.e., this method is "site specific."

         1. The _____ of fluorine in groundwater is based on local conditions and varies from one area to another.

2. Comparing bones from different localities is _____.

d. As in other relative techniques, actual _____ in years can not be obtained.

D. Chronometric (absolute) dating

1. Chronometric dating provides an estimate of age in years and is based on

_____ decay.

a. Certain radioactive isotopes of elements are unstable and they disintegrate to

form an isotope of another _____.

b. This disintegration occurs at a constant rate.

1. By _____ the amount of disintegration in a particular

sample, the number of years it took for the amount of decay may be

calculated.

2. The time it takes for one-half of the original amount of the isotope to

decay into another isotope is referred to as the _____ - _____.

2. Uranium 238 decays with a half-life of 4.5 billion years to form lead. This

chronometric technique has been used to date the age of the _____ .

3. Potassium/argon (K/Ar) dating involves the decay of _____

into argon gas.

a. K/Ar has a half-life of 1.3 _____ years.

b. This technique can only be done on _____ matrix; it will not work on

organic material such as bone.

1. However, fossil bones are often associated with matrix and can be indirectly

dated by its association.

2. The best type of rock to perform K/Ar dating on is _____ rock.

a. When the lava is laid down in its molten state, the _____ gas

present is driven off. After solidification any argon that has been

trapped in the rock is the result of potassium decay.

b. To obtain the date of the rock, it is reheated and the escaping argon is

_____.

4. _____ _____ is a radiometric method commonly used by archeologists.

a. Carbon 14 has a half-life of 5,730 years.

b. This method can be used to date _____ materials from less than 1,000 years old to 75,000 years.

c. The _____ of Carbon 14 decreases after 40,000 years.

5. Each of the chronometric techniques has its own problems and none of these methods is precise. Analysis provides _____ dates with a standard deviation that provides a time range.

E. Application of dating methods: examples from Olduvai

1. The first use of _____ - _____ at a paleoanthropology site was at Olduvai.

a. "Zinj" (OH 5) was dated at 1.75 million years; this K/Ar date for it was more than twice the age depth previously assumed for the entire Pleistocene.

b. As a result of this one monumental date, the entire history of the _____ and our corresponding interpretations of hominid evolution had to be rewritten.

c. As a result of the success at Olduvai, K/Ar dating has been widely used in areas containing suitable _____ deposits.

d. Due to potential sources of error, K/Ar dating must be _____ -checked using other independent methods.

2. Fission-track dating

a. Uranium 238 decays at a constant rate through spontaneous fission. This spontaneous fission leaves microscopic _____ .

b. By _____ tracks, i.e., the fraction of uranium atoms that have fissioned, the age of a mineral can be estimated.

    c. One of the earliest uses of uranium 238 dating was at Olduvai, which yielded a date of 2.30 (±.28) m.y.a., compatible with the K/Ar dates.

3. Another important means of cross-checking dates is _____.

    a. This technique is based on the constantly shifting nature of the earth's _____ pole.

    b. The earth's magnetic field, currently oriented in a northern direction, periodically _____.

    c. Paleomagnetic dating involves taking samples of sediment that contains magnetically _____ particles.

        1. Magnetically charged particles _____ towards the magnetic pole.

        2. These particles will be oriented towards the direction of the magnetic pole that existed when they were incorporated into rock; thus these particles serve as a "fossil _____ ."

    d. The paleomagnetic sequence is then compared against the K/Ar dates to _____ if they agree.

4. _____ _____, or biostratigraphy, is another method for cross-checking the other methods.

    a. This involves correlating the evolutionary stages of well-_____ mammals from one site to another; some of these stages are very brief and such an animal serves as an "index fossil."

    b. When these animals are found at sites with chronometric dates, _____ ages can be assigned to sites where no suitable materials for dating are present.

5. Because each dating technique has problems, it is important to use several in conjunction with one another in order to cross-check the various methods.

V. EXCAVATIONS AT OLDUVAI

A. The 70 miles of exposed vertical surface at Olduvai has provided several dozen

_____ sites.

1. An incredible amount of paleoanthropological information has come from these

excavated areas.

2. The data has been organized into three broad categories of site types (see below),

depending on implied _____ .

B. "_____" localities are sites that contain one or only a few individuals

of a single species of large mammals associated with a scatter of archeological traces.

C. Quarry localities

1. These sites are areas where early hominids extracted their _____

resources and initially fashioned their tools.

2. There are usually thousands of small stone fragments of a particular type of rock

at _____ localities, but no or very little bone refuse.

D. _____ localities (AKA camp sites)

1. These are _____ -purpose areas where hominids possibly ate, slept,

and put the finishing touches on their tools.

2. The _____ of living debris, including broken animal

bones and many broken stones is a basic human pattern.

3. One of the multipurpose areas excavated at Olduvai is over 1.8 million years

old. This site has a _____ of large stones forming what was at one time

thought to be a base for a windbreak; however, this interpretation is now

considered unlikely.

4. The types of _____ carried out at multipurpose sites remain

open to speculation.

a. Many archeologists had thought that these sites functioned as

"_____."

b. Some, such as Binford, suggest that these sites are the result of

_____ activities, such as the remains of carnivore meals.

c. Potts has suggested that these sites were _____ (collecting points)

for some tools.

E. Context and association

1. Archeologists derive their information from more than just the analysis of

_____ .

2. It is the context and association of objects that give archeologists the data they

require to understand the _____ patterns of ancient human

populations.

a. _____ refers to where the objects are found.

b. _____ refers to what the object is found with.

VI. DIET OF EARLY HOMINIDS

A. One of the goals of paleoanthropological research is to _____

the biology and behavior of our ancestor.

B. An important question regarding ancestral humans is what was their _____?

1. Broken _____ bones provide some direct evidence regarding one aspect

of early human dietary behavior.

2. Modern analogs, hunter-gatherer peoples such as the South African San, eat

_____ food as a large part of their diet.

a. Such foods leave _____ trace in the archeological record.

b. Such foods probably made up a _____ part (perhaps the majority) of

the caloric intake of early hominids.

3. Using a simple _____ _____ as a tool, hominids living 2-1

m.y.a. were able to exploit a variable diet that probably ranged from vegetable

foods to small animals.

a. Olduvai has shown that a range of _____ resources was exploited in

earlier beds (1.85-1.0 m.y.a.).

b. Evidence for fish eating is found in the form of fish bones contained within

human _____ (fossilized feces) from Omo, Ethiopia.

c. By 1 m.y.a., some _____ of large mammals may have provided

important meat resources as demonstrated by the *Pelorovis* butchering site at

Olduvai.

KEY TERMS

absolute dating techniques: see chronometric dating techniques.

accuracy: refers to how close a measured quantity is to the true value of what is being measured. Generally, the true value is represented by a standard.

artifacts: material remnants or traces of hominid behavior. Very old artifacts are usually made of stone or, occasionally, bone.

association: what an artifact or archeological trace is found with.

biostratigraphy: dating method based on evolutionary changes within an evolved lineage.

chronometric dating techniques: dating techniques that give an estimate in actual number of years, based on radioactive decay. AKA absolute dating.

context: the environmental setting where an archeological trace is found. *Primary* context is the setting in which the archeological trace was originally deposited. A *secondary* context is one to which the archeological trace has been moved by some force such as the action of a stream.

faunal analysis: see biostratigraphy.

fluorine analysis: a relative dating technique in which the amount of fluorine deposited in bones is compared. Bones with the most fluorine are the oldest.

geomorphology: changes in the form of the earth's land, such as rifting of land, mountain building, development of ravines and canyons, etc.

half-life: in chronometric dating, the amount of time that it takes for one-half of the original (parent) isotope to decay into its daughter isotope.

mosaic evolution: the evolutionary pattern in which different characteristics evolve at different rates.

paleoecology: the study of fossil communities and environments.

paleomagnetism: dating methods based on the earth's shifting magnetic poles.

paleontology: the recovery and study of ancient organisms.

palynology: the study of fossil spores, pollen, and other microscopic plant parts.
precision: refers to the closeness of repeated measurements of the same quantity to each other.
protohominid: the earliest members of the hominid lineage. No fossils of this hypothetical
    group have yet been found.
relative dating: a type of dating in which objects are ranked by age. Thus, some objects can
    be said to be older than other objects, but no actual age in years can be assigned.
stratigraphy: study of the sequential layering of deposits.
taphonomy: the study of how bones and other materials came to be buried and preserved as
    fossils.

FILL-IN QUESTIONS

1. At the earliest stages of the hominid lineage, skeletal evidence for _____

    _____ is the only truly reliable indicator of hominid status.

2. The evolutionary pattern seen in hominids, in which the locomotor system evolved at a

    different rate than that of the dentition or the brain, is an example of _____

    _____.

3. When compared to other animals, our most distinctive behavioral feature is our extraor-

    dinary elaboration of and dependence on _____.

4. In addition to material culture such as tools, culture integrates an entire _____

    _____ involving cognitive, political, social, and economic components.

5. The earliest hominids, who lived between 7 and 5 m.y.a., are referred to as

    _____. As yet, they are not represented in the fossil record.

6. The task of recovering and interpreting all the clues left by early hominids is the work of

    _____.

7. Behavioral clues are also referred to in paleoanthropology as _____.

8. The discipline that studies how bones and other materials came to be deposited in the

    earth and preserved as fossils is _____.

9. A member of the genus *Homo* is killed by a leopard one million years ago in East Africa.

    Much of the skeletal remains are destroyed by weathering, but the skull becomes

    fossilized. 100,000 years ago a flash flood uncovers the skull and carries it several miles away. We then say that this last site to which it was moved is of _____

_____.

10.   One of the major paleoanthropologist sites in the world is _____ _____.
It is located along the East African Rift Valley system in northern Tanzania and provides
a record of hominid evolution over the last two million years.

Three important results of geological rifting are very important from the perspective of
paleoanthropology. These are,

11.   _____.

12.   _____

_____.

13.   _____

_____.

14.   At the very foundation of all paleoanthropological research is a well-established
_____ context.

15.   Dating techniques that provide an estimate of age in actual number of years are referred
to as _____ dating techniques.

16.   A _____ dating technique involves a comparison of objects which results in
an ordering of those objects that are older and those which are younger.

17.   Stratigraphy is based on the law of _____ .

18.   _____ _____ was used to help expose the Piltdown hoax.

19.   The amount of time required for one-half of a parent (original) isotope to decompose
into a daughter isotope, e.g., uranium 238 into lead, is called the _____ - _____.

20.   The age of the earth has been dated by the dating technique that uses the isotope
_____ _____.

21.   A useful chronometric technique employed by archeologists because its range goes from
about 1,000 years ago to as old as 75,000 years is the _____ _____ method.

22. None of the chronometric techniques is _____ , and each is beset with problems that must be considered during collection and analysis.

23. Due to potential sources of error, potassium-Argon (K/Ar) dating must be _____-_____ using other independent methods.

24. One independent dating method that has been used at Olduvai to cross-check the potassium-argon (K/Ar) method is _____ .

25. The dating technique that calibrates changes in the earth's geomagnetic pole is _____ .

26. An excavated area at Olduvai that contains one or only a few individuals of a single species of large mammal, associated with archeological trace, is referred to as a "_____" locality.

27. A *Homo habilis* skull is found with several stone tools and some *Deinotherium* bones. Archeologists refer to these objects being found together as _____.

28. Evidence for fish eating among early humans comes from the presence of fish bones in human _____.

MULTIPLE CHOICE QUESTIONS

1. Evolution in which structures evolve at different rates is termed
    A. convergent evolution.
    B. parallel evolution.
    C. mosaic evolution.
    D. punctuated equilibrium.

2. Human evolution can be characterized as
    A. parallel.
    B. convergent.
    C. homologous.
    D. mosaic.

3. Which of the following is an aspect of material culture that would be a vestige of the earliest hominids?
    A. a fragment of a stone tool
    B. cognitive abilities
    C. economic systems
    D. social systems

4. Initial surveying and locating potential hominid sites is the primary task of
    A. physical anthropologists.
    B. geologists.
    C. paleoecologists.
    D. archeologists.

5. The primary task of an archeologist at a paleoanthropological site is to
    A. search for hominid "traces."
    B. reconstruct the ancient environment of the site.
    C. establish the relationships of any fossil humans recovered.
    D. perform dating techniques to establish the time period.

6. The earliest documented artifact site is
    A. Laetoli at 3.4 m.y.a.
    B. Omo at 2.4 m.y.a.
    C. Olduvai at 1.85 m.y.a.
    D. Taung at 1 m.y.a.

7. The first artifact that we can say is an actual hominid-made tool is made of
    A. wood.
    B. bone.
    C. horn.
    D. stone.

8. The archeological setting where an artifact is found is called the
    A. association.
    B. context.
    C. quarry site.
    D. monolith.

9. Which of the following does a paleoanthropologist **not** use in the concluding stages of a site interpretation?
    A. information pertaining to dating
    B. paleoecology
    C. information from linguists
    D. anatomical evidence from hominid remains

10. The paleoanthropologist who discovered the best preserved *Proconsul* skull ever found and also discovered "Zinj," was
    A. Louis Leakey.
    B. Mary Leakey.
    C. Jane Goodall.
    D. Meg Weigel.

11. The earliest stone tool industry found at Olduvai is called
   A. Acheulean.
   B. Chellean.
   C. Oldowan.
   D. Developed Oldowan.

12. Which of the following statements is **not** correct?
   A. Earth disturbances may shift geological strata making the strata unusable for strati-graphic dating.
   B. Fluorine analysis can only be done on bones that come from the same location.
   C. Chronometric dating techniques are precise and lack the confounding factors that beset relative dating techniques.
   D. Chronometric techniques are based on the phenomenon of radioactive decay.

13. A disadvantage to fluorine analysis is that it
   A. can only be done on volcanic beds.
   B. can only be done on bones found in the same area.
   C. is not effective for materials older than 50,000 years.
   D. has a range of error of 12,000 years.

14. Chronometric techniques are based on
   A. radioactive decay.
   B. superposition.
   C. stratigraphy.
   D. the works of Oldowan Kanobe.

15. A half-life
   A. differs for the isotopes of different elements.
   B. is the amount of time it takes for the original amount of an isotope to decay into another isotope.
   C. is set at 5,730 years for K/Ar.
   D. Both A and B are correct.

16. The dating technique used extensively in paleoanthropology for the time period 5-1 m.y.a. is
   A. uranium 238.
   B. carbon 14.
   C. fluorine analysis.
   D. potassium-argon.

17. Chronometric dates are accompanied with a
   A. standard deviation.
   B. mean.
   C. analysis of covariance.
   D. regression slope.

18. If you found a fossil in East Africa and you suspected that it might be over a million years old, what type of dating technique would you use to obtain an actual date?
    A. carbon 14 dating
    B. biostratigraphy
    C. potassium-argon
    D. stratigraphy

19. Several different dating techniques are used to cross-check the age of a paleoanthropological site because
    A. there are gaps in the periods covered.
    B. sources of error differ in the various techniques.
    C. because the techniques are all done on the same material duplication adds reliability.
    D. spectrophotometers must be transported to field sites where field conditions can cause error.

REFER TO THIS ILLUSTRATION TO ANSWER QUESTIONS 20-27.

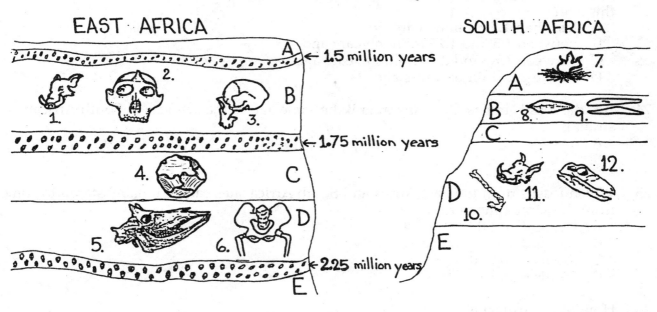

KEY
    Fossils: 1 = *Mesochoerus africanus* (pig species that only existed for about 100,000 years)
    2 = *A. boisei* skull   3 = *H. habilis* skull   4 = Oldowan tool   5 = giraffe molar
    6 = hominid femur   7 = charcoal from fire   8 = stone spear point   9 = blade tool
    10 = hominid femur   11 = *Mesochoerus africanus*   12 = crocodile skull

20. How were the dates arrived at that appear on the right hand side of the East African site?
    A. carbon 14 dating
    B. potassium-argon dating
    C. stratigraphy
    D. fluorine analysis
    E. the historical records left by Oldowan Kanobe

21. We would like to get a date for the charcoal in South Africa strata A. Assuming that this material lies within the dating range for an absolute dating technique, which technique should we use?
     A. carbon 14 dating
     B. potassium-argon dating
     C. uranium 238 dating
     D. fission track dating

22. How old is fossil 6?
     A. less than 1.5 million years old
     B. between 1.5 and 1.75 million years old
     C. between 1.75 and 2.25 million years old
     D. older than 2.25 million years old
     E. It is not possible to give an age range for this fossil.

23. Based on the information from the East African site, when was *Homo habilis* present at this site?
     A. less than 1.5 million years ago
     B. between 1.5 and 1.75 million years ago
     C. between 1.75 and 2.25 million years ago
     D. before 2.25 million years ago

24. Are the fossils in East African strata B the same age as the artifacts in South African strata B?
     A. Yes
     B. No

25. Which fossils from the East Africa and South Africa sites can be reliably stated to come from the same time period?
     A. fossils 4 and 8
     B. fossils 3 and 8
     C. fossils 2 and 10
     D. fossils 6 and 11

26. How old is artifact 8?
     A. less than 1.5 million years old.
     B. between 1.5 and 1.75 million years old.
     C. between 1.75 and 2.25 million years old.
     D. older than 2.25 million years.

27. In which strata do we find the most recent fossil or artifact?
     A. East Africa strata B
     B. East Africa strata C
     C. South Africa strata A
     D. South Africa strata D
     E. It is not possible to say which is most recent because two different sites are being compared.

28. Areas from which early hominids extracted stone for their tools are referred to as
    A. butchering localities.
    B. quarry localities.
    C. multipurpose localities.
    D. campsites.

29. A type of locality where, it is believed by some, hominids ate, slept, and made tools is a
    A. butchering locality.
    B. quarry locality.
    C. multipurpose locality.
    D. assembly point.

30. Which of the following is **not** a type of evidence that paleoanthropologists use for attempting to reconstruct the diet of early hominids?
    A. scattered broken bone debris at a hominid site
    B. using modern hunter-gatherers such as the San of South Africa as models
    C. using modern industrialized humans such as Americans as models
    D. Neither B or C are used to help reconstruct early hominid diet.

31. *Eoanthropus dawsoni*, commonly known as "Piltdown Man," was
    A. demonstrated to be the oldest human ancestor found in Europe through fluorine analysis.
    B. reclassified *Australopithecus dawsoni*.
    C. the invention of Sir Arthur Conan Doyle in the Sherlock Holmes mystery, "The Giant Rat of Sumatra."
    D. a complete and deliberate hoax.

ANSWERS TO FILL-IN OUTLINE

I. DEFINITION OF HOMINID
   A. 1. brain
      2. toolmaking
      3. bipedal
   B. 1. simultaneously
      2. rates
      3. bipedal locomotion
         b. indicator
      4. mosaic
   C. 1. culture
      2. a. adaptive strategy
         b. culture
      3. material
         a. earliest
         b. hard
            1. tools
      4. cognitive
         a. 1. time

   2. not
      a. protohominids
      b. chimpanzees
   b. several
      1. developed
      2. neural
      3. intelligence
      4. biocultural

II. THE STRATEGY OF PALEOANTHROPOLOGY
   A. hominids
      1. paleoanthropology
      2. multidisciplinary
   B. 1. geologists
      2. age
   C. 1. archeologist
      2. occupied
         a. artifacts
         b. cultural

        c. stone
            1. transported
            3. Omo
    D. 2. reconstruct
        3. paleoecological
        4. a. 1. geological
                2. paleontological
                3. geophysical
            b. 1. paleontology
                2. palynology
                3. geomorphology
                4. taphonomy
            c. behavior
            d. anatomical
        5. ancestor
            a. primatologists
            b. cultural
III. PALEOANTHROPOLOGY IN ACTION—
      OLDUVAI GORGE
    A. Olduvai Gorge
        2. hominid
            a. two
            b. savanna
        3. a. Rift
            b. 1. faulting
                2. preservation
                3. datable
    B. two
        1. geological context
        2. animals
            a. ecological
            c. bone-processing
        3. a. 1.85
                1. Oldowan
                2. Developed
            b. tool
                1. bifacial
                2. Acheulian
        4. hominids
IV. DATING METHODS
    A. chronological
    B. relative, chronometric
    C. 1. years
        2. stratigraphy
            a. superposition
            b. 1. disturbances
                2. time

    3. a. bones
        b. fluorine
            1. longer
            2. older
        c. location
            1. amount
            2. impossible
        d. age
    D. 1. radioactive
            a. element
            b. 1. measuring
                2. half-life
        2. earth
        3. potassium
            a. billion
            b. rock
                2. volcanic
                    a. argon
                    b. measured
        4. carbon 14
            b. organic
            c. precision
        5. approximate
    E. 1. potassium-argon
            b. Pleistocene
            c. volcanic
            d. cross
        2. a. tracks
            b. counting
        3. paleomagnetism
            a. magnetic
            b. shifts
            c. charged
                1. orient
                2. compass
            d. check
        4. faunal correlation
            a. known
            b. approximate
V. EXCAVATIONS AT OLDUVAI
    A. hominid
        2. function
    B. butchering
    C. 1. stone
        2. quarry
    D. multipurpose
        1. general

2. accumulation
3. circle
4. activities
   a. campsites
   b. nonhominid
   c. caches
E. 1. objects
   2. behavioral
      a. context
      b. association

VI. DIET OF EARLY HOMINIDS
   A. reconstruct
   B. diet
      1. animal
      2. vegetable
         a. little
         b. large
      3. digging stick
         a. meat
         b. coprolites
         c. hunting

ANSWERS & REFERENCES TO FILL-IN QUESTIONS

1. bipedal locomotion, p. 326
2. mosaic evolution, p. 326
3. culture, p. 326
4. adaptive strategy, p. 327
5. protohominids, p. 327
6. paleoanthropologists, p. 330
7. artifacts, p. 330
8. taphonomy, p. 331
9. secondary context, p. 331
10. Olduvai Gorge, pp. 332-333

The answers for questions 11-13 need not be in the exact order.
11. faulting, that exposes geological beds near the surface, p. 333
12. rapid sedimentation from volcanic activity that aids in preservation of bone and artifacts, p. 333
13. volcanic material that provides materials for chronometric dating, p. 333
14. geological, p. 334
15. chronometric, p. 337
16. relative, p. 337
17. superposition, p. 337
18. fluorine analysis, p. 338
19. half-life, p. 340
20. uranium 238, p. 341
21. carbon 14, p. 341
22. precise, p. 341
23. cross-checked, p. 342
24. Actually several methods have been used, so any of the following are correct: fission-track dating, paleomagnetism, and biostratigraphy, pp. 342-344.
25. paleomagnetism, pp. 342-343
26. butchering, p. 345
27. association, p. 345
28. coprolites, p. 347

ANSWERS & REFERENCES TO MULTIPLE CHOICE QUESTIONS

1. C, p. 326
2. D, p. 326
3. A, p. 327
4. B, p. 330
5. A, p. 330
6. B, p. 331
7. D, p. 331
8. B, p. 331
9. C, p. 332
10. B, pp. 336-337
11. C, p. 337
12. C, p. 341
13. B, p. 339
14. A, p. 340
15. D, pp. 341 & 342
16. D, p. 341
17. A, p. 342, Box 13-3
18. C, p. 342
19. B, p. 344
20. B, p. 341
21. A, p. 341. Carbon 14 must be used on traces that are organic, such as this charcoal. In order for carbon 14 dating to be effective this charcoal must have come from within the last 75,000 years.
22. C, p. 341. Fossil 6 is in between two volcanic tuffs which are datable. The fossil is not datable itself and this is referred to as indirect dating. What we do know is that the fossil lies between two layers that are dated 1.75 million years and 2.25 million years. In the illustration it appears that the fossil lies closer to 2.25 million years, but sedimentation takes place at different rates and the proximity of the fossil to the tuff may not reflect the actual distance in time.

23. B, p. 341. This is answered in the same way as question 25.
24. B. Strata are assigned names by geologists at a particular site. There is no reason to believe that these two strata are from the same time period merely because they are both strata Bs. As we will see in the subsequent questions, there is evidence that these two strata are not from the same time period.
25. C, p. 344. The key to answering this question is the pig species found at both sites. It is stated in the key to the illustrations that this pig existed for only 100,000 years. Because the pig fossils are found in East Africa strata B and South Africa strata D those strata must be from the same time period (unless one of the sites has been disturbed in some way that we do not know about).
26. A, p. 337. Artifact 8 does not have any datable material with it. However, we know that South Africa strata D is of a comparable age to East Africa strata B which does have a date assigned to it. Artifact 8, however, is in a higher strata. Thus, we know it is younger than strata D, based on stratigraphy. From the information at hand, all we can say is that it is less than 1.5 million years old. If someone were to date the charcoal in strata A we could get a range for artifact 8.
27. A
28. B, p. 345
29. C, pp. 345-346
30. C, p. 346
31. D, p. 349 b

CHAPTER 14

PLIO-PLEISTOCENE HOMINIDS

LEARNING OBJECTIVES

After reading this chapter you should be able to:
- list the benefits associated with bipedalism. (p. 354)
- explain the effects of bipedalism on human body structure. (pp. 355-358)
- list the major features of human bipedalism. (pp. 356-358)
- explain what is meant by habitual and obligate bipedalism. (p. 358)
- discuss bipedalism in reference to the early hominids of East and South Africa. (pp. 358-359)
- review the earliest East African hominids. (pp. 361-368)
- discuss the evidence for bipedalism in the earliest hominids. (pp. 363-371)
- comment on the cranial capacities of the earliest hominids. (pp. 368-370)
- compare and contrast the different types of humans found at Olduvai and Lake Turkana. (pp. 373-378)
- explain why the of the South African hominid finds were so important. (pp. 380-382)
- compare and contrast the "robust" and "gracile" australopithecines from South Africa. (pp. 383-386)

FILL-IN OUTLINE

Introduction

   In the past, various researchers attempted to define hominids based mainly on dental characteristics or toolmaking behavior. Neither of these criteria work when applied to the earliest hominids. In chapter 14, the large collections of early hominids recovered from East and South Africa encompassing the period from just before 4 m.y.a. to 1 m.y.a. are reviewed. Analysis of these several thousand specimens has led paleoanthropologists to conclude that bipedalism represents the primary functional adaptation that best distinguishes the hominid lineage.

I. THE BIPEDAL ADAPTATION

A. Efficient bipedalism among primates is found only among _____.

B. Advantages of bipedalism

   1. frees the _____ for carrying objects and making and using simple tools

   2. Standing upright provides a _____ view of the surroundings, enabling a biped to detect predators earlier.

   3. _____ walking is an efficient means of covering long distances.

   4. We do not know what _____ bipedalism, but all of the above factors probably played a role in its evolution.

C. The process of bipedal walking

   1. To walk bipedally a human must _____ on the "stance" leg while the "swing" leg is off the ground.

   2. During normal walking, both feet are simultaneously on the ground only about _____% of the time.

D. Structural/anatomical modifications for bipedalism

   1. To maintain a _____ center of balance-many drastic anatomical modifications in the basic primate quadrupedal pattern are required.

   2. The most dramatic changes occur in the hominid _____ and its associated musculature.

     a. Compared to a chimpanzee's pelvis, the hominid pelvis is _____ and _____ and extends to the side.

       1. This configuration helps to stabilize the line of _____ _____ from the lower back to the hip joint.

       2. The result of the broadening of the two sides of the pelvis is to produce a _____-_____ structure that helps to support the abdominal organs.

   b. Hominid pelvic modifications also _____ the attachments of several key muscles that act on the hip and leg, changing their mechanical function.

      1. The _____ _____, the major muscle in bipedal walking, is the largest muscle in humans (but not so in quadrupeds).

      2. The gluteus maximus is a _____ extensor of the thigh and provides additional force, particularly during running and climbing.

3. The foramen magnum has been repositioned under the cranium so that the head _____ on the spine. This arrangement also removes the need for robust neck muscles to hold the head erect.

4. The rib cage has been _____ and breathing is no longer tied to movements of the forelimbs.

5. Unlike the straight great ape vertebral column, the human spine has _____ that keep the trunk centered above the pelvis. This stabilizes weight transmission.

6. The human hind limb is increased in _____, increasing stride length.

7. The femur is angled _____.

   a. This arrangement keeps the legs more directly _____ the body.

   b. Also, the knees and feet are brought _____ together under the body.

8. There are several structural changes made in the human foot.

   a. The big toe is realigned so that it is _____ with the other toes, losing its opposability.

   b. A longitudinal _____ develops which helps to absorb shock and adds a propulsive spring.

9. For these major anatomical changes to have been selected, there must have been a tremendous _____ advantage to bipedalism.

    a. It bears repeating that we do not know what conditions led to bipedalism.

    b. The various ideas of what led to bipedalism should be considered

        _____ rather than hypotheses; we do not have sufficient data

        to test any of these ideas.

E. In structural modifications such as seen in bipedalism, form follows _____.

    1. During evolution, organisms do not undergo significant _____

        change (i.e., form) unless these changes assist individuals in some functional

        capacity.

    2. Evolutionary changes such as bipedalism do not occur all at once, but probably

        evolve over a fairly long period of time.

F. Hominid bipedalism is habitual and obligate.

    1. _____ bipedalism means that hominids move bipedally as their

        standard and most efficient mode of locomotion.

    2. _____ bipedalism means they hominids cannot locomote efficiently

        in any other manner.

    3. When examining the earliest hominids, it is crucial to identify those anatomical

        features that indicate _____ and to what degree these organisms

        were committed to _____.

        a. All the _____ structural changes required for bipedalism are seen in early

            hominids from East and South Africa.

        b. In particular, the _____ shows dramatic remodeling to support weight

            in a bipedal stance.

        c. Other human structural characteristics are also present in these early hominids.

            1. The vertebral column shows the same _____ as in modern humans.

            2. The lower _____ were lengthened to almost the same degree as in

               modern humans (although the arms were longer).

3. The carrying _____ of weight support from the hip to the knee was also very similar to modern humans.

d. Early hominid foot structure is known from sites in both South and East Africa.

1. These specimens indicate that the _____ and longitudinal _____ were well adapted for a bipedal gait.

2. Some paleontologists suggest, however, that the great toe was _____ unlike the pattern seen in later hominids.

a. This would have aided the foot in _____ , enabling early hominids to more effectively exploit arboreal habitats.

b. This type of foot would not have been as efficient as a stable _____ during bipedal locomotion.

c. Consequently, some researchers believe that early hominids were not necessarily _____ bipeds.

1. They believe that these early humans spent considerable amount of time in the _____.

2. Nevertheless, all the early hominids that have been identified from Africa are thought by _____ researchers to have been both habitual and obligate bipeds.

II. EARLY HOMINIDS IN THE PLIO-PLEISTOCENE

A. The beginnings of hominid differentiation have their roots in the late _____ (c. 15-10 m.y.a.)

1. Sometime during the period 8-5 m.y.a., hominids began to adapt more fully to a _____ - _____ niche

2. Unfortunately, fossil recovery for this time period is scant, creating a significant 3 million year _____.

B. The human fossil record increases beginning around _____ m.y.a.

    1. This encompasses the Pliocene and the earliest stages of the _____

       (5-1 m.y.a.)

    2. This span of time is usually referred to as the _____-_____.

III. THE EAST AFRICAN RIFT VALLEY

A. The Great _____Valley of Africa is a stretch of 1,200 miles (see map, Fig. 14-6)

    1. This area has experienced active geological processes over the last several

       _____ years in which the area is being rifted (separated).

    2. Because of this geological activity, earlier sediments are thrown to the _____

       where they become exposed and can be located by a paleoanthropologist.

B. Rifting has stimulated _____ activity.

    1. Volcanic sediments provide a valuable means for _____

       dating many sites in East Africa.

    2. The datable hominid sites along the Rift Valley have yielded crucial information

       concerning the precise _____ of early human evolution.

IV. THE EARLIEST EAST AFRICAN HOMINIDS

A. Earliest Traces

    1. The oldest specimen that is believed to be a hominid comes from Lothagam,

       Northern Kenya.

       a. This specimen is very _____ and consists of only a lower jaw.

       b. Several other fragmentary specimens from around the same area of East Africa

         have also been found. All are represented by only a _____ specimen.

    2. These early specimens all come from the time period _____ m.y.a.

B. Aramis

1. This site has been radiometrically dated at 4.4 m.y.a., making the group of fossils from this site the oldest _____ (rather than single specimens) of hominids yet discovered.

2. Remains recovered include jaws, teeth, partial crania and upper limb bones, hand and foot bones. In addition, 40% of a complete _____ skeleton has recently been recovered.

3. Because many of the discoveries have only been partially described, only provisional interpretations are possible at this time.

    a. If these forms are hominids, they are quite _____.

        1. The _____ teeth are fairly large.

        2. A sectorial premolar, with which the upper canine shears, is present. This is similar to the condition found among _____.

        3. The base of the _____ is chimpanzee-like.

    b. There is anatomical evidence of _____, the criterion for hominid status.

        1. The _____ _____ is positioned further forward than in quadrupeds.

        2. Features of the humerus suggest that the forelimb was not _____ - _____.

        3. Morphology of the _____ is consistent with bipedalism.

4. Tim White and his co-workers has suggested that the _____ hominids be assigned to a new genus and species, *Ardipithecus ramidus*. The basis for this recognition of a new genus is that

    a. these specimens are much more _____ than *Australopithecus* (the other hominid genus closest to this time period).

b. _____ enamel caps on the molars in contrast to the thicker enamel caps of *Australopithecus.*

c. *Ardipithecus* may represent the "sister-group" and _____ species for all later hominids.

C. Kanapoi and Allia Bay (East Turkana)

1. These hominid sites had been dated between _____ m.y.a.

2. Material from these sites exhibit primitive _____ and the facial features also appear to be quite primitive.

   a. However, the _____ enamel on the molars conform to the condition found in *Australopithecus.*

   b. It has been suggested that these specimens be assigned to the genus *Australopithecus*, but to a separate species, i.e., *A. anamensis.*

D. Laetoli

1. K/Ar dating for Laetoli provides a date of _____ m.y.a.

2. Most of the recovered material from this site consists of jaws and teeth.

3. A rare find was fossilized hominid _____ imprinted into volcanic tuff.

   a. These footprints are directly dated at _____ m.y.a.; thus, we know for certain that there were bipedal hominids walking in East Africa by this time.

   b. One group of footprints suggests _____, possibly, _____ individuals. Analysis of the footprints indicate one individual was 4' 9" and the other was 4' 1".

   c. Despite agreement that these individuals were bipedal, some researchers feel they were _____ bipedal in the same way as modern humans. They suggest that the Laetoli hominids moved in a "strolling" fashion with a short stride.

E. Hadar (Afar Triangle)

1. Hadar has produced at least _____ individual hominids.

2. The most recent dating calibrations suggest a range of dates from 3.9-____ m.y.a.

3. Two of the most extraordinary discoveries of human paleontology were found at Hadar.

   a. _____ percent of an *Australopithecus afarensis* female, nicknamed "Lucy," was recovered here. This is one of the two most complete humans from before 100,000 years ago.

   b. The "first family"

      1. A group of bones representing at least 13 individuals, including 4 _____, was found at Hadar.

      2. It has been suggested that these individuals represented a single _____ _____ that died at the same time in a catastrophe.

         a. These individuals have been nicknamed the "first family."

         b. The precise _____ of the site has not been completely explained and the assertion that these individuals were contemporaries must be viewed tentatively.

   c. Considerable cultural material has been recovered. Some stone tools may be 2.5 million years old, making them the _____ cultural evidence yet found.

V. HOMINIDS FROM LAETOLI AND HADAR

A. The hominids from Laetoli and Hadar are assigned to *Australopithecus* _____.

B. *A. afarensis* is more _____ than any of the later species of *Australopithecus*.

   1. By "primitive" we mean that *A. afarensis* is less evolved in any particular _____ than are the later occurring hominid species.

      a. *A. afarensis* shares more primitive features with other early _____ (such as *Sivapithecus*) and living pongids than with later hominids.

b. Derived traits seen in later hominids are _____ present in *A. afarensis*.

2. The teeth of *A. afarensis* are quite _____ .

   a. The _____ are often large, pointed teeth that overlap.

   b. The lower first _____ is semisectorial (i.e., it provides a shearing surface for the upper canine).

   c. The tooth rows are _____.

3. The cranial parts that are preserved also exhibit several primitive _____ features.

   a. *A. afarensis* displays a compound _____ /_____ crest in the back.

   b. Cranial capacities are difficult to estimate but they seem to range from _____ cm³ to 500 cm³.

      1. It appears that the smaller cranial capacities are for the _____ and the larger cranial capacities are for _____.

      2. One thing that is certain is that *A. afarensis* had a _____ brain, the mean for the species is probably 420 cm³.

4. Postcrania

   a. Relative to the lower limbs, the upper limbs are _____ than found in modern humans.

      1. This is also a _____ hominoid condition.

      2. Note that this does not mean that the arms were longer than the legs.

   b. Wrist, hand, and foot bones show several _____ from modern humans.

5. Stature has been estimated.

   a. *A. afarensis* was _____ than modern humans.

b. There appears to have been considerable sexual _____. If this is true,

    1. _____ were between 3 1/2 to 4 feet tall.

    2. males could be up to _____ feet tall.

    3. *A. afarensis* may have been as sexually dimorphic as _____ living primate.

6. *A. afarensis* is so primitive in the majority of dental and cranial features that if it were not for evidence of _____, this primate would not be classified as a hominid.

    a. The _____ teeth are actually reminiscent of Miocene hominoids.

    b. However, two hominid-derived features are the position of the _____ _____ (indicating bipedalism) and _____ enamel on the molars.

C. Locomotion of *Australopithecus afarensis*

1. Stern and Sussman have analyzed the _____ anatomy of *A. afarensis*.

    a. *A. afarensis* differs from modern _____ in such features as long, curved fingers and toes, long upper limbs and short lower limbs, the position of the hip and knees, and pelvic orientation.

    b. Stern and Sussman conclude that

        1. *A. afarensis* was capable of efficient _____ and probably spent considerable time in the trees.

        2. On the ground, *A. afarensis* was a _____ biped but walked with a much less efficient bent-hip, bent-knee gait than that seen in modern humans.

2. The conclusions of Stern and Sussman have themselves been challenged.

    a. Lovejoy and his associates see _____ that suggests *A. afarensis* was arboreal or that they were not efficient obligate bipeds.

b. While other researchers have noted differences between *A. afarensis* and the later australopithecines, some have pointed out that the hands and pelves are _____ in both.

c. Several researchers have suggested that *A. afarensis* may have been an efficient biped and also competent in the _____ .

VI. LATER EAST AFRICAN HOMINID SITES

A. There are 10 different hominid sites from 3-1 m.y.a. now known in East Africa. We focus on three.

B. East Lake Turkana (Koobi Fora)

1. The time period covered at _____ _____ ranges from 1.8-1.3 m.y.a.

2. The specimens recovered at Koobi Fora represent at least _____ individuals.

3. Next to Olduvai, Koobi Fora has yielded the most information concerning the _____ of early hominids.

   a. One of the archeological sites discovered is a "butchering" site.

   b. _____ _____ are similar to the Oldowan industry (with which it is contemporaneous).

C. West Lake Turkana

1. This site has yielded one of the most spectacular fossil finds, a nearly _____ skeleton of a 1.6 million-year-old *Homo erectus* adolescent.

2. Another important find was a well-preserved cranium, nicknamed "_____ _____ _____."

   a. This find dated to _____ million years ago.

   b. "The black skull" has caused a major _____ of Plio-Pleistocene hominid evolution.

D. Olduvai Gorge has produced the remains of about 50 individuals covering the period from 1.85 m.y.a. to _____ years ago.

VII. HOMINIDS FROM OLDUVAI AND LAKE TURKANA

A. The hominids from Olduvai and Lake Turkana represent _____ taxa.

   1. These include _____ different genera and up to six different species.

   2. The term "_____" is an anatomical descriptive term that paleoanthropologists have historically used to describe a heavy or "stout" framed australopithecine. "_____" has been applied to the lighter framed australopithecines.

   3. The _____ representative of the robust group is WT 17,000 ("the black skull").

     a. With a cranial capacity of 410 cm^3, WT 17,000 has the _____ definitely ascertained brain volume of any hominid yet found.

     b. WT 17,000 also has other primitive traits reminiscent of *A. afarensis*. These include

       1. compound _____ in the back of the skull.

       2. _____ upper face.

       3. upper dental row _____ in back.

       4. _____ base is extensively pneumatized (contains air pockets).

     c. _____ is a mosaic of primitive traits and very derived traits.

       1. These features seem to place it between _____ _____ and the later robust species.

       2. WT 17,000 has been placed in a separate species, *Australopithecus* _____.

   4. By 2 m.y.a., even more _____ members of the robust lineage were on the scene in East Africa. Robust australopithecines have

     a. _____ cranial capacities (510-530 cm^3).

     b. very large, broad _____.

     c. _____ back teeth and lower jaws.

    d. the larger (probably male) individuals possess a _____ crest.

    e. these East African robust hominids are assigned to *Australopithecus* _____.

B. Early Homo

1. The earliest appearance of our genus, _____, may be as ancient as the robust australopithecines.

    a. The earliest evidence of *Homo* is a skull fragment from _____ m.y.a.

    b. These earliest humans are already beginning to _____ .

2. *Homo* _____ at Olduvai ranges in time from 1.85-1.6 m.y.a.

    a. *H. habilis* differs from *Australopithecus* in cranial _____ and cranial _____ .

        1. The estimated _____ cranial capacity for *H. habilis* is 631 cm^3.

        2. The _____ in cranial capacity is at a minimum 20% greater over the australopithecines.

    b. *H. habilis* has larger front teeth _____ to back teeth and narrower premolars.

    c. When Louis Leakey named these specimens _____ _____ (which means "handy man") it was meaningful from two perspectives:

        1. It inferred that *Homo habilis* was the early Olduvai _____.

        2. By calling this group *Homo*, Leakey was arguing for at least _____ separate branches of hominid evolution in the Plio-Pleistocene. By calling one group *Homo*, Leakey was guessing at which group led to us.

    d. A problem with the validity of *Homo habilis* is the difficulty in distinguishing between this species and the _____ australopithecines from South Africa.

3. ER 1470 is an early *Homo* from Koobi Fora, dating between 1.8-1.6 m.y.a..

    a. It has a _____ _____ of 775 cm^3.

b. The _____ vault and face are not australopithecine-like.

c. However, the face is quite _____ .

d. The _____ teeth were quite large.

4. From the evidence available, it appears that one or more species of early *Homo* were present in East Africa probably by _____ m.y.a.

a. They would have developed in _____ with at least one line of australopithecines.

b. These hominid lines lived _____ for at least one million years.

1. After this time, the _____ lineage became extinct.

2. The early *Homo* line evolved into a later form, *Homo erectus*, which itself eventually evolved into *H. sapiens*.

VIII. CENTRAL AFRICA

A. A hominid mandible was discovered in Chad dating from _____ - _____ m.y.a.

B. Preliminary analysis suggests that this fossil's closest affinities is to _____ _____.

IX. SOUTH AFRICA: EARLIEST DISCOVERIES

A. Darwin had predicted that the earliest humans would be found in Africa.

B. The first australopithecine described was discovered in South Africa.

1. This was a child from a quarry at _____.

2. Raymond Dart, the researcher who analyzed this fossil, observed several features that suggested that this child was a _____.

a. The foramen magnum was farther _____ than in modern apes (although not as far forward as in modern humans).

b. The slant of the forehead was not as _____ as in apes.

c. The milk _____ were exceedingly small and the first molars were large, broad teeth.

d. In all respects, this fossil resembled a hominid, rather than a pongid, with the glaring exception of the very small _____ .

3. Dart named this species _____ _____ and he believed it represented a "missing link" between the apes and the humans.

a. This was not well received.

b. The major objection to *A. africanus* as a hominid was the _____ brain size.

1. At this time (the 1920s) anthropologists believed that the primary functional adaptation distinguishing humans was a _____ brain.

2. The _____ hoax fit the preconceived ideas of the time with a large brain, but ape-like jaw and teeth.

X. FURTHER DISCOVERIES OF SOUTH AFRICAN HOMINIDS

A. More _____ discoveries were made during the 1930s and 1940s.

1. Additional sites include Sterkfontein, Kromdraai, Swartkrans, and Makapansgat.

2. As the number of discoveries accumulated, it became increasingly difficult to insist that the australopithecines were simply aberrant _____ .

a. Among the fossils recovered were postcranial bones that indicated bipedalism in these hominids.

b. With the exposure of the _____ Hoax in the 1950s, scientists came to accept the australopithecines as hominids.

B. The acceptance of the australopithecines as hominids required revision of human evolutionary theory.

1. It had to be recognized that the greatest hominid brain expansion came

    _____ earlier changes in teeth and locomotor anatomy.

2. The _____ nature of human evolution had to be recognized.

XI. HOMINIDS FROM SOUTH AFRICA

A. The Plio-Pleistocene hominids discoveries from South Africa are most significant.

1. They were the _____ hominid discoveries in Africa and helped

    direct paleontologists to this continent and the later discoveries in East Africa.

2. The presence of South African hominids provide another group by which to

    compare the East African hominids.

    a. They are _____ in broad appearance, but with several distinctive

        features.

    b. These differences argue for separation, at least at the _____ level.

3. There is a large _____ of hominid fossils from South Africa,

    adding to our "fleshing out" of our ancestors.

4. The most meaningful remains are those of the _____, which indicates

    bipedalism, that most important of human characteristics.

B. "Robust" australopithecines

1. A robust species, *Australopithecus* _____ , is found in South Africa.

2. *A. robustus* is similar to the East African robust forms in

    a. _____ cranial capacities (the average is 530 cm^3).

    b. large, broad _____ .

    c. very _____ premolars and molars (although not as massive as in the

        East African robust forms).

3. The South African robust forms differ from the East African robust forms in dental

    proportions and facial architecture. This justifies separate _____ status

    for *A. robustus* and its contemporary East African robust form, *A. boisei*.

4. All members of the robust lineage appear to be specialized for a diet of _____ food items, such as seeds and nuts.

   a. The (male?) robust australopithecines have a _____ crest.

   b. The sagittal crest serves as additional attachment area for the large temporalis muscle, the primary _____ operating the massive jaw (see Fig. 14-26)

C. "Gracile" australopithecines

   1. The gracile australopithecines are only known from _____ _____.

   2. These hominids are also small-brained, but the _____ are not as large as the found in the robust varieties. This is the species named by Dart, *Australopithecus africanus*.

   3. Historically, it had been thought that there was significant differences in _____ _____ between the gracile and robust forms.

      a. It is now understood that there is not much difference in body size between the gracile and robust forms.

      b. Most of the differences between the two types of australopithecines are found in the _____ and in the _____ .

   4. The face structure of the gracile australopithecine is _____ built and somewhat dish-shaped compared to the robust species.

      a. The most distinctive difference between the gracile and robust australopithecines is in the _____.

      b. The back teeth of _____ forms are relatively large compared to modern humans, but definitely hominid in pattern.

      c. The dental complex of the _____ forms are extremely derived.

         1. They exhibit deep _____ .

         2. Much-enlarged _____ teeth, particularly the molars.

3. There is severe crowding of the _____ teeth (incisors and canines) and the canine is very reduced in size.

4. The first premolar is a much larger tooth than the small _____ (about twice as large), whereas in the gracile specimens the premolar is only about 20 percent larger than, good-sized canine.

   d. The differences in the relative proportions of teeth and jaws noted above best define a _____ , as compared to a robust australopithecine.

   e. Most differences in skull shape can be attributed to contrasting _____ function in the two forms: the sagittal crest and the broad vertical face of the robust species are related to the muscles and biomechanical requirements of the extremely large-tooth-chewing adaptation of this animal.

D. Early *Homo* in South Africa

1. Early members of _____ have also been found in South Africa, apparently living at the same time as the australopithecines.

2. The specimen Stw 53 is almost _____ to the OH 24 *Homo habilis* from Olduvai.

3. There is disagreement whether South African *Homo* such as Stw 53 (and even the East African OH 24) should be included with _____ _____ , or deserve separate species designations.

XII. PLIO-PLEISTOCENE HOMINIDS OUTSIDE AFRICA

A. It has been assumed, until recently, that hominids not only originated in Africa, but were confined there until about _____ years ago.

1. It now appears that some hominids had already reached _____ by 1.8 m.y.a. and perhaps _____ prior to 1.5 m.y.a.

2. It has always been presumed that the first hominid migrants were the later and more derived _____ _____. Now this assumption is being challenged.

B. Early hominids in central China

1. New finds from Longgupo Cave, China, have been provisionally interpreted by the primary researchers as not belonging to *Homo erectus*. These hominids are more analogous to _____ _____ from East Africa.

2. The age of this site is estimated as between _____ - _____ m.y.a., clearly making these Chinese specimens contemporaries of East African early *Homo*.

KEY TERMS

Ardipithecus ramidus : a provisional species of the most primitive hominid yet discovered. It dates from 4.4 million years ago.

australopithecine: the common name for members of the genus *Australopithecus*. Originally this term was used as a subfamily designation. North American researchers no longer recognize this subfamily, but the term is well established in usage.

Australopithecus : a genus of Plio-Pleistocene hominids with at least five species. The genus is characterized by bipedalism, a relatively small brain, and large back teeth.

"the black skull": a fossil cranium, designated WT 17, 000, that was recovered from West Lake Turkana. This member of the robust group has been provisionally assigned to *Australopithecus aethiopicus* and lived about 2.5 million years ago.

endocast: a solid impression of the inside of the skull, showing the size, shape, and some details of the surface of the brain.

family, the: a collection of the remains of at least 13 *Australopithecus afarensis* individuals who may have been contemporaries.

foramen magnum: the large opening at the base of the cranium through which the spinal cord passes and where the vertebral column joins the skull.

gracile australopithecine: the South African species, *Australopithecus africanus*, that is more lightly built than the stouter species inhabiting the same area.

habitual bipedalism: refers to the usual mode of locomotion of the organism. Used in reference to humans in the text, there are other habitual bipedal animals (e.g., large terrestrial flightless birds and kangaroos), although many hop rather than walk.

Homo habilis: a species of early *Homo*, well known in East Africa, but also perhaps from other regions.

"Lucy": a female *Australopithecus afarensis* for which 40 percent of the skeleton was recovered.

obligate bipedalism: refers to the fact that the organism cannot use any other form of locomotion efficiently.

os coxa: the structure that consists of three bones (fused together in the adult) that, together with another ox coxa and the sacrum, constitutes the pelvis. It is also referred to as the coxal by some anatomists and as the innominate bone by an earlier generation of anatomists.

robust australopithecine: any of the three species of *Australopithecus* that are characterized by a stouter body frame, larger back teeth relative to front teeth, a more vertical face, and sometimes a sagittal crest.

sagittal crest: a ridge of bone running along the midline (i.e., sagittal plane) of the cranium. The temporalis muscle, used in chewing, attaches to the sagittal crest in those mammals that possess this structure.

sectorial premolar: a premolar with a bladelike cutting edge that sections food by shearing against the cutting edge of the upper canine. The shearing action also sharpens both teeth.

Now take the Fill-in and Multiple Choice tests. Do not guess. Following completion of the tests, correct them. The correct answers and textbook page references are at the end of this study guide chapter. Note your strong areas and your weak areas to guide you in your continuing study.

FILL-IN QUESTIONS

1. _____ as the primary form of locomotion is seen only in hominids.

2. To become bipedal required a number of drastic anatomical changes in the hominid body. The most dramatic changes are found in the _____.

3. The muscle that is a powerful extensor of the thigh and forms the bulk of the buttocks in humans is the _____ _____.

4. The opening at the base of the cranium through which the spinal passes into the vertebral column is called the _____ _____. This opening has become positioned more directly underneath the skull in humans for balancing the head as one of the modifications to accommodate bipedalism.

5. Humans are committed to bipedalism and cannot locomote efficiently in any other manner. This is referred to as _____ _____.

6. It was in the late _____ that hominid differentiation began and our ancestors began to adapt more fully to their terrestrial niche.

7. The East African Plio-Pleistocene fossil-bearing sites are all part of a massive geological feature, the _____ _____ _____ of Africa.

8. The oldest specimen discovered so far, that is considered by some to be a probable hominid, dates from 5-4 m.y.a. and was found at _____ .

9. The earliest collection of hominids, dating at 4.4 m.y.a., come from the site at _____.

10. According to Tim White and his associates, _____ may form the root species for the hominids that followed it.

11. The early hominid that is the only hominid to have **thin** enamel on its molars is _____ .

12. *Australopithecus anamensis* comes from the sites at _____ and _____.

13. The individuals who made the footprints preserved at Laetoli were _____ in stature.

14. One of the most complete hominid fossils ever discovered is that of an *Australopithecus afarensis* women nicknamed "_____."

15. The word "_____ ," as used by evolutionary biologists, means that an organism is less evolved in any particular direction than later occurring organisms. It does not carry a judgment value and does not mean inferior.

16. The tooth rows of *A. afarensis* are primitive and can best be described as _____.

17. A primitive cranial feature of *A. afarensis* is the compound _____ /_____ crest.

18. A major characteristic of *A. afarensis*, that is quite unhominid-like, is extreme _____ _____ in body size between the males and the females, as much as seen in any living primate.

19. _____ _____ is a measure of brain size or volume.

20. Cranial capacity estimates for australopithecines fall within the range of most modern _____ _____.

21. A very important find, a nearly complete skeleton of a 1.6-million-year-old *Homo erectus* boy, was found at _____ _____ _____.

22. A well-preserved cranium, 2.5 million years old, that was found at West Lake Turkana, has caused a major reevaluation of Plio-Pleistocene hominid evolution. This skull is nick-named "_____ _____ _____."

23. The hominids that have massive back teeth and a vertical face are the _____ australopithecines.

24. A hominid belonging to the genus _____ was living in East Africa at the same time as *Australopithecus boisei*.

25. From all the evidence, it appears that there was at least two hominid lines living in East Africa from 2.4 million years ago, and that these two lines lived together for at least _____ _____ years.

26. A fossil _____ is a rock impression of the inside of the skull, showing the size, shape, and some details of the surface of the brain.

27. The first australopithecine was discovered by Raymond Dart and is called the _____ child.

28. Most human evolutionists did not accept Dart's *Australopithecus africanus* as a hominid because it did not have a _____ _____ .

29. *Australopithecus africanus* was finally accepted by most human evolutionary biologists by the 1950s. The final piece of evidence was actually the exposure of the _____ _____.

30. The australopithecine from South Africa that has smaller teeth and a dish-shaped face is referred to as a "_____" australopithecine.

31. Stw 53 from Sterkfontein, South Africa, is nearly identical to at least one of the _____ _____ specimens from East Africa.

MULTIPLE CHOICE QUESTIONS

1. An advantage conferred by bipedalism is
   A. a biped can get a wider view of the surroundings, enabling it to detect danger more quickly.
   B. it is a form of locomotion that increases the speed of the animal.
   C. the feet become specialized and can be used to make tools.
   D. greater distances can be covered more quickly; this explains the rapid expansion of humans throughout the world.

2. What factor led to humans becoming bipedal?
    A. Protohominids started standing upright in order to free the hands for carrying objects and making tools.
    B. Being bipedal reduced the amount of solar radiation hitting the skin and prevented protohominids from overheating.
    C. Protohominids stood bipedally to get a view over the tall grasses of the savanna in order to detect predators.
    D. We do not know what the initiating factor for bipedalism was.

3. The gluteus maximus is the largest muscle in the human. Why?
    A. It provides a "cushion" for when we sit.
    B. It is a powerful muscle for throwing and was selected for in our spear-throwing ancestors.
    C. It is an important muscle in bipedal walking and is a powerful extensor of the upper leg.
    D. Its main purpose is energy storage in the form of fat. This would have been strongly selected for in our ancestors who lived through periods of food scarcity.

4. Which of the following is **not** a major feature of hominid bipedalism?
    A. development of curves in the human vertebral column
    B. the "straightening" of the human fingers from the curved condition found in the apes
    C. the forward repositioning of the foramen magnum underneath the cranium
    D. the modification of the pelvis into a basin-like shape

5. The standard, and most efficient, mode of locomotion of humans is bipedalism. This is called
    A. saltation.
    B. obligate bipedalism.
    C. habitual bipedalism.
    D. rumination.

6. Which of the following statements is true?
    A. The human vertebral column is fairly straight.
    B. The earliest hominid, *Homo erectus*, is completely bipedal.
    C. All the major structural changes required for bipedalism are seen in the early hominids from East and South Africa.
    D. The earliest hominids have all the major features of bipedalism, except that the os coxa is long and bladelike.

7. The central task in trying to understand the earliest members of the hominid family is to
    A. interpret their degree of bipedality.
    B. determine their cranial capacity.
    C. delineate the hominid, as compared to pongid, characteristics of the brain.
    D. determine how dependent they were on material culture.

8. A foot that is highly capable of grasping and climbing is less capable as a stable platform during bipedal locomotion. This is because anatomical remodeling is limited by functional
   A. contingencies.
   B. constraints.
   C. paradoxes.
   D. drift.

9. One of the reasons that East Africa is such excellent area for following the evolution of humans is
   A. the soil is acidic, making preservation of fossils more likely.
   B. it was once a sea and the fossilization of the shells of marine organisms provide for excellent stratigraphy.
   C. there is a great deal of commercial development occurring and these developers find fossil remains and alert paleoanthropologists.
   D. there is a great deal of geological activity, which not only churns up earlier sediments but also provides datable material.

10. Which of the following is **not** a characteristic of *Ardipithecus ramidus*?
    A. large canines
    B. a sectorial premolar
    C. The foramen magnum is positioned forward, consistent with bipedalism.
    D. The pelvis is narrow with a long iliac blade.

11. Which hominid species has been recovered from Aramis?
    A. *Ardipithecus ramidus*
    B. *Australopithecus aethiopicus*
    C. *Australopithecus africanus*
    D. *Homo habilis*

12. What is the good hard evidence from Laetoli that hominids were bipedal by 3.5 m.y.a.?
    A. a fossilized foot
    B. fossilized footprints imprinted in volcanic tuff
    C. the forward position of the foramen magnum on a cranium that has been recovered.
    D. a fossil pelvis

13. Which of the following sites would you **least** expect to find fossil remains of *Australopithecus afarensis?*
    A. Hadar
    B. Laetoli
    C. Olduvai
    D. Any of these sites could yield an *A. afarensis* fossil.

14. Which of the following was found at Hadar?
    A. "Lucy"
    B. the "Family"
    C. the "Black Skull"
    D. "Zinj"
    E. Both A and B were found at Hadar.

15.   Excluding the proposed *A. anamensis*, the most primitive *Australopithecus* species is
      A. *A. afarensis.*
      B. *A. aethiopicus.*
      C. *A. boisei.*
      D. *A. africanus.*
      E. *A. robustus.*

16.   Which of the following has a sectorial or semisectorial premolar?
      A. *Ardipithecus*
      B. *Australopithecus afarensis*
      C. *Australopithecus aethiopicus*
      D. *Australopithecus robustus*
      E. Both A and B are correct.

17.   Which of the following is **not** a characteristic of *Australopithecus afarensis*?
      A. small stature
      B. small brain, averaging around 420 cm^3
      C. longer upper limbs, relative to lower limbs
      D. reduced canine size relative to the other teeth

18.   What makes *A. afarensis* a hominid?
      A. large thickly enameled molars
      B. Lucy's pelvis
      C. the front teeth are hominid
      D. the presence of a sagittal crest

19.   Which of the following statements **cannot** be attributed to Stern and Sussman?
      A. *A. afarensis* was capable of efficient climbing and probably spent considerable amounts of time in the trees.
      B. *A. afarensis* could have been quite at home in the trees as well as being an efficient terrestrial biped.
      C. On the ground, *A. afarensis* walked with a much less efficient bent-hip, bent-knee gait than we see in modern humans.
      D. *A. afarensis* was a habitual biped.

20.   The earliest species of robust australopithecine is
      A. *Australopithecus boisei.*
      B. *Australopithecus robustus.*
      C. *Australopithecus aethiopicus.*
      D. *Australopithecus africanus.*

21.   The smallest ascertained cranial capacity in a hominid is found in
      A. *Australopithecus boisei.*
      B. *Australopithecus robustus.*
      C. *Australopithecus aethiopicus.*
      D. *Australopithecus africanus.*

22. Which of the following exhibits more primitive traits than the other hominids?
    A. *Australopithecus boisei*
    B. *Australopithecus robustus*
    C. *Australopithecus aethiopicus*
    D. *Homo habilis*

23. Early *Homo* is distinguished from the australopithecines largely by
    A. larger cranial capacity.
    B. shorter stature.
    C. larger back teeth.
    D. the presence of a chin.

24. L. S. B. Leakey's explanation for tools associated with *A. boisei* ("Zinj") is that
    A. this species made tools.
    B. this species was dinner for the tool maker.
    C. these were specialized tools used for breaking open nuts and crushing seeds.
    D. they were the result of geological processes, not intentional hominid modification.

25. By assigning certain specimens to the genus *Homo*, L. S. B. Leakey was
    A. stating that these hominids were more closely related to the South African australopithecines than to the East African australopithecines.
    B. arguing for at least two separate branches of hominid evolution in the Plio-Pleistocene.
    C. indicating that this was the only species making tools in East Africa.
    D. Both B and C are correct.

26. You have measured the cranial capacity of a East African hominid from around 1.7 m.y.a. The measurement you obtained is 775 cm^3. Which species below does your specimen most likely belong to?
    A. *Australopithecus robustus*
    B. *Australopithecus boisei*
    C. *Australopithecus africanus*
    D. *Homo habilis*

27. Which of the following hominids is found in South Africa?
    A. *Australopithecus boisei*
    B. *Australopithecus afarensis*
    C. *Australopithecus aethiopicus*
    D. *Australopithecus africanus*

28. Raymond Dart's claim that *Australopithecus africanus* was a hominid was rejected by many human evolutionary biologists because they expected early members of the human family to have
    A. long faces, stabbing canines, and small brains.
    B. large brains, modern teeth, modern faces.
    C. apelike jaws and teeth, large brains.
    D. manufactured stone tools.
    E. apelike jaws and teeth, small brains.

29. The acceptance of the australopithecines as hominids by the scientific community required a complete revision of the thinking of the time, namely that
    A. large brains have always been part of the hominid line.
    B. the manufacture and use of stone tools and dental modifications occurred simultaneously.
    C. the brain expanded after modifications in the dental and locomotor systems.
    D. to be human requires a minimal cranial capacity of 750 cm^3.

30. Pitting and scratches, revealed under electron microscopy, indicates that *A. robustus* was consuming a diet of
    A. fruit.
    B. insects.
    C. meat.
    D. tough, fibrous vegetation.

31. Compared to *A. africanus*, *A. robustus*
    A. was larger, weighing up to 300 pounds (about the size of a gorilla).
    B. had smaller grinding teeth (molars).
    C. had a sagittal crest and large projecting canines.
    D. probably did more heavy chewing.
    E. had a relatively larger brain.

32. The sagittal crest present in the robust australopithecines functions as
    A. additional buttressing protecting the skull from heavy blows.
    B. a structure used in head-butting during competition for females.
    C. additional surface area for attachment of a large temporalis muscle.
    D. an area where brain expansion occurred.

33. An early *Homo*, similar to that in East Africa, has been found in
    A. Ericsberg, Minnesota.
    B. Longgupo Cave, China.
    C. Tirana, Albania.
    D. Niah Cave, Borneo.

Answers to Fill-in Outline

I. THE BIPEDAL ADAPTATION
    A. hominids
    B. 1. hands
        2. broader
        3. bipedal
        4. initiated
    C. 1. balance
        2. 25
    D. 1. stable
        2. pelvis
            a. shorter, broader
                1. weight transmission
                2. basin-shaped
            b. reposition
                1. gluteus maximus
                2. powerful
        3. balances
        4. reshaped
        5. curves
        6. length
        7. inward
            a. under
            b. closer
        8. a. parallel
            b. arch
        9. adaptive
            b. scenarios
    E. function
        1. structural
    F. 1. habitual
        2. obligate
        3. bipedalism, bipedalism
            a. major
            b. pelvis
            c. 1. curves
                2. limbs
                3. angle
            d. 1. heel, arch
                2. divergent
                    a. grasping
                    b. platform
                    c. obligate
                        1. trees
                        2. most

II. EARLY HOMINIDS IN THE PLIO-PLEISTOCENE
     A. Miocene
         1. ground-living
         2. gap
     B. 4.5
         1. Pleistocene
         2. Plio-Pleistocene

III. THE EAST AFRICAN RIFT VALLEY
     A. Rift
         1. million
         2. surface
     B. volcanic
         1. chronometrically
         2. chronology

IV. THE EARLIEST EAST AFRICAN HOMINIDS
     A. 1. a. fragmentary
             b. single
         2. 5-4
     B. 1. collection
         2. adult
         3. a. primitive
                1. canine
                2. apes
                3. cranium
             b. bipedalism
                1. foramen magnum
                2. weight-bearing
                3. pelvis
         4. Aramis
             a. primitive
             b. thin
             c. root
     C. 1. 4.3-3.9
         2. teeth
             a. thick
     D. 1. 3.7-3.5
         3. footprints
             a. 3.5
             b. two, three
             c. not
     E. 1. 40
         2. 3.0
         3. a. 40
             b. 1. infants
                2. social unit
             b. deposition
             c. oldest

V. HOMINIDS FROM LAETOLI AND HADAR
   A. *afarensis*
   B. primitive
      1. direction
         a. hominoids
         b. not
      2. primitive
         a. canines
         b. premolar
         c. parallel
      3. hominoid
         a. sagittal/nuchal
         b. 375
            1. females, males
            2. small
      4. a. longer
            1. primitive
         b. differences
      5. a. shorter
         b. dimorphism
            1. females
            2. five
            3. any
      6. bipedalism
         a. front
         b. foramen magnum, thick
   C. 1. postcranial
         a. humans
         b. 1. climbing
            2. habitual
      2. a. nothing
         b. similar
         c. trees

VI. LATER EAST AFRICAN HOMINID SITES
   B. 1. Koobi Fora
      2. 100
      3. behavior
         b. stone tools
   C. 1. complete
      2. the black skull
         a. 2.5
         b. reevaluation
   D. 50,000

VII. HOMINIDS FROM OLDUVAI AND LAKE TURKANA
   A. multiple
      1. two

      2. robust, gracile
      3. earliest
         a. smallest
         b. 1. crest
            2. projecting
            3. converges
            4. cranial
         c. WT 17,000
            1. *Australopithecus afarensis*
            2. *aethiopicus*
      4. derived
         a. small
         b. faces
         c. massive
         d. sagittal
         e. *boisei*
   B. 1. *Homo*
         a. 2.4
         b. diversify
      2. *habilis*
         a. capacity, shape
            1. average
            2. increase
         b. relative
         c. *Homo habilis*
            1. toolmakers
            2. two
         d. gracile
      3. a. cranial capacity
         b. skull
         c. robust
         d. back
      4. 2.4
         a. parallel
         b. contemporaneously
            1. australopithecine

VIII. CENTRAL AFRICA
   A. 3.5-3.0
   B. *Australopithecus afarensis*

IX. SOUTH AFRICA: EARLIEST DISCOVERIES
   B. 1. Taung
      2. hominid
         a. forward
         b. receding
         c. canines
         d. brain

3. *Australopithecus africanus*
   b. small
     1. large
     2. Piltdown

X. FURTHER DISCOVERIES OF SOUTH AFRICAN HOMINIDS
  A. australopithecine
    2. apes
     b. Piltdown
  B. 1. after
    2. mosaic

XI. HOMINIDS FROM SOUTH AFRICA
  A. 1. earliest
    2. a. similar
     b. species
    3. assemblage
    4. pelvis
  B. 1. *robustus*
    2. a. small
     b. faces
     c. large
    3. species
    4. hard
     a. sagittal
     b. muscle

C. 1. South Africa
   2. teeth
   3. body size
    b. face, dentition
   4. lightly
    a. dentition
    b. both
    c. robust
     1. jaws
     2. back
     3. front
     4. canine
    d. gracile
    e. jaw
D. 1. *Homo*
   2. identical
   3. *Homo habilis*

XII. PLIO-PLEISTOCENE HOMINIDS OUTSIDE AFRICA
  A. 1 million
    1. Asia, Europe
    2. *Homo erectus*
  B. 1. early *Homo*
   2. 1.9-1.7

ANSWERS & REFERENCES TO FILL-IN QUESTIONS

1. bipedalism, p. 354
2. pelvis, p. 355
3. gluteus maximus, p. 355
4. foramen magnum, p. 358
5. obligate bipedalism, p. 358
6. Miocene, p. 360
7. Great Rift Valley, p. 360
8. Lothagam, p. 361
9. Aramis, p. 361
10. *Ardipithecus*, p. 364
11. *Ardipithecus*, p. 364
12. Kanapoi, Allia Bay, p. 364
13. small, p. 365
14. Lucy, p. 366
15. primitive, p. 368
16. parallel, p. 368
17. sagittal/nuchal, p. 368
18. sexual dimorphism, p. 370
19. cranial capacity, p. 370
20. great apes, p. 370
21. West Lake Turkana, p. 373
22. the black skull, p. 373
23. robust, p. 374
24. *Homo*, p. 375
25. one million, p. 378
26. endocast, p. 379
27. Taung, p. 380
28. large brain, p. 381
29. Piltdown forgery, p. 382
30. gracile, p. 383
31. *Homo habilis*, p. 386

ANSWERS & REFERENCES TO MULTIPLE CHOICE QUESTIONS

1. A, p. 354
2. D, p. 354. Answers A through C are certainly advantages that bipedalism conferred and these have all been offered as speculations as to why humans became bipedal. However, we can not make observations of early hominids and it is difficult to test any of these speculations. The initiating factor, or factors, is probably one of those questions that is unanswerable and will forever remain a mystery.
3. C, p. 355
4. B, p. 358, Box 14-1
5. C, p. 358
6. C, p. 358
7. A, p. 358
8. B, p. 359
9. D, pp. 359-360
10. D, p. 363
11. A, pp. 362-364
12. B, p. 365
13. C. Both Hadar and Laetoli have yielded *A. afarensis* fossils. Olduvai has not, nor is it likely to. The geological deposits at Olduvai range in time from 1.85 m.y.a. to 50,000 years ago, long after the time period we would expect to find *A. afarensis*.
14. E, p. 366
15. A, p. 368
16. E, pp. 363 & 368
17. D, p. 368
18. B, i.e., evidence that these hominids were bipedal, p. 371
19. B, p. 371. This statement reflects the views of McHenry and Wolpoff.
20. C, p. 374
21. C, p. 374
22. C, p. 374. The robust group is more derived than the gracile line. Nevertheless, *A. aethiopicus* still has a number of primitive traits including a large sagittal crest and nuchal crest, a projecting face, convergent dental rows, and an extensively pneumatized cranial base.
23. A, p. 375
24. B, p. 375
25. B, p. 375
26. D, p. 376
27. D, p. 380
28. C, p. 381
29. C, p. 382
30. D, p. 383
31. D, pp. 383 & 385
32. C, p. 385
33. B, p. 387

CHAPTER 15

PLIO-PLEISTOCENE HOMINIDS: ORGANIZATION AND INTERPRETATION

LEARNING OBJECTIVES

After reading this chapter you should be able to:
- understand the geological complexities and resultant dating problems in South Africa. (pp. 392-394)
- understand the biological implications in making a genus-level or species-level distinction in interpreting fossil relationships. (pp. 394-400)
- know the steps necessary to interpret fossil remains. (pp. 395-396)
- discuss the current consensus in taxonomic interpretation for the Plio-Pleistocene hominids. (pp. 396-400)
- recount the four broad groupings for the Plio-Pleistocene African hominids as an alternative to a proposed phylogeny. (pp. 400-401)
- interpret various proposed phylogenies. (pp. 401-402)

FILL-IN OUTLINE

Introduction

The previous chapter looked at the history, context, and basic morphology of the large collection of Plio-Pleistocene hominid material from South and East Africa. This chapter explores the difficulties of trying to interpret this vast array of fossil materials is explored. The broader areas of interpretation where a general consensus can be found and the more specific interpretations of proposed phylogenies are all discussed.

I. INTRODUCTION

A. In the past few years a lot of _____ _____ have been made.

B. We now have specimens representing over _____ individuals from South Africa.

C. There are many complications when it comes to _____.

D   The fossil record is _____.

E. From all the African sites we have about _____ total individuals ranging from _____ to _____ m.y.a.

F. We want to know why some continued to evolve and others _____ _____.

II. GEOLOGY AND DATING PROBLEMS IN SOUTH AFRICA

A. In South Africa there are _____ early hominid sites.

B. South African sites are _____ complex.

C. The South African sites have a _____ of caves and fissures.

D. It is likely that none of the South African australopithecine sites are _____ hominid localities.

E. At Swartkrans, Sterkfontein and Kromdraai the fossil bones were probably accumulated by _____ animals.

F. Tools made of bone, tooth and horn are called _____.

G. So little is left of the Taung site that an _____ reconstruction is not possible.

H. The best dating that can be done for South Africa is to correlate _____ _____ from East Africa.

I. All the South African sites have been dated after *Australopithecus* _____.

III. INTERPRETATIONS: WHAT DOES IT ALL MEAN?

A. Numbering fossil specimens is an attempt to keep designations _____.

B. Formal _____ comes later.

C. Using taxonomic nomenclature implies an interpretation of fossil _____.

D. The distinction between groups implies a basic difference in _____ level.

E. The first step in interpreting hominid evolutionary events is to _____ and _____ a site.

F. Hominids that are on an evolutionary side branch from human ancestors must have become _____.

IV. CONTINUING UNCERTAINTIES—TAXONOMIC ISSUES

A. Plio-Pleistocene hominids come from _____ and _____ Africa.

B. The Plio-Pleistocene hominids span from _____ to _____ m.y.a.

C. Researchers generally agree to a _____-level assignment for most Plio-Pleistocene hominids.

D. At the _____-level, very little consensus can be found.

E. Evolution is not a _____ process.

F. _____ is at the heart of scientific research.

G. *Ardipithecus* is

   1. _____ million years old.

   2. from _____.

   3. known to have had thin _____ on the back teeth.

   4. different looking from any known _____ species.

H. At Hadar and Laetoli,

   1. some paleoanthropologists think that at least _____ species exist.

   2. it is clear that australopithecines were highly _____.

   3. it is good practice not to overly _____ fossil samples.

I. *Australopithecus anamensis*

   1. fossils have been quite _____.

2. anatomical differences compared to *Australopithecus afarensis* are not _____.

J. Regarding the number of genera of *australopithecus:*

1. In the _____ and _____ , most researchers lumped all forms into the genus *Australopithecus.*

2. In the last decade, there has been an increasing tendency to split the _____ group into a separate clade.

3. The robust forms have been generically termed _____.

4. The robust forms include _____, _____ and _____.

5. This text continues to lump these closely related taxa because it simplifies _____.

K. Regarding the number of species of early *Homo:*

1. The current debate will not likely be _____ soon.

2. The key issue is whether the variation we see is _____ or _____ specific.

3. One species implies extreme intraspecific _____.

4. The pattern of variation seen among early *Homo* _____ fit the pattern seen intraspecifically among extant primate species.

5. How much _____ _____ did *Homo habilis* display?

6. There is a growing consensus that there was more than _____ species.

7. Early *Homo* overlaps in time with _____ _____.

V. PUTTING IT ALL TOGETHER

A. A diagram of a family tree is called a _____.

B. Plio-Pleistocene hominid material has been divided into _____ broad groupings.

1. Set I dates to around _____ m.y.a. and includes _____ _____.

  2. Set II dates from _____ to _____ m.y.a. and includes *Australopithecus*

      _____ and *Australopithecus* _____.

  3. Set III dates from _____ to _____ m.y.a. and includes remains from

      both _____ and _____ Africa.

  4. Set IV dates from _____ to _____ m.y.a. and includes early _____.

C. More than _____ fossils from East Africa are currently in the descriptive stage.

VI. INTERPRETING THE INTERPRETATIONS

  A. All proposed phylogenies in the text postdate _____.

  B. Proposed phylogenies prior to this date did not include _____

      _____.

  C. The new finds, _____ and _____ _____

      need to be incorporated into these proposed phylogenies.

KEY TERMS

breccia: a cement matrix comprised of sand, pebbles and soil.
osteodontokeratic: Tools made from bone, tooth and horn.
phylogeny: a diagram depicting a family tree, usually in chronological order.

Now take the Fill-in and Multiple Choice tests. Do not guess. Following completion of the tests, correct them. The correct answers and textbook page references are at the end of this study guide chapter. Note your strong areas and your weak areas to guide you in your continuing study.

FILL-IN QUESTIONS

  1. In the past few years many new fossil discoveries have been made bringing the current

      total of hominid fossils for the Plio-Pleistocene period to around _____.

  2. The Plio-Pleistocene hominids date to around _____ to _____ m.y.a.

  3. Only a few of the _____ African hominids have been thoroughly studied.

  4. Some of the ancient fossils from this time period are undoubtedly those of our _____.

5. In examining early hominids we want to know how they lived and what kinds of _____ and _____ adaptations they made.

6. The East African sites are _____ and _____ straightforward.

7. The South African sites were discovered by _____ _____ activity which sometimes destroyed the site.

8. In South Africa fossil remains are found in limestone cliffs, _____, fissures, and _____.

9. In South Africa bones either fell or were carried through _____ shafts and _____ cave openings.

10. Primary hominid localities are those where the early hominids organized activities or _____.

11. The high proportion of _____ _____ suggests that they were near primate _____ sites.

12. _____ _____ suggested that early hominids at Makapansgat regularly used bone, tooth, and horn as tools—a tool technology he termed _____.

13. In South Africa it appears that large animals (presumably carnivores) could have entered but not _____ these deep caverns.

14. _____ at the South African sites has been a difficult problem.

15. The best dating technique for the South African early hominid sites is to correlate faunal sequences from _____ _____ where the dates are better known.

16. Faunal sequencing has included animals such as _____, bovids such as _____ and Old World _____.

17. Dating of the South African sites is still _____ and at times _____.

18. The formal naming of fossils has biological _____.

19. Taxonomic nomenclature implies fossil _____.

20. The steps necessary to interpret hominid evolution ideally should include seven steps.

These steps include selecting and surveying the site, _____ sites and recovering

_____ _____, designating _____ _____, cleaning,

preparing, studying and describing fossils, _____ fossil variation with

_____ ranges of variation and lastly, assigning _____ _____ to

the fossil material.

21. For the Plio-Pleistocene fossils we have a large number of fossils from a _____

    geographical area.

22. For the Plio-Pleistocene fossils we have a large number of fossils from a _____

    time period.

23. Plio-Pleistocene hominid fossils span _____ million years dating from _____ to

    _____ m.y.a.

24. We have good evidence for _____ _____ of the body.

25. All of the Plio-Pleistocene hominid fossils were well-adapted _____.

26. Making species-level designations has resulted in _____ and _____.

27. The only evidence we have thus far regarding *Ardipithecus* comes from the _____

    and _____ _____.

28. Although there is much argument among paleoanthropologists regarding the number of

    species from Hadar and Laetoli, it is clear that all _____ were variable.

29. We only have fragmentary evidence for _____ _____.

30. In the 1960s and 1970s, most of the forms of *Australopithecus* were _____ under

    this genus.

31. The genus *Homo* is recognized as being present in the _____.

32. In the last decade many paleoanthropologists have separated the robust forms of

    Australopithecus and assigned them to the genus _____.

33. The robust forms of *Australopithecus* include _____, _____ and

    _____.

34. Early *Homo* either exhibited dramatic _____ _____ or more than one species is represented.

35. A diagram of a family tree showing ancestor-descendant relationships, usually in chronological order, is called a _____.

36. To avoid the problems associated with phylogenetic relationships the Plio-Pleistocene hominid material has been broadly divided into _____ groupings.

37. One of the problems in attempting to create a human phylogeny at present is that so much material has been discovered so _____.

38. The proposed phylogenies postdate 1979 because that was when _____ _____ was suggested as the common ancestor of all later hominids.

MULTIPLE CHOICE QUESTIONS

1. Plio-Pleistocene hominid specimens from South Africa
   A. represent close to 500 individuals.
   B. are fragmentary.
   C. are relatively complete.
   D. were uncovered many years ago.

2. The five South African early hominid sites were discovered
   A. by the same scientist.
   B. after tedious and lengthy excavation.
   C. by commercial quarrying activity.
   D. accidentally by local fishermen.

3. South African cave fissures
   A. were subjected to erosive forces from above and below.
   B. were preserved in sediment.
   C. have preserved hominid bones that were deliberately buried.
   D. were permanently sealed thousands of years ago.

4. The remains at Makapansgat were accumulated
   A. through a narrow shaft entrance.
   B. through a broad cave entrance.
   C. near a hearth.
   D. near the surface.

5. Accurate paleontological reconstruction is not possible at which site?
    A. Swartkrans
    B. Kromdraai
    C. Makapansgat
    D. Taung

6. The best dating technique arrived at for the South African sites is
    A. paleomagnetism.
    B. biostratigraphy.
    C. radiocarbon.
    D. dendrochronology.

7. The Plio-Pleistocene hominid fossils from Africa
    A. range from 6 m.y.a. to 1.5 m.y.a.
    B. are widely dispersed geographically.
    C. span 3.4 million years.
    D. None of the above are correct.

8. Regarding the Plio-Pleistocene hominid fossils from Africa,
    A. researchers don't agree as to their locomotion.
    B. researchers generally agree to a genus-level distinction.
    C. not all researchers agree that they are members of the family Hominidae.
    D. more complete specimens are needed.

9. The species-level distinctions of the African Plio-Pleistocene hominids
    A. are fairly clear.
    B. are the subject of ongoing disputes.
    C. are being resolved through dating.
    D. require immediate splitting.

10. *Ardipithecus*
    A. resembles most *Australopithecus* species.
    B. shows distinct evidence of sexual dimorphism.
    C. shows thin enamel on the back teeth.
    D. may not have been bipedal.

11. *Australopithecus afarensis*
    A. is found in both East and South Africa.
    B. might represent one highly dimorphic species.
    C. is actually three different species.
    D. is only represented by fragmentary remains.

12. *Australopithecus anamensis*
    A. is not much different than *A. afarensis* anatomically.
    B. has been represented by an almost complete skeleton.
    C. requires further study and analysis before it can be confirmed as a separate species.
    D. Both A and C are correct.

13. The australopithecines are
    A. sometimes divided into two different genera.
    B. are clearly one genus.
    C. sometimes divided into four different genera.
    D. very similar in their adaptive levels.

14. The key issue with early *Homo* is
    A. dating.
    B. evaluating intraspecific variation.
    C. evaluating interspecific variation.
    D. evaluating the observed variation as being either intraspecific or interspecific.

15. In examining the variation seen among the *H. habilis* fossils
    A. we find that it is similar to that among gorillas.
    B. we find that the pattern does not fit the intraspecific variation found among any extant species.
    C. we find that it is well within an acceptable range for one species.
    D. we see relatively mild sexual dimorphism.

16. A phylogeny is
    A. a grouping into which early hominids are placed.
    B. a diagram representing ancestor-descendant relationships.
    C. a branch on a family tree.
    D. All of the above are correct.

17. Basal hominids
    A. are represented by *Ardipithecus ramidus*.
    B. are represented by *Australopithecus afarensis*.
    C. are represented by *Australopithecus africanus*.
    D. are represented by the robust Australopithecines.

18. Solid opinions regarding human evolution
    A. should be arrived at soon.
    B. are premature since more than 300 fossils have recently been found in East Africa.
    C. are overdue since no new fossils have been found in recent years.
    D. can generally be divided into two camps.

ANSWERS TO FILL-IN OUTLINE

I. INTRODUCTION
   A. New discoveries
   B. 200
   C. Interpretation
   D. Incomplete
   E. 500, 4.4-1.0
   F. Died out

II. GEOLOGY AND DATING PROBLEMS IN SOUTH AFRICA
   A. Five
   B. Geologically
   C. Maze
   D. Primary
   E. Carnivorous
   F. Osteodontokeratic
   G. Accurate
   H. The faunal sequences
   I. *afarensis*

III. INTERPRETATIONS: WHAT DOES IT ALL MEAN?
   A. Neutral
   B. Naming
   C. Relationships
   D. Adaptive
   E. Select, survey
   F. Extinct

IV. CONTINUING UNCERTAINTIES—TAXONOMIC ISSUES
   A. South, East
   B. 4.4, 1.0
   C. Genus
   D. Species
   E. Simple
   F. Debate

G. 1. 4.4
   2. Aramis
   3. Enamel
   4. *Australopithecus*
H. 1. Two separate
   2. Variable
   3. Split
I. 1. Fragmentary
   2. Striking
J. 1. 1960s, 1970s
   2. Robust
   3. *Paranthropus*
   4. *aethiopicus, boisei, robustus*
   5. Terminology
K. 1. Resolved
   2. Intra, inter
   3. Variation
   4. Does not
   5. Sexual dimorphism
   6. One
   7. *Homo erectus*

V. PUTTING IT ALL TOGETHER
   A. Phylogeny
   B. Four
      1. 4.4, *Ardipithecus ramidus*
      2. 4.2, 3.0 *afarensis, anamensis*
      3. 2.5, 1.0, South, East
      4. 2.4, 1.8, *Homo*
   C. 300

VI. INTERPRETING THE INTERPRETATIONS
   A. 1979
   B. *Australopithecus afarensis*
   C. *Ardipithecus, Australopithecus anamensis*

ANSWERS & REFERENCES TO FILL-IN QUESTIONS

1. 500, p. 392
2. 4.4, 1.0, p. 392
3. East, p. 392
4. ancestors, p. 392
5. physical and cultural, p. 392
6. geologically and archeologically, p. 392
7. commercial quarry, p. 392
8. caves, sinkholes, p. 392
9. vertical, horizontal, p. 392
10. scavenged food, p. 393
11. primate remains, sleeping, p. 393
12. Raymond Dart, osteodontokeratic, p. 393
13. departed, p. 393

14. dating, p. 394
15. East Africa, p. 394
16. pigs, antelopes, monkeys, p. 394
17. tenuous, ambiguous, p. 394
18. implications, p. 395
19. relationships, p. 395
20. excavating, fossil hominids, specimen numbers, comparing, known, taxonomic names, p. 396
21. restricted, p. 396
22. concentrated, p. 396
23. 3.4, 4.4 to 1.0, p. 396
24. most parts, p. 396
25. bipeds, p. 396
26. disputes, disagreements, pp. 396-397
27. cranium, upper limb, p. 397
28 Australopithecines, p. 397
29 *A. anamensis*, p. 397
30. lumped, p. 397
31. Plio-Pleistocene, p. 397
32. *Paranthropus*, p. 398
33 *aethiopicus, boisei, robustus*, p. 398
34. sexual dimorphism, p. 398
35. phylogeny, p. 400
36. four, p. 400
37. recently, p. 401
38. *A. afarensis*, p. 401

ANSWERS & REFERENCES TO MULTIPLE CHOICE QUESTIONS

1. B, p. 392
2. C, p. 392
3. A, p. 393
4. A, p. 393
5. D, p. 394
6. B, p. 394
7. C, p. 396
8. B, p. 396
9. B, p. 396
10. C, p. 397
11. B, p. 397
12. D, p. 397
13. A, pp. 397-398
14. D, p. 398
15. B, p. 398
16. B, p. 400
17. A, p. 400
18. B, p. 401

CHAPTER 16

HOMO ERECTUS

LEARNING OBJECTIVES

After reading this chapter you should be able to:
- discuss the temporal and geographic distribution of *Homo erectus*. (p. 408)
- briefly describe the time frame and glacial movements of the Pleistocene. (p. 412)
- describe the physical characteristics of *Homo erectus*. (pp. 412-415)
- discuss scientists and the *erectus* finds they are associated with. (pp. 415-419)
- describe the fossil remains and related archeological evidence of Java, China and Africa. (pp. 415-428)
- compare African and Asian *erectus* fossils. (pp. 415-425)
- describe the cultural stages of *Homo erectus*. (pp. 425-428)
- understand some of the disputes in interpreting *erectus* fossils and archeological evidence. (pp. 408-429)
- analyze the technological advances reflected in the *erectus* tool kit. (pp. 425-427)

FILL-IN OUTLINE

Introduction

The previous chapters looked at early hominid evolution by examining the genera *Australopithecus* and early *Homo*. This chapter moves on chronologically to examine *Homo erectus*, believed by most to be the ancestor of modern *Homo sapiens*. Regarding *erectus*, their geographic and temporal distribution, physical characteristics, the history of their discoveries, variation exhibited by African and Asian *erectus* fossils, and the technological advances made by them over approximately 1.5 million years are all discussed.

I. INTRODUCTION

   A. Hominid evolution has been characterized by _____ _____.

II. *HOMO ERECTUS*—TERMINOLOGY AND GEOGRAPHICAL DISTRIBUTION

   A. The name first given for the Javanese fossils was _____.

   B. After _____ _____ ___ the previous taxonomic splitting was combined under the classification *Homo erectus*.

   C. Finds in E. Africa have been radiometrically dated to _____ m.y.a.

   D. Two sites in _____ have dates that compare to those in E. Africa.

   E. Evidence indicates that hominids left Africa before _____ m.y.a.

   F. A likely route that can be reconstructed for the *Homo erectus* migration out of Africa would be _____.

   G. The fossil remains from the Gran Dolina site in Spain are approximately _____ years old.

III. THE PLEISTOCENE (1.8 M.Y.A. – 10,000 Y.A.)

   A. Also known as the "_____ _____ _____" or "_____ _____"

   B. _____ _____ was covered with ice.

   C. New evidence indicates approximately _____ major cold periods and _____ minor advances.

   D. *H. erectus* _____ and _____ during the Pleistocene.

IV. THE MORPHOLOGY OF *HOMO ERECTUS*

   A. Brain Size

      1. In *Homo erectus* ranges from _____ to _____ cm^3.

      2. Has a mean of _____ cm^3 in *H. erectus*.

      3. Is related to overall _____ _____.

   B. Body Size

1. *H. erectus* displays a dramatic _____ in body size.

2. Adults are estimated to have weighed on average over _____ pounds.

3. Average adult height is estimated at _____.

C. Cranial Shape

1. Has a distinctive _____.

2. Thick cranial bones are found in the _____ specimens.

3. Supraorbital tori refer to _____ _____.

4. The forehead is _____ _____ _____ _____.

5. Maximum breadth is _____ _____ _____ _____.

D. Dentition

1. _____-_____ incisors are a typical characteristic.

V. HISTORICAL OVERVIEW OF *HOMO ERECTUS* DISCOVERIES

A. Java

1. _____ was the first laboratory scientist to go to work in the field.

2. The first fossils unearthed were a _____ and a _____.

3. These fossils were classified as _____ _____.

4. _____ evolved before the enlargement of the brain.

B. *Homo erectus* from Java

1. All the fossils from Java have come from _____ sites.

2. _____ is a problem because of complex Javanese geology.

3. New dating techniques have revealed dates ranging from _____ m.y.a. to _____ m.y.a.

4. No _____ have been found that can be associated with *H. erectus*.

C. Peking

1. "_____ _____" were known to be used as medicine and as aphrodisiacs.

2. Near the village of _____ a remarkable fossil skull was found.

3. The bones from Peking (Beijing) were packed for shipment and _____.

D. Zhoukoudian *Homo erectus*

1. More than _____ male and female adults and children have been found.

2. Features include the _____ _____ behind.

3. The skull is keeled by a _____ _____.

4. Cultural Remains

a. More than _____ artifacts have been unearthed.

b. The site was inhabited intermittently for almost _____ years.

c. Occupation has been divided into _____ cultural stages.

d. Early tools are _____ and _____.

e. Materials used to make tools include _____, _____ and _____.

f. Drinking bowls were made out of _____ _____.

g. Food included _____, _____, _____, _____, _____ and _____.

h. It is _____ that they used language.

E. Other Chinese Sites

1. Chenjiawo and Gongwangling are often referred to as "_____."

2. Lontandong Cave is often referred to as "_____."

3. The Chenjiawo find is provisionally dated at _____-_____ y.a.

4. Gongwangling finds are provisionally dated at _____ m.y.a.

5. In the Lontandong Cave, a _____ was found exhibiting several _____ _____.

F. East Africa

1. Olduvai

a. _____ _____ unearthed OH9.

b. OH9 dates to _____ m.y.a.

c. OH9 is the _____ of the African *H. erectus* finds.

2. East Turkana

a. ER 3733 is an almost complete _____.

b. ER 3733 dates to _____ m.y.a.

c. Not many _____ have been found.

3. West Turkana

a. WT 15,000 is the most complete *H. erectus* _____ ever found.

b. WT 15,000 dates to _____ m.y.a.

c. WT 15,000 was a boy about _____ years old.

d. If WT 15,000 had grown to his full height he would have been _____.

e. WT 15,000's adult cranial capacity would have been _____.

4. Ethiopia

a. An abundance of _____ tools have been found.

b. A robust mandible has been found dating to _____ m.y.a.

c. E. African *H. erectus* finds show several _____ from the Java and Chinese fossils.

d. E. African specimens exhibit _____ _____ crania.

e. Some scientists would argue that the African and Asian *H. erectus* finds should be classified as _____ _____.

5. South Africa

a. Disagreement exists over how to classify the _____ found at Swartkrans.

6. North Africa

a. Remains are almost entirely made up of _____ _____ _____ _____.

b. Tenerife remains are quite _____.

    c. Tenerife remains date to _____ y.a.

    d. Moroccan material is less _____ than that from Tenerife.

VI. TECHNOLOGICAL AND SOCIAL TRENDS IN THE MIDDLE PLEISTOCENE

  A. Technological Trends

    1. _____ exists over the physical and cultural changes of *H. erectus*.

    2. The text takes a _____ _____ regarding changes.

    3. A core stone that was worked on both sides is called a _____.

      a. These tools are commonly called _____ _____ and _____.

    4. The _____ stone tool was an all purpose *erectus* tool for more than a million years.

      a. it has been found in _____, _____, and later in _____ _____.

      b. it has never been found in _____ _____ or _____ _____.

    5. Early toolmakers used a hammer made of _____.

    6. Later toolmakers began using _____ and _____.

      a. which gave them more _____

    7. Widespread evidence for _____ exists.

      a. thousands of Acheulian hand axes have been found in association with _____ ____ _____ _____.

  B. Social Trends

    1. *H. erectus* had a penchant for _____.

    2. Hunters-scavengers and gatherers are _____.

    3. *H. erectus* was committed to a _____ way of life.

KEY TERMS

Acheulian: a tool technology from the lower and middle Pleistocene characterized by bifacial tools usually made of stone.

artifacts: objects or materials made or modified for use by hominids.

biface: a stone tool consisting of a core stone worked on both sides. Commonly called hand axes and cleavers. Associated with *H. erectus* in Africa, W. Asia and W. Europe.

biocultural: An approach to the study of human evolution taking into account the interaction between morphological evolution and cultural changes.

contemporaneous: living at the same time.

encephalization: the relationship between brain size and overall body size.

mandible: jaw bone.

morphology: refers to the form or shape of anatomical structures or an entire organism.

Nariokotome: also known as WT 15,000. Refers to an almost complete skeleton of a 12-year-old boy from West Lake Turkana in Kenya classified as *H. erectus*.

nuchal torus: large muscle attachment at the base of the skull.

Pleistocene: the epoch of the Cenozoic dating from 1.8 m.y.a. to 10,000 y.a. characterized by continental glaciations of the northern latitudes. Frequently referred to as the "Age of Glaciers" or the "Ice Age."

postcranial: refers to the skeleton. Anything **except** the cranium.

sagittal ridge: a ridge of bone running along the center of the skull (like parting the hair down the middle) where chewing muscles attach.

supraorbital torus: heavy browridge.

taxonomy: the science of classifying organisms based on evolutionary relationship.

temporal: refers to either time or a cranial bone.

Zhoukoudian: A village near Peking famous for a cave that has yielded rich fossil remains of *H. erectus*.

Now take the Fill-in and Multiple Choice tests. Do not guess. Following completion of the tests, correct them. The correct answers and textbook page references are at the end of this study guide chapter. Note your strong areas and your weak areas to guide you in your continuing study.

FILL-IN QUESTIONS

1. Prior to World War II a variety of _____ _____ were proposed for

   fossils that were later lumped under the classification of *Homo erectus.*

2. Reclassifying fossils and shifting away from taxonomic splitting was a benefit to

   paleoanthropology because it refocused the research away from arguments regarding

   classification to broader _____, _____ and _____

   considerations.

3. We now have growing evidence of the early dispersal of hominids out of _____.

4. Some evidence from China may indicate that members of the genus *Homo* migrated out of _____ prior to the appearance of _____ _____.

5. The Boxgrove site in _____ _____ dates to _____ y.a.

6. The _____ _____ site in northern Spain dates to 780,000. If the dating can be further corroborated, these finds would be ____ _____ _____ years older than any other Western European hominid finds.

7. The "Age of Glaciers" or the "Ice Age" refers to the epoch of the Cenozoic known as the _____ which dates from _____ m.y.a. to _____ y.a.

8. The Pleistocene was characterized by 15 major cold periods and 50 minor advances. This computes out to approximately one major cold period every _____ years.

9. By the end of the Pleistocene _____ _____ had appeared.

10. Many scholars believe that there were more than _____ species of *Homo* in Africa 2 m.y.a.

11. The relationship of brain size to overall body size is referred to as _____.

12. The Nariokotome skeleton indicates a dramatic increase in _____ _____ for *H. erectus*.

13. A robust body build is typical of hominid evolution until the appearance of _____ _____ _____ when a more gracile skeleton appears.

14. *Homo erectus* is said to have a distinctive cranial shape. The characteristics that give *H. erectus* this distinct shape include _____, _____, _____, _____, and _____ _____.

15. *H. erectus* dentition is similar to that of *Homo sapiens* however early *H. erectus* finds exhibit _____ _____ teeth.

16. The incisors of *H. erectus* exhibit a unique characteristic which is _____-_____.

17. The first *H. erectus* find comes from _____.

18. Eugene Dubois left Holland for Sumatra in 1887 in search of "_____ _____".

19. After Dubois published his findings from Java he was criticized. How did he combat this criticism and what was the result? _____

_____.

20. The similarities between Dubois' Java fossils and those of Beijing were obvious. How did Dubois respond to these similarities? _____

_____.

21. Java has a complex geology, making accurate dating difficult. However, it is generally accepted that the approximate dates for the majority of fossils from Java date to less than _____ y.a.

22. Zhoukoudian Cave in China, near Peking (Beijing) was inhabited off and on for around _____ years.

23. The Zhoukoudian Cave has yielded the remains of _____ individuals and over _____ artifacts have been found.

24. The Zhoukoudian Cave has been divided into three cultural stages. The Earliest Stage dates from _____ to _____ y.a. and its tools are _____ and made of _____ _____.

25. The Middle Stage of the Zhoukoudian Cave dates from _____ to _____ and its tools are _____ than those from the Earliest Stage.

26. The Final Stage of the Zhoukoudian Cave dates from _____ to _____ y.a. and its tools are _____ _____ and made of _____ _____.

27. Peking Man (the term often used when referring to the Zhoukoudian Cave fossils) exploited various sources in the environment for subsistence including _____, _____, _____, _____, and _____.

28. *H. erectus* from Zhoukoudian probably _____ have articulated speech.

29. Although the life span of *H. erectus* is unknown, nearly 40% of the bones found at Zhoukoudian Cave belonged to individuals _____ years or younger and only 2.6% belonged to individuals in the _____ to _____ age range.

30. A partial cranium discovered at _____ may be the oldest known Chinese *H. erectus* find.

31. In 1960, Louis Leakey found the largest African *H. erectus* specimen at _____.

32. ER 3733 is a skull without a mandible that has a cranial capacity of 848cm^3 which is at the _____ _____ end of the range for *H. erectus* cranial capacity.

33. WT 15,000 from Nariokotome, Kenya is _____

_____

_____.

34. The Acheulian stone tools found in Ethiopia were primarily bifaces and picks and were made of _____, _____, _____, _____,

_____, _____, _____.

35. Bernard Wood proposes that African and Chinese *H. erectus* finds are _____ species.

36. By using different methodologies to analyze data, scientists have reached different conclusions regarding whether the _____ and _____ characteristics of *H. erectus* populations underwent many changes.

37. The biface, an Acheulian stone tool became the all-purpose *H. erectus* tool for more than _____ years.

38. At the Olorgesailie site in Kenya, dated at around 800,000 y.a. thousands of _____ _____ _____ have been recovered associated with large animal remains.

39. *H. erectus* loved to travel. In a million years they dispersed to north and south Africa as well as into _____.

MULTIPLE CHOICE QUESTIONS

1. New dates from two sites in Java indicate that
   A. *H. erectus* may have originated in Asia.
   B. the Java finds are as old as the East African finds.
   C. the Java finds are much more recent than the East African finds.
   D. *H. erectus* arrived in Java one million years later than previously thought.

2. Currently, it is believed that the first hominids left Africa
   A. between 1.5 and 2 m.y.a.
   B. due to a geologic catastrophe.
   C. around 500,000 y.a.
   D. and went first to Western Europe.

3. A physical characteristic distinct to *H. erectus* that distinguishes it from other hominids is
   A. cranial height.
   B. alveolar prognathism.
   C. large teeth.
   D. the cranial breadth is below the ear.

4. The importance of WT 15,000, found at Nariokotome on the west side of Lake Turkana, is
   A. the remarkable old age of the specimen at death.
   B. the completeness of the skeleton.
   C. the estimated stature of a 12 year old boy.
   D. Both B and C are correct.

5. Which of the following traits is not characteristic of *H. erectus*?
   A. supraorbital torus
   B. shovel-shaped incisors
   C. gracile muscle attachments
   D. pentagonal contour to the cranium

6. Given *H. erectus* dates and sites, it appears probable that *H. erectus*
   A. originated in Africa.
   B. migrated from Africa to southwestern Asia.
   C. moved into Europe about a million years ago.
   D. All of the above are correct.
   E. Both A and B are correct.

7. An all purpose *H. erectus* tool was the
   A. biface.
   B. burin.
   C. side scraper.
   D. pebble tool.

8. The Pleistocene
    A. is also known as the "Ice Age."
    B. had 15 major cold periods.
    C. saw the appearance of *H. erectus*.
    D. saw the disappearance of *H. erectus*.
    E. All of the above are correct.

9. *H. erectus* cranial capacity
    A. shows considerable enlargement.
    B. relative to its body size was less encephalized than archaic *sapiens*.
    C. does not indicate enlargement when compared to overall body size.
    D. Both A and B are correct.

10. The cranial shape of *H. erectus*
    A. is distinctive.
    B. has large browridges.
    C. has a projecting nuchal torus.
    D. All of the above are correct.
    E. Both A and C are correct.

11. The dentition of *H. erectus*
    A. exhibits large cheek teeth.
    B. has thin enamel.
    C. is much like *Homo sapiens*.
    D. All of the above are correct.

12. The first *H. erectus* find was in
    A. Peking.
    B. Java.
    C. Africa.
    D. Europe.

13. The first *H. erectus* find consisted of
    A. a skullcap.
    B. a clavicle.
    C. a tibia.
    D. a femur.

14. Zhoukoudian Cave
    A. was discovered after Europeans had heard about "dragon bones."
    B. shows evidence of a bear cult.
    C. has firm evidence of cannibalism.
    D. was inhabited intermittently for almost 250,000 years.
    E. Both A and D are correct.

15. The cultural remains at Zhoukoudian Cave
    A. are minimal.
    B. are limited to hearths.
    C. consist of over 100,000 artifacts.
    D. enable archaeologists to easily reconstruct a day in the life of *H. erectus*.

16. It appears that *H. erectus* exploited
    A. primarily meat sources.
    B. primarily fruits.
    C. meat, fruit, eggs and seeds.
    D. marine life.

17. Of the fossil remains at Zhoukoudian,
    A. 40% belonged to individuals 14 years old and younger.
    B. 2.6% belonged to individuals 50-60 years old.
    C. nuclear families were clearly represented.
    D. All of the above are correct.
    E. Both A and B are correct.

18. Which of the following advanced characteristics was found on the cranium from Lontandong Cave which dates to 250,000 y.a.?
    A. Reduced postorbital constriction
    B. Temporal characteristics
    C. Occipital characteristics
    D. All of the above are correct.

19. OH9 found in 1960 by Louis Leakey at Olduvai
    A. is dated at 1.4 m.y.a.
    B. has a massive cranium.
    C. is gracile.
    D. Both A and B are correct.

20. WT 15,000 from Nariokotome, Kenya
    A. is the most complete *H. erectus* skeleton every found.
    B. exhibits very primitive characteristics.
    C. has a huge cranial capacity.
    D. dates to 1.6 m.y.a.
    E. Both A and D are correct.

21. Bernard Wood suggested that
    A. African *H. erectus* finds should be named *Homo ergaster*.
    B. Asian *H. erectus* finds should retain the name *Homo erectus*.
    C. both African and Asian *H. erectus* finds should be reclassified.
    D. Both A and B are correct.

22. The Acheulian stone biface was a standard tool for *H. erectus* for over a million years and was
    A. never found in Africa.
    B. never found in West Asia.
    C. never found in East Asia.
    D. found in abundance in eastern Europe.

23. Wood and bone allowed toolmakers to
    A. have more control.
    B. leave shallower scars.
    C. create sharper edges.
    D. All of the above are correct.
    E. Both A and B are correct.

24. *H. erectus* was
    A. sedentary.
    B nomadic.
    C. not very successful.
    D. None of the above are correct.

ANSWERS TO FILL-IN OUTLINE

I. INTRODUCTION
   A. biocultural interaction

II. *HOMO ERECTUS*—TERMINOLOGY AND GEOGRAPHICAL DISTRIBUTION
   A. *Pithecanthropus*
   B. World War II
   C. 1.8
   D. Java
   E. 1
   F. To South and North Africa, southern and northeaster Asia and perhaps Europe
   G. 780,000

III. THE PLEISTOCENE (1.8 M.Y.A. - 10,000 Y.A.)
   A. Age of Glaciers, Ice Age
   B. Northern Hemisphere
   C. 15, 50
   D. appeared, disappeared

IV. THE MORPHOLOGY OF *HOMO ERECTUS*
   A. 1. 750, 1250^3
      2. 1000
      3. body size
   B. 1. increase
      2. 100
      3. 5'6"
   C. 1. shape
      2. Asian
      3. large browridges
      4. receding with little development
      5. below the ear opening
   D. 1. shovel-shaped

V. HISTORICAL OVERVIEW OF *HOMO ERECTUS* DISCOVERIES
   A. 1. Eugene Dubois
      2. skullcap and femur
      3. *Pithecanthropus erectus*
      4. bipedalism
   B. 1. six
      2. dating
      3. 1.8, 1.6
      4. artifacts
   C. Peking
      1. dragon bones
      2. Zhoukoudian
      3. never been found (lost or stolen)
   D. 1. 40
      2. nuchal torus
      3. sagittal ridge
      4. cultural remains

a. 100,000
b. 250,000
c. three
d. crude, shapeless
e. stone, bone, horn
f. deer skulls
g. deer, horse, fruits, berries, eggs, seeds, herbs, tubers
h. unlikely

E. 1. Lantian
   2. Hexian
   3. 600,000-500,000
   4. 1.15
   5. cranium, advanced features

F. 1. Olduvai
      a. Louis Leakey
      b. 1.4
      c. largest
   2. a. skull
      b. 1.8
      c. tools
   3. a. skeleton
      b. 1.6
      c. 12
      d. more than 6 ft.
      e. 909 cm^3
   4. a. Acheulian
      b. 1.3

c. differences
d. less robust (not as strongly buttressed, do not have thick cranial bones)
e. Separate species

5. a. mandible
6. a. mandibles and mandible fragments
   b. robust
   c. 700,000
   d. robust

VI. TECHNOLOGICAL AND SOCIAL TRENDS IN THE MIDDLE PLEISTOCENE

A. 1. dispute
   2. moderate position
   3. biface
      a. hand axes, cleavers
   4. biface
      a. Africa, Asia, western Europe
      b. eastern Europe, East Asia
   5. stone
   6. wood, bone
      a. control
   7. butchering
      a. remains of large animals

B. 1. travel
   2. nomadic
   3. cultural

ANSWERS & REFERENCES TO FILL-IN QUESTIONS

1. taxonomic names, p. 408
2. populational, behavioral, ecological, p. 408
3. Africa, p. 409
4. Africa, *H. erectus*, p. 409
5. southern England, 500,000, p. 409
6. Gran Dolina, at least 250,000, p. 409
7. Pleistocene, 1.8, 10,000, p. 412
8. 100,000, p. 412
9. modern humans, p. 412
10. one, p. 412
11. encephalization, p. 413
12. body size, p. 413
13. most modern populations, p. 413
14. supraorbital tori, nuchal torus, long and low vault, receding forehead, maximum breadth below the ear opening, pp. 414-415.

15. somewhat larger, p. 415
16. shovel-shaped, p. 415
17. Java, p. 415
18. the missing link, p. 416
19. He elaborated on certain points and showed the actual fossil material. Many opponents became sympathetic (started to change their minds), p. 417
20. He refused to recognize the connection referring to them as "degenerate Neanderthaler," p. 418
21. 800,000, p. 418
22. 250,000, p. 420
23. 40, 100,000, pp. 419-420
24. 460,000, 420,000, large, soft stone, p. 420
25. 370,000, 350,000, smaller, p. 420
26. 300,000, 230,000, still small finer quartz and flint, p. 420
27. deer, horses, fruits, berries, eggs, seeds, herbs, tubers, p. 421
28. did not, p. 421
29. 14, 50, 60, p. 421
30. Gongwangling, p. 422
31. Olduvai, p. 423
32. lower end, p. 423
33. The almost complete skeleton of a 12 year old boy classified as *H. erectus*, dated to 1.6 m.y.a., who was 5'3" and had a cranial capacity of 880cm3 at death. It is estimated that his adult height would have been over 6' and his cranial capacity would have been approximately 909 cm3, pp. 416 & 424.
34. quartz, quartzite, volcanic rock, cobbles, blocks, cores, flakes, p. 424.
35. Separate, p. 424
36. physical, cultural, p. 425
37. 1,000,000, p. 427
38. Acheulian hand axes, p. 427
39. Asia, p. 428

ANSWERS & REFERENCES TO MULTIPLE CHOICE QUESTIONS

1. B, p. 409
2. A, p. 409
3. D, p. 415
4. D, p. 413
5. C, pp. 413, 415
6. E, p. 409
7. A, p. 427
8. E, p. 412
9. D, pp. 412-413
10. D, p. 414
11. C, p. 415
12. B, p. 415
13. A, p. 416
14. E, pp. 418, 420
15. C, p. 420
16. C, p. 421
17. E, p. 421
18. D, p. 422
19. D, p. 423
20. E, p. 424
21. D, p. 424
22. C, p. 427
23. D, p. 427
24. B, p. 428

CHAPTER 17

NEANDERTALS AND OTHER ARCHAIC
HOMO SAPIENS

LEARNING OBJECTIVES

After reading this chapter you should be able to:
- see the morphological changes from *H. erectus* to archaic *H. sapiens*. (pp. 436-443)
- know the geographic distribution of archaic *sapiens*. (pp. 436-443)
- discuss specific fossils of archaic *sapiens* and their distinguishing characteristics. (pp. 437-443, 446-455)
- compare the tool technology of archaic *sapiens* to that of *H. erectus* and early modern *H. sapiens*. (pp. 440-452, 455-456, 459)
- discuss the physical characteristics of classic Neandertals. (pp. 446-449)
- discuss specific Neandertal finds and their distinguishing characteristics. (pp. 446-455)
- describe Neandertal shelters, subsistence and burials. (pp. 456-460)
- have an understanding of the confusion surrounding the origins and disappearance of Neandertal. (p. 458)

FILL-IN OUTLINE

Introduction

    The previous chapter examined *Homo erectus*, believed by most to be the ancestor of modern *Homo sapiens*. This chapter looks at archaic *Homo sapiens* from Europe, Africa, China and Java who display both *H. erectus* and *H. sapiens* characteristics. Neandertals, including their physical characteristics, culture, technology, settlements, subsistence patterns and burials are also examined. A discussion on the confusion surrounding Neandertal origins as well as their disappearance is included.

  I. INTRODUCTION

    A. Some fossils from Europe, Africa, China and Java display both *H. erectus* and

    _____ _____ characteristics.

B. They are referred to as _____ *H. sapiens* because they exhibit certain _____ traits.

C. Some populations of *erectus* continued to evolve and emerge as _____ forms between V*erectus* and *H. sapiens sapiens*.

II. EARLY ARCHAIC *H. SAPIENS*

A. exhibit _____ characteristics like brain expansion.

B. have been found on _____ continents including _____, _____ and _____.

C. The most well-known from Europe are the _____.

D. Africa

   1. The Broken Hill cranium has a very heavy _____ _____.

   2. The Bodo skull contains the first evidence of _____.

   3. In Africa the archaic *H. sapiens* are morphologically similar which may signify a close _____ relationship.

E. Asia

   1. Certain *H. erectus* features can be found in modern Chinese such as a _____ _____ and flattened _____ bone.

   2. This could indicate that modern Chinese evolved from a separate _____ _____ lineage in _____.

F. Europe

   1. _____ _____ exist to prove that *H. erectus* lived in Europe.

   2. Early archaic *H. sapiens* from Europe show *H. erectus* characteristics like a _____ mandible.

   3. Later archaics from Europe show derived characteristics like a _____ occipital area and reduced _____ size.

4. The Petralona, Greece skull is _____ because it exhibits characteristics from Neandertal, Broken Hill and *H. erectus.*

5. The later group of European archaics may have given rise to _____.

6. The largest sample of archaic *H. sapiens* comes from _____ , _____.

III. A REVIEW OF MIDDLE PLEISTOCENE EVOLUTION (CIRCA 400,000-125,000 Y.A.)

A. Fossils from Europe, Africa and China exhibit a _____ of traits from both *H. erectus* and *H. sapiens.*

B. The earlier European forms are more _____.

C. The later European forms are more like _____.

D. African and Asian forms begin exhibiting a more _____ ___ _____ pattern.

IV. MIDDLE PLEISTOCENE CULTURE

A. The basic tools are _____ and _____ _____.

B. African and European archaics invented the _____ technique for tool making.

C. This technique indicates an increased _____ ability.

D. Acheulian tools are associated with _____ _____.

E. We see _____ tool traditions in some areas.

F. Archaic *H. sapiens* lived in _____ and _____-_____ sites.

G. Chinese archaeologists insist that humans _____ control fire.

H. The Lazaret Cave shelter was supported by _____ and large _____.

1. Inside were two _____.

2. The people exploited _____ fish.

I. At Terra Amata we have found evidence of short-term, _____ visits.

J. To hunt large prey, early *H. sapiens* probably drove the animals _____ _____.

V. NEANDERTALS: LATE ARCHAIC *H. SAPIENS* (130,000-35,000 Y.A.)

A. Neandertals are _____.

B. _____ Neandertals dated from around 75,000 y.a. to 10,000 y.a. and are from _____ Europe.

C. Modern *H. sapiens* brain size is around _____ cm³.

D. Neandertal brain size was around _____ cm³.

   1. This may be associated with _____ in cold weather.

E. The Neandertal cranium is large _____ and _____.

   1. The forehead begins to _____ more vertically.

   2. Over the orbits we see _____ _____ instead of a supraorbital torus.

F. Postcranially Neandertals are very _____.

G. Neandertals lived in Europe and Western Asia for around _____ years.

H. France and Spain

   1. In La Chapelle-aux-Saints in S.W. France, a nearly complete skeleton was found _____.

      a. It was turned over to _____ _____ for analysis.

      b. He depicted this find as a _____, bent-kneed, not fully erect _____.

      c. This resulted in a general misunderstanding that Neandertals were highly _____.

      d. In fact, the skeleton was of an older male suffering from _____ _____.

      e. This individual is not a _____ Neandertal.

      f. He is unusually _____.

   2. If the date for the Zafarraya Cave in southern Spain is correct, it would make this the most _____ of Neandertal fossils.

   3. It appears that Neandertals and modern *H. sapiens* _____ _____ _____ _____ for several thousand years.

I. Central Europe

   1. Krapina, Croatia

      a. has remains of up to _____ individuals.

      b. has 1,000 _____ tools.

      c. dates to _____ y.a.

      d. has one of the oldest intentional _____ to _____ on record.

J. Western Asia

   1. Israel

      a. Tabun

         1. yielded a female skeleton dated at _____ y.a..

         2. if the dating is correct it indicates that _____ and modern _____ _____ lived contemporaneously.

      b. Kabara

         1. the most complete Neandertal _____ was found here.

         2. yielded the first ever _____ bone.

            a. important to reconstruct _____ capabilities.

   2. Iraq

      a. Shanidar

         1. yielded the remains of _____ individuals.

            a. _____ of them were deliberately buried.

         2. Shanidar 1 was a _____ to _____ year old male.

            a. his stature is estimated at _____.

            b. he exhibited extreme injuries that he _____.

K. Central Asia

   1. Uzbekistan

      a. is the _____ Neandertal discovery.

      b. is a _____ year-old _____.

VI. CULTURE OF NEANDERTALS

    A. The stone tool industry associated with Neandertals is the _____.

        1. which extended geographically into _____, _____,

        _____, _____, _____,

        _____ and perhaps even _____.

    B. Technology

        1. Neandertals improved on the previous _____ techniques.

        2. We see some indication of _____ of tools.

    C. Settlements

        1. Neandertals lived in _____ _____, _____ and _____ _____.

        2. On the tundra there is some evidence of _____ _____ _____.

        3. Archeologists found traces of an oval ring of _____ bones.

        4. Inside the ring they found traces of a number of _____.

        5. _____ was in general use by this time.

    D. Subsistence

        1. Neandertals were successful _____.

        2. After the beginning of the Upper Paleolithic (around 40 k.y.a.) the _____ _____ or _____ was invented.

        3. The pattern of trauma found among Neandertals is similar to modern day _____ _____.

        4. Besides meat, Neandertals also ate _____, _____ and other _____.

        5. Since it was so cold we assume that Neandertals _____ _____.

    E. Symbolic Behavior

        1. We believe that Neandertals _____ capable of speech.

        2. We have a problem explaining _____ _____ to Neandertals.

        3. Neandertals are being viewed as an _____ dead end.

F. Burials

   1. Some form of deliberate and consistent disposal of the dead dates back to _____ y.a. from the Atapuerca, Spain site.

     a. This is seen in Western Europe long before it appears in either _____ or _____ _____.

   2. After 35,000 y.a. with *H. sapiens sapiens* we see deliberate burials containing grave goods like _____ and _____ _____.

   3. In Neandertal burials the bodies were put in a _____ position.

VII. CONCLUSION: EVOLUTIONARY TRENDS IN THE GENUS *HOMO*

A. _____ major transitions have taken place.

B. The first transition was from early _____ to _____ _____.

   1. This was geographically limited to _____.

   2. It occurred quite _____.

C. The second transition was _____ _____ grading into _____ _____ _____.

   1. It _____ geographically limited.

   2. It occurred slowly and _____.

   3. Interpretations are _____.

   4. Many populations could have been _____ and small.

D. The third transition was from _____ _____ _____ to _____ _____ _____.

   1. It was _____ than the second transition.

KEY TERMS

archaic *Homo sapiens*: earlier forms of *Homo sapiens*, including but not limited to Neandertals, that come after *H. erectus* but before modern humans.
Chatelperronian: a tool industry created from Neandertals modifying technology borrowed from anatomically modern humans.
flexed: the position in which bodies were found in Neandertal burials. The arms and legs are drawn up to the chest.
hearth: floor of a fireplace.
Levallois: a technique for the manufacture of tools by striking flakes from a flat flint nodule.
Mousterian: the stone tool technology associated with Neandertals and some modern *H. sapiens* groups.
transitional forms: fossils that have both primitive and derived characteristics. They are not fully one form but rather exhibit traits from two different species, i.e., *erectus/sapiens* or Neandertal/moderns.

Now take the Fill-in and Multiple Choice tests. Do not guess. Following completion of the tests, correct them. The correct answers and textbook page references are at the end of this study guide chapter. Note your strong areas and your weak areas to guide you in your continuing study.

FILL-IN QUESTIONS

1. The earliest members of our species that date from around 400,000 to 130,000 y.a. are

    called _____.

2. These early human forms exhibited both derived characteristics like those found in modern

    humans as well as primitive characteristics typical of either *H. erectus* or Neandertal. The

    presence of both the primitive and derived characteristics suggest that these are

    _____ forms.

3. Early archaic humans exhibit morphological changes more derived than _____ _____.

4. Some of the derived characteristics present in archaic *H. sapiens* include _____,

    _____, _____ and a general

    decrease in cranial and post cranial _____.

5. The Broken Hill skull exhibits both primitive and derived characteristics. The cranial base

    is _____ _____ although it dates from 150,000 to 125,000 y.a.

6. No _____ have been found in Africa or Eastern Asia.

7. Chinese paleoanthropologists interpret the presence of _____ _____ and _____ _____ _____ in both modern Chinese people and Chinese *H. erectus* populations to be evidence that modern Chinese evolved from a specific lineage of *H. erectus* in China.

8. The skeletal remains from Jinniushan in N.E. China dates to around 200,000 y.a. and exhibits an unusually large _____ _____ for an individual this old.

9. In 1982, a partial skull was found in the Narmada Valley of _____.

10. It is difficult to accurately interpret European archaic *H. sapiens* because _____ _____ and/or _____ _____ are lacking.

11. We have no definite fossil evidence that puts _____ _____ in Central or Western Europe.

12. Archaic *H. sapiens* from Europe exhibit *erectus* characteristics such as _____ cranial bones and heavy _____ torus but they also exhibit *H. sapiens* characteristic like reduced tooth size or a more rounded _____ area.

13. At Atapuerca, in northern Spain, the site dates to 300,000 y.a. yet the morphological characteristics are similar to Neandertal. Specifically, these fossils exhibit arching _____ and a _____ midface.

14. The mosaic Chinese fossils are/are not similar to the African or European mosaic finds.

15. In China the _____ _____ is rare in the Middle Pleistocene.

16. Although bone is a very useful material from which to make tools _____ ____ _____ did not seem to use it.

17. The Levallois technique for manufacturing tools required several _____ _____ suggesting an increase in cognitive abilities among archaic *H. sapiens*.

18. Although the Acheulian tool assemblages have been found in a wide geographical range, it is important to consider the intra-regional _____ of the tools.

19.   At the Lazaret Cave in southern France the hearth charcoal indicates that the occupants burned oak and boxwood. The advantages of these woods are that they are _____ _____ and _____ _____ _____.

20.   At the Channel Island of Jersey off the west coast of France remains of large _____ and _____ _____ have been found associated with stone flakes.

21.   In the text the bulk of information on Neandertals comes from Western Europe and dates from 75,000 to around 30,000 y.a. These specimens are usually referred to as "_____" Neandertals.

22.   The climate in Eastern Europe and western Asia was not as cold as Western Europe during the last glaciation which may explain why Neandertal skeletons from there are _____ _____ as their W. European relatives.

23.   Neandertals are well-known for their large brain. Among modern populations we find this same characteristic as an adaptation to _____ climates.

24.   Neandertals lived in _____ and _____ _____ for about 100,000 years.

25.   Neandertal get its name from the Neander Valley in _____ where the first fossil was found in 1856.

26.   The first Neandertal skeleton was atypical as to its size and the health of the individual. It was unusually _____ exhibiting a cranial capacity of _____ cm³ and immense _____ _____. The 40+ year old man had suffered from spinal osteoarthritis giving him a _____ _____ _____ posture.

27.   It appears that Neandertals and modern *H. sapiens* lived near each other for several thousand years. The _____ tool tradition is the result of the blending of their technologies.

28.   The Krapina fossils are similar to the classic Neandertals of Western Europe although they are less _____.

29. In Israel, although the overall pattern of the fossils is Neandertal, they display

_____ features and are _____ robust than classic Neandertals of Europe.

30. One of the most impressive Neandertal finds is the Shanidar 1 male who was between

30-45 years old, 5'7" tall and had terrible injuries that he had survived for years. His

injuries were numerous including _____,

_____, _____,

_____, _____

and _____.

31. In order for Shanidar 1 to survive his injuries _____.

32. A 9-year-old boy who was deliberately buried is the easternmost Neandertal discovery

in _____.

33. Evidence exists that Neandertal developed specialized tools for skin and meat preparation,

_____, _____ and _____.

34. In the cold tundra, evidence suggests that Neandertal _____ _____.

35. Because of the level of their tool technology, it appears that Neandertal was still required

to get up close when hunting large animals. An analysis of the pattern of _____

(particularly _____) in Neandertals found that they were most like contemporary

rodeo performers.

36. One of the greatest mysteries is "What happened to Neandertals?" Paleoanthropologists

are suggesting that _____ differences between Neandertals and anatomically

modern *H. sapiens* must account for our survival and the demise of Neandertal.

37. It appears that _____ burial was practiced among Neandertals.

38. Three major transitions have taken place in human evolution over the last 2 million years.

They are (1) from _____ to _____; (2) _____ to

_____; and (3) _____ to _____.

MULTIPLE CHOICE QUESTIONS

1. Archaic *H. sapiens* refer to
   A. Neandertals.
   B. Broken Hill.
   C. *H. erectus.*
   D. All of the above are correct.
   E. Both A and B are correct.

2. Derived morphological changes found in archaic *H. sapiens* include all but which of the following?
   A. brain expansion
   B. increase in molar size
   C. increased parietal breadth
   D. decreased robusticity

3. The archaic *H. sapiens* finds from South and East Africa
   A. are similar to Broken Hill.
   B. are very different from Broken Hill.
   C. indicate a lot of genetic variation.
   D. exhibit Neandertal characteristics.

4. Neandertals are found in
   A. Africa.
   B. Eastern Asia.
   C. Europe.
   D. Java.
   E. Both A and C are correct.

5. Modern Chinese populations exhibit certain archaic *H. sapiens* traits including
   A. a sagittal ridge.
   B. flattened nasal bones.
   C. post orbital constriction.
   D. All of the above are correct.
   E. Both A and B are correct.

6. European archaic *H. sapiens* fossils
   A. contain strong evidence that *H. erectus* inhabited Europe around 250,000 y.a.
   B. have problems with dating.
   C are sketchy.
   D. All of the above are correct.
   E. Both B and C are correct.

7. The earliest archaic *H. sapiens* from Europe
   A. exhibit Neandertal characteristics.
   B. exhibit primarily *H. sapiens* characteristics.
   C. exhibit both *H. erectus* and *H. sapiens* traits.
   D. have a more gracile cranium.

8. Many archaic *H. sapiens* finds
    A. exhibit mosaic traits.
    B. appear to be transitional forms from *H. erectus* to modern *H. sapiens*.
    C. exhibit Neandertal and modern *H. sapiens* traits.
    D. All of the above are correct.
    E. Both A and B are correct.

9. Mosaic forms from China
    A. are surprisingly similar to those from W. Europe.
    B. are not the same as those from Europe and Africa.
    C. exhibit many Neandertal characteristics.
    D. All of the above are correct.

10. The Levallois technique for tool manufacturing
    A. arose in both Africa and Europe.
    B. enabled the toolmaker to control flake size and shape.
    C. required coordinated steps.
    D. All of the above are correct.

11. The stone tool tradition referred to as Acheulian
    A. exhibits considerable intra-regional diversity.
    B. has been found in E. Asia.
    C. is uniform throughout Europe and Africa.
    D. is associated with Neandertals.

12. All but which of the following was found in or around the Lazaret Cave in southern France?
    A. a lot of stone waste
    B. rock and large bone supports
    C. two hearths
    D. evidence of a framework of poles

13. The majority of Neandertal fossils have been found in
    A. Africa.
    B. Israel.
    C. Europe.
    D. Asia.

14. Average brain size among Neandertals
    A. is larger than modern humans.
    B. may be related to metabolic efficiency in cold climates.
    C. is close to that of modern Inuit (Eskimo) brain size.
    D. All of the above are correct.
    E. Both A and B are correct.

15. All but which of the following is typical of a Neandertal cranium?
    A. long and low
    B. arched browridges
    C. sharply angled occipital bone
    D. forehead begins to appear

16. The LaChapelle-aux-Saints burial in southwest France was buried with
    A. nonhuman long bones over the head.
    B. a bison leg.
    C. food.
    D. flowers.
    E. Both A and B are correct.

17. The skeleton from the LaChapelle-aux-Saints burial
    A. was a gracile, adult female.
    B. was an arthritic older male.
    C. was larger than the "typical" Neandertal.
    D. showed evidence of trauma.
    E. Both B and C are correct.

18. If the date is accurate, the most recent Neandertal find comes from
    A. Southwestern France.
    B. Spain.
    C. Iran.
    D. Croatia.

19. The Krapina, Croatia Neandertal finds
    A. include fragments of up to 70 individuals.
    B. date to around 30,000 y.a.
    C. are particularly robust.
    D. have very few tools associated with them.
    E. All of the above are correct.

20. The Tabun Neandertal finds
    A. are less robust than the classic finds from Europe.
    B. date to around 110,000.
    C. were contemporaneous with modern *H. sapiens*.
    D. All of the above
    E. Both A and C are correct.

21. The Shanidar 1 male
    A. was obviously high ranking.
    B. was unusually large and robust.
    C. exhibited evidence of extreme trauma.
    D. was around 25 years old when he died.

22. The tool industry associated with Neandertals is
    A. Mousterian.
    B. Levallois.
    C. Chatelperronian.
    D. All of the above are correct.

23. Neandertal hunting
    A. included spears.
    B. included bows and arrows.
    C. probably required close contact with the prey.
    D. was not very successful.

24. The evolution of the genus *Homo* over the last 2 million years
    A. can be divided into at least three major transitions.
    B. has been fairly steady.
    C. has been uniform over the different geographic regions.
    D. can be clearly interpreted.

ANSWERS TO FILL-IN OUTLINE

I. INTRODUCTION
   A. *H. sapiens*
   B. archaic, derived
   C. transitional

II. EARLY ARCHAIC *H. SAPIENS*
   A. derived
   B. three, Africa, Asia, Europe
   C. Neandertals
   D. 1. supraorbital torus
      2. scalping
      3. genetic
   E. 1. sagittal ridge, nasal
      2. *H. erectus*, China
   F. 1. no fossils
      2. robust
      3. rounded, tooth
      4. mosaic
      5. Neandertals
      6. Atapuerca, Spain

III. A REVIEW OF MIDDLE PLEISTOCENE EVOLUTION (CIRCA 400,000-125,000 Y.A.)
   A. mosaic
   B. robust
   C. Neandertals
   D. modern *H. sapiens*

IV. MIDDLE PLEISTOCENE CULTURE
   A. choppers, chopping tools
   B. Levallois
   C. cognitive
   D. hand axes
   E. different
   F. caves, open-air

G. did
H. rocks, bones
   1. hearths
   2. freshwater
I. seasonal
J. off cliffs

V. NEANDERTALS: LATE ARCHAIC *H. SAPIENS* (130,000-35,000 Y.A.)
   A. misfits
   B. classic
   C. 1400
   D. 1520
      1. metabolic efficiency
   E. long, low
      1. rise
      2. arched browridges
   F. robust
   G. 100,000
   H. 1. buried
      a. Marcellin Boule
      b. brutish, biped
      c. primitive
      d. spinal osteoarthritis
      e. typical
      f. robust
      2. recent
      3. lived in close proximity
   I. 1. Krapina, Croatia
      a. 70
      b. stone
      c. 130,000, 110,000
      d. burials
   J. 1. a. 1. 110,000
            2. Neandertals, *H. sapiens*
         b. 1. pelvis

2. hyoid
  a. language (speech)
2. a. 1. 9
    a. four
  2. 30, 45
    a. 5'7"
    b. survived
3. a. 1. easternmost
  2. 9, boy

VI. CULTURE OF NEANDERTALS
  A. Mousterian
    1. Europe, North Africa, former Soviet Union, Israel, Iran, Uzbekistan, China
  B. 1. Levallois
    2. specialization
  C. 1. open sites, caves, rock shelters
    2. building of structures
    3. mammoth
    4. hearths
    5. Fire
  D. 1. hunters
    2. spear thrower, atlatl
    3. rodeo performers

4. berries, nuts, plants
5. wore clothing
E. 1. were
  2. what happened
  3. evolutionary
F. 1. 300,000
    a. Africa, eastern Asia
  2. bone, stone tools
  3. flexed

VII. CONCLUSION: EVOLUTIONARY TRENDS IN THE GENUS *HOMO*
  A. Three
  B. *Homo, H. erectus*
    1. Africa
    2. rapidly
  C. *H. erectus*, archaic *H. sapiens*
    1. was not
    2. unevenly
    3. ambiguous
    4. isolated
  D. archaic *H. sapiens*, modern *H. sapiens*
    1. faster

ANSWERS & REFERENCES TO FILL-IN QUESTIONS
1. archaic *H. sapiens*, p. 436
2. transitional, p. 436
3. *H. erectus*, p. 436
4. Brain expansion, increased parietal breadth, decrease in the size of the molars, decreased skeletal robusticity, p. 436
5. essentially modern, p. 437
6. Neandertals, p. 437
7. sagittal ridge, flattened nasal bones, p. 437
8. cranial capacity, p. 440
9. India, p. 440
10. Definite dates, adequate remains, p. 441
11. *H. erectus*, p. 441
12. thick, supraorbital, occipital, p. 441
13. browridges, projecting, p. 443
14. are not, p. 443
15. hand ax, p. 444
16. Archaic *H. sapiens*, p. 444
17. coordinated steps, p. 444
18. diversity, p. 444
19. Slow burning, easy to rekindle, p. 445
20. mammoth, woolly rhinoceros, p. 446

21. classic, p. 446
22. less robust, p. 446
23. cold, p. 446
24. Europe, western Asia, p. 449
25. Germany, p. 449
26. large, 1620, supraorbital ridges, not fully erect, p. 449
27. Chatelperronian, p. 452
28. robust, p. 453
29. modern, less, p. 454
30. Blow to the left side of the head, probably blind in the left eye, blow to the right side of the body leaving a withered right arm (probably amputated later), atrophied shoulder blade, collar bone and upper right arm, damaged lower right leg, pathology in the right knee and left leg, p. 455
31. he had to be helped by others, p. 455
32. Uzbekistan, p. 455
33. hunting, woodworking, hafting, p. 456
34. built structures, p. 456
35. trauma, fractures, p. 457
36. behavioral, p. 458
37. deliberate, p. 459
38. early *Homo*, *H. erectus*, *H. erectus* to archaic *H. sapiens*, archaic *H. sapiens*, modern *H. sapiens*, pp. 460-461

ANSWERS & REFERENCES TO MULTIPLE CHOICE QUESTIONS

1. E, pp. 436-437	9. B, p. 443	17. E, p. 449
2. B, p. 436	10. D, p. 444	18. B, p. 452
3. A, p. 437	11. A, p. 444	19. A, p. 452
4. C, p. 437	12. A, p. 445	20. D, p. 454
5. E, p. 437	13. C, p. 446	21. C, p. 455
6. E, p. 441	14. D, p. 446	22. D, pp. 452, 455, 456
7. C, p. 441	15. C, p. 447	23. C, p. 457
8. D, pp. 442-443	16. E, p. 449	24. A, p. 460

CHAPTER 18

HOMO SAPIENS SAPIENS

LEARNING OBJECTIVES

After reading this chapter you should be able to:
- compare the three basic hypotheses for the origin and dispersal of anatomically modern humans. (pp. 468-473)
- discuss the earliest evidence of modern *H. sapiens sapiens* including geographic distribution, technology and art. (pp. 472-491)
- distinguish between the cultural periods of the Upper Paleolithic. (pp. 481-491)
- describe early art from Europe and Africa. (pp. 482-490)
- evaluate the various hypotheses attempting to interpret Upper Paleolithic art. (pp. 484-488)

FILL-IN OUTLINE

Introduction
The previous chapter looked at archaic *Homo sapiens* including Neandertals. This chapter arrives at anatomically modern humans. The problems in attempting to determine when, where, and how modern *H. sapiens* first appeared and the three basic hypotheses that attempt to answer these questions are discussed. Modern *H. sapiens* fossils, technological artifacts, and art in a wide range of geographic locations are examined.

I. INTRODUCTION

    A. It is difficult to say when modern *H. sapiens* first appeared due to ongoing

        _____ in dating.

    B. It appears that the dispersal of modern humans in the Old World was _____.

II. THE ORIGIN AND DISPERSAL OF *HOMO SAPIENS SAPIENS* (ANATOMICALLY MODERN HUMAN BEINGS)

A. The Recent Replacement Model (Recent African Evolution)

1. This hypothesis was developed by _____ and _____ (1988).

2. According to this theory, moderns originated in _____ within the last _____ years.

3. Moderns then migrate out of _____ and into _____ and _____.

    a. Where they _____ the existing populations

4. This theory does not explain the transition from _____ to modern *H. sapiens* anywhere except Africa.

5. The appearance of moderns is seen as a biological _____ event.

    a. which means that moderns could not _____ with any of the local populations

6. The evidence used to support this theory comes from _____ obtained from living peoples.

    a. Specifically, DNA found in the cytoplasm, called _____ DNA (mtDNA).

    b. which is only inherited through the _____.

7. Using the mtDNA scientists at Berkeley have constructed "trees" and concluded that the world's population descended from a _____ African _____.

8. Other scientists, using the same mtDNA material, have constructed different "trees" and found that some of them have no _____.

B. The Partial Replacement Model (African-European *H. sapiens* Hypothesis)

1. Modern *H. sapiens* populations first evolved in _____.

2. The earliest dates for African modern *Homo sapiens* is _____ y.a.

3. This theory is proposed by _____ from University of Hamburg.

4. The initial dispersal out of South _____ was a _____ process.

5. Moderns then moved into _____ where they _____ with local archaic *H. sapiens* populations.

    a. Eventually moderns _____ archaic populations.

C. The Regional Continuity Model (Multiregional Evolution)

   1. This model is proposed by _____ and his associates.

   2. They propose that some local archaic populations in _____, _____ and _____ continued on their indigenous evolutionary paths.

    a. Some of these archaic populations evolved into _____.

   3. Moderns are not considered to be a separate species because some

    _____ (migration) occurred between archaic populations.

III. The Earliest *Homo sapiens sapiens* Discoveries

A. Africa

   1. Fully anatomically modern forms date to _____ y.a.

   2. Problems exist with dating, provenience and _____ of the evidence.

B. Near East

   1. In Israel at least 10 individuals have been found in the _____ at Mt. Carmel.

    a. This site is close to the _____ site of Tabun.

    b. It has been dated at _____ y.a.

   2. The Qafzeh Cave in Israel has yielded the remains of at least _____ individuals.

    a. Some exhibit certain archaic (_____) features

    b. It has been dated at _____ y.a.

    C. Central Europe

        1. At many sites the fossils display both Neandertal and _____ features.

           a. This would support the _____ hypothesis.

        2. From Mladec, in the Czech Republic moderns have been found that date to

            _____.

           a. They exhibit a great deal of _____.

           b. Although modern, all but one crania exhibit a _____.

    D. Western Europe

        1. Previously, theories on human evolution were based almost exclusively on

            _____ material.

        2. The best known of the W. European modern fossil finds is from the

            _____ site.

           a. Discovered in _____

           b. In a _____ shelter in southern France

           c. The tool industry is known as _____

           d. The site dates to _____ y.a.

    E. Asia

        1. Ordos (from Dagouwan, Inner Mongolia) is probably the oldest anatomically

           modern find in _____ dating to at least _____ y.a.

        2. Chinese paleoanthropologists see a continuous evolution in their geographic

           area from _____ to _____ to anatomically modern

           humans.

    F. Australia

        1. _____ refers to the area including New Guinea and Australia.

        2. Some archeological sites in Australia date to _____.

        3. Human fossils date to _____.

4. The Kow Swamp people date to _____ y.a. and exhibit certain
    _____ traits such as a receding forehead.

G. The New World

1. Humans entered the New World over the _____.

2. Although debates continue, at present, the only direct evidence we have of
    hominids in the New World date to about _____.

IV. TECHNOLOGY AND ART IN THE UPPER PALEOLITHIC

A. Europe

1. The Upper Paleolithic began approximately _____ y.a. in western Europe.

    a. It has been divided into _____ cultural periods based on
        _____ technologies.

2. A warming trend lasting _____ years began around _____ y.a.

    a. which resulted in the growth of _____ plants and other
        _____.

    b. _____ animals lived off of the new vegetation;

        1. and _____ animals lived off of them.

    c. It became a hunter's _____.

    d. For the first time humans also began to regularly eat _____ and
        _____.

3. Clothing is better fitting now because it is _____.

4. Around 20,000 y.a. the weather became _____ in Europe and Asia.

5. Around 20,000 y.a. the weather became _____ in Africa.

6. Humans had an advantage to changing conditions due to _____.

7. Humans began inventing new and _____ tools.

8. _____ tools were the finest stone tools known.

9. The _____ is the last stage of the Upper Paleolithic stone tool industry.

10. To catch fish, a _____ was used.

11. We begin to see a reduction in _____ size.

12. The lower face of moderns is less _____ compared to archaics.

13. We begin to see the distinctive characteristic of modern humans, the _____.

14. For the first time we begin to see "symbolic representation" in the form of _____.

15. Paleolithic art covered _____ years and is found in Europe, _____, North and South _____ and _____.

16. Bone and ivory _____ and _____ was improved with the use of specialized tools.

17. The first use of ceramics dates to _____ y.a.

18. The majority of cave art comes from _____ and _____.

19. In 1994 the _____ cave in France was discovered.

    a. It dates to _____ y.a.

    b. It contains images of _____, _____ and _____ which have never been seen in cave art before.

    c. On the floor there are footprints of _____ and _____.

20. A common motif in cave art is _____.

21. The partial sculpting of a rock face is termed _____;

    a. which were found in areas thought to be _____.

    b. the subjects of this type of art include _____ and one human.

22. The themes in portable art are _____ and _____.

23. In caves, the themes are _____ and _____.

24. Women are always painted in _____.

25. Most of the cave art in southwestern France and northern Spain was created

around _____ y.a.

B. Africa

1. Rock art is found in southern Africa dating to _____ y.a.

2. Personal adornment dates back to _____ y.a. in the form of _____

made from _____.

3. In central Africa _____ and _____ were used to make tools.

4. Harpoons from Katanda of eastern Zaire are made from _____ or long

bone _____ of large _____.

5. The Katanda sites date between _____ and _____ y.a.

V. SUMMARY OF UPPER PALEOLITIC CULTURE

A. For most of the Pleistocene change was very _____.

B. In Europe and central Africa, cultural innovations were dramatic including big game

hunting, new _____, body _____ and _____

clothing.

KEY TERMS

Aurignacian: an Upper Paleolithic stone tool assemblage dating to around 30,000 y.a. and associated with Cro-Magnon

Chatelperronian: an Upper Paleolithic stone tool assemblage dating to around 35,000 y.a. and associated with Neandertals. It appears that Neandertals modified technology borrowed from anatomically modern humans thus creating a new tool technology.

Cro-Magnon: A term commonly used when referring to early modern humans from Europe. It comes from a specific find in southern France which dates to around 30,000 y.a. where eight skeletons were found in 1868. The skeletons included three adult males, one adult female and four young children.

Gravettian: An Upper Paleolithic stone tool assemblage dating to around 27,000 y.a.

Magdalenian: The final stage of the Upper Paleolithic stone tool assemblage dating to around 17,000 y.a.

Salutrean: An Upper Paleolithic stone tool assemblage dating to around 21,000 y.a. Considered to be the most highly developed stone tool industry.

Upper Paleolithic: refers to a cultural period of early modern humans distinguished by innovative stone tool technologies. Dates from around 40,000 to 10,000 y.a. It is further divided into five different cultural periods associated with stone tool technology. These five cultural periods (from the oldest to the most recent) are Chatelperronian, Aurignacian, Gravettian, Solutrean and Magdalenian.

Now take the Fill-in and Multiple Choice tests. Do not guess. Following completion of the tests, correct them. The correct answers and textbook page references are at the end of this study guide chapter. Note your strong areas and your weak areas to guide you in your continuing study.

FILL-IN QUESTIONS

1. Taxonomically, anatomically modern humans are known as _____ _____ _____.

2. The subject of considerable debate is whether modern humans evolved solely in _____ or from archaic *H. sapiens* in _____ _____.

3. Three hypotheses have been proposed to explain the origins of modern humans. These three include the _____ _____ model (recent African evolution), the _____ _____ model (African-European *H. sapiens* hypothesis) and the _____ _____ _____ (multiregional evolution).

4. The complete replacement model holds that modern humans originated in _____, migrated out and later completely _____ populations in Europe and Asia.

5. One of the problems with the complete replacement model is that it does not take into account any transitions from _____ _____ to _____ _____ anywhere except _____.

6. An important aspect of this theory is that _____ _____ are a different species.

7. Mitochondrial DNA (mtDNA) are _____ found in the cytoplasm (not the nucleus) and genetically passed on only by the _____.

8. To test their theory scientists from Berkeley took mtDNA from different populations and constructed _____ (something like a family tree). Based on this research they concluded that the world's population descended from a single _____ _____.

9. Other scientists, using the same mtDNA and the same methodology have constructed different _____ that show _____ _____ _____.

10. The use of mtDNA as evidence for proving genetic relatedness among contemporary populations remains controversial. Many paleoanthropologists are _____ of the conclusions drawn from such data.

11. The partial replacement model has been proposed by Gunter Bräuer of the University of _____.

12. The partial replacement model holds that modern *Homo sapiens* first evolved in _____ around _____ _____ y.a.

13. Bräuer's theory is that early modern *H. sapiens* gradually migrated out of South Africa as the result of _____ and _____ conditions.

14. The partial replacement model has modern *H. sapiens* moving into Eurasia (from Africa) where they mated with resident _____ groups resulting in a _____ which eventually replaced the local archaic populations.

15. The partial replacement model explains the disappearance of archaic *H. sapiens* as being partly due to _____ (moderns breeding with archaics) and _____.

16. The regional continuity model holds that some local populations of archaic *H. sapiens* in Europe, Asia and Africa continued on independent _____ paths and developed into _____ _____ _____.

17. This model holds that archaic *H. sapiens* did not evolve exclusively in _____.

18. This model further holds that since a certain amount of breeding (gene flow/migration) probably took place between archaic populations, modern *H. sapiens* would not be considered a separate _____.

19. This genetic mixing would result in humans being a single _____ species.

20. Although there is some dispute as to dates, it appears that the earliest modern *H. sapiens* evidence comes from _____.

21. Three sites in Africa have yielded very old fossils of early modern *H. sapiens*. These sites are _____ _____ _____, _____ _____ and _____ _____ which date to between _____ y.a.

22. The Skhūl Cave at Mt. Carmel in Israel is very near the Neandertal site of Tabun. The fossil remains from this site, although fully modern, exhibit certain _____/ _____ characteristics.

23. The dating at Tabun indicates that Neandertals and modern *H. sapiens* _____ in their occupation of this area.

24. At Mladec, in the Czech Republic, the modern *H. sapiens* remains date to around _____ y.a. and although fully modern, exhibit prominent _____ _____, an archaic trait.

25. Most of our evidence for early modern *H. sapiens* comes from western Europe for two reasons:

    (1) _____; and

    (2) _____.

26. Until recently, most of our theories on human evolution have been based on the fossils and evidence from _____ _____.

27. The Cro-Magnon site in southern France includes _____ skeletons and dates to _____ y.a.

28. Cro-Magnon is associated with the _____ tool assemblage.

29. The most modern looking of the crania discovered at the Cro-Magnon site is that of the _____. Her more gracile features may be the result of _____ _____.

30. The blending of Neandertal and modern *H. sapiens* characteristics found at the Mladec, Vindija and Israel sites suggests _____ between the two groups.

31. The two most important sites in China for early modern *H. sapiens* are the Upper Cave at _____ and _____ at Dagouwan, _____.

32. _____ may be the oldest site with modern fossils, dating to _____ y.a. or more.

33. Chinese paleoanthropologists contend that in China evolution of the genus *Homo* has been continuous from Chinese *H. erectus* to archaic *H. sapiens* to modern *H. sapiens*. They further state that their fossils have features typical of their geographic region and these features are definitely not _____.

34. In Sri Lanka, modern *H. sapiens* remains have been found that date to _____ y.a.

35. Although the oldest human fossil remains from Australia only date to _____ y.a., archeological evidence dates to at least _____ y.a.

36. The oldest Australian fossils are two burials dating from _____ y.a. and _____ y.a. The crania of these finds are _____.

37. The Kow Swamp people with the relatively recent date of 14,000 and 9,000 y.a. exhibit some surprisingly archaic traits on the crania. Specifically, they have _____ foreheads, heavy _____ _____ and _____ _____.

38. Debates continue over when modern humans first entered the New World. Although some claims date prior to 15,000 y.a. and geographically they range from the Yukon to Pennsylvania and Peru, the first direct evidence for modern humans in the New World dates to about _____ y.a.

39. Scholars agree that modern humans entered the New World through the _____ _____ _____ that connected Asia and Alaska.

40.   The Upper Paleolithic in Europe began around 40,000 y.a. It has been divided into five cultural periods based on _____ _____ technologies.

41.   Due to the warming trend that occurred around 30,000 y.a. and lasted several thousand years the food chain underwent dramatic changes. Vegetation became more diverse and abundant therefore the numbers and variety of herbivores increased which in turn gave rise to the number of carnivores that could eat the herbivores. It became a _____ paradise.

42.   During this time humans _____ new and specialized _____.

43.   Perhaps because of the increased use of tools in processing food, selective pressures were relaxed for large front (anterior) _____ resulting in reduced prognathism and the appearance of the _____.

44.   During this warming trend we also begin to see _____.

45.   Art takes many forms including _____ paintings, _____ on tools and tool handles, our first evidence of _____ dating back to 27,000 y.a. and _____ figurines.

46.   Cave art is found in France and Spain. The themes in cave art include _____, stylized _____ and human _____.

47.   We also begin to see bas-relief art which is a partial _____ of a rock face. These are generally found in close association with _____ _____ (first interior decorators?).

48.   Many attempts have been made to _____ ancient art.

49.   In Africa, the first evidence of personal _____ is found in the form of beads made from ostrich egg shells.

MULTIPLE CHOICE QUESTIONS

1. The dispersal of anatomically modern *H. sapiens*
   A. was a relatively rapid event.
   B. was a relatively slow event.
   C. is agreed upon by scientists to have occurred 175,000 y.a.
   D. is agreed upon by scientists to have occurred from Africa into Europe.

2. Regarding the evolution of anatomically modern humans, scientists
   A. agree that it took place in Africa.
   B. agree that it took place in China.
   C. debate regarding both geography and dates.
   D. debate regarding dates but not necessarily geography.

3. The three hypotheses explaining the origins and dispersal of anatomically modern humans include all but which of the following?
   A. the partial replacement model
   B. the regional continuity model
   C. the regional replacement model
   D. the complete replacement model

4. The model also known as the "Recent African Evolution" is
   A. based on the origin of modern humans in Africa and their interbreeding with local African populations.
   B. based on the origin of modern humans in Africa and their replacement of local populations in Europe and Asia.
   C. based on the origin of modern humans in China and their relatively recent evolution in Africa.
   D. based on the origin of modern humans simultaneously in Africa and China.

5. According to the model also known as the African-European *H. sapiens* Hypothesis,
   A. modern humans evolved in Africa and Europe at the same time.
   B. archaic *H. sapiens* evolved into modern *H. sapiens* in southern Africa.
   C. the dispersal of modern humans was relatively rapid.
   D. moderns did not breed with archaics in Eurasia.

6. According to the model also known as the multiregional evolution model,
   A. anatomically modern humans originated exclusively in Africa.
   B. archaic *H. sapiens* were a separate species.
   C. some local populations of archaic *H. sapiens* in Europe, Asia and Africa evolved into moderns.
   D. Both A and B are correct.

7. Although not everyone agrees on dates, current evidence strongly indicates that
   A. modern *H. sapiens* evolved simultaneously in Africa, Europe and Asia.
   B. modern *H. sapiens* arose from Neandertals.
   C. modern *H. sapiens* arose in western Europe.
   D. modern *H. sapiens* arose in Africa.

8. Provenience refers to
    A. a geographic region in western Europe.
    B. the specific location of an archeological discovery.
    C. a dating technique.
    D. a fossil find in western Asia.

9. The Skhūl Cave at Mt. Carmel, Israel,
    A. has yielded more than 20 individuals.
    B. is very near the Neandertal site of Tabun.
    C. has yielded purely modern looking fossils.
    D. has yielded purely archaic looking fossils.

10. At the Vindija site in Croatia,
    A. typical Neandertals were found in early contexts.
    B. no modern/Neandertal mixtures were found.
    C. late *H. erectus* is found overlapping with archaics.
    D. evidence of art is abundant.

11. The area of the world from which the most early modern *H. sapiens* evidence has come is
    A. Africa.
    B. Western Asia.
    C. China.
    D. Western Europe.

12. Cro-Magnon is
    A. typical of the European "races" of early modern *H. sapiens.*
    B. a site from southern France.
    C. a site yielding eight individuals.
    D. Both B and C are correct.

13. Aurignacian refers to a(n)
    A. tool assemblage associated with France's earliest anatomically modern humans.
    B. site in western Europe yielding 10 skeletons.
    C. archeologist who uncovered a rich site in northern Spain.
    D. tool tradition associated with archaic *H. sapiens* in western Asia.

14. The Mladec and Vindija fossils
    A. date to around 100,000 y.a.
    B. are rich and numerous.
    C. indicate a combination of both modern and Neandertal characteristics.
    D. show evidence of social stratification.

15. The Upper Cave at Zhoukoudian
    A. dates to between 18,000 and 10,000 y.a.
    B. has yielded fossils that exhibit both modern and Neandertal characteristics.
    C. may be the oldest anatomically modern find.
    D. has evidence of burials.

16. The oldest anatomically modern find in Asia may be
    A. Vindija.
    B. Zhoukoudian.
    C. Ordos.
    D. Batadomba.

17. In Australia,
    A. the oldest fossils date to 55,000 y.a.
    B. the oldest fossils date to 30,000 y.a.
    C. archeological sites date to 80,000 y.a.
    D. evidence of body adornment was found.

18. The Kow Swamp people
    A. date to 14,000 to 9,000 y.a.
    B. date to about 30,000 y.a.
    C. exhibit archaic traits on their cranial skeleton.
    D. Both A and C are correct.

19. Modern humans entered the New World
    A. prior to 15,000 y.a.
    B. about 12,000 y.a.
    C. by boat.
    D. on horses.

20. In the former Soviet Union,
    A. storage pits have been found.
    B. evidence of social status distinctions were found.
    C. the first evidence of language has been found.
    D. Both A and B are correct.

21. Magdalenian refers to
    A. the first evidence of religion.
    B. a geographic region in western Asia.
    C. the final phase of the stone tool tradition in the Upper Paleolithic in Europe.
    D. a type of facial structure found among early moderns.

22. Paleolithic art has been found in all but which of the following locations?
    A. Australia
    B. Siberia
    C. North America
    D. South Africa

23. Dolni Vestonice and Predmosti from the Czech Republic yielded the
    A. first documented use of ceramics.
    B. first documented use of metal.
    C. first documented use of controlled fire.
    D. first documented use of buttons.

24. Solutrean refers to
    A. a cultural period of the Upper Paleolithic.
    B. an archeological methodology for cleaning artifacts.
    C. a famous paleoanthropologist working in Western Europe.
    D. the cranial structure typical of early moderns in Western Asia.

25. The partial sculpting of a rock face is called
    A. knapping.
    B. pressure-engraving.
    C. punch technique.
    D. bas-relief.

26. In Africa, we find the first evidence of
    A. ceramics.
    B. personal adornment.
    C. use of fire.
    D. cave paintings.

27. In Paleolithic art, women are
    A. always depicted alone.
    B. always depicted in groups.
    C. usually depicted with animals.
    D. not depicted.

28. During the Magdalenian,
    A. European prehistoric art reached its climax.
    B. we begin to see carvings on tools.
    C. ceramics are numerous.
    D. we begin to see burins.

29. The fossils from the Upper Cave at Zhoukoudian
    A. share similarities with the African moderns.
    B. share similarities with the African archaics.
    C. do not share features with Africa.
    D. do not exhibit features that are regional.

30. Prehistoric art
    A. has a common theme over a vast geographic region.
    B. shows strong signs of ritual significance.
    C. ranged from 35,000 to 10,000 y.a.
    D. was limited to cave paintings.

Answers To Fill-in Outline

I. Introduction
   A. Ambiguities
   B. Rapid

II. The Origin and Dispersal of *Homo sapiens sapiens* (Anatomically Modern Human Beings)
   A. 1. Stringer, Andrews
      2. Africa, 200,000
      3. Africa, Europe, Asia
      4. Archaic *Homo sapiens*
      5. Speciation
         -breed
      6. Genetic data
         -mitochondrial
         -mother
      7. Single, lineage
      8. African roots
   B. The Partial Replacement Model (African-European *sapiens* Hypothesis)
      1. Africa
      2. Over 100,000
      3. Gunter Brauer
      4. Africa, gradual
      5. Eurasia, hybridized
         -replaced
   C. The Regional Continuity Model (Multiregional Evolution)
      1. Milford Wolpoff
      2. Europe, Asia, Africa
         -anatomically modern
      3. Gene flow

III. The Earliest *Homo sapiens sapiens* Discoveries
   A. Africa
      1. About 120,000-80,000
      2. Differing interpretations]
   B. Near East
      1. Skhul Cave
         -Neandertal
         -115,000
      2. 20
         -Neandertal
         -about 100,000
   C. Central Europe
      1. Modern
         -Regional continuity
      2. 33,000 y.a.

      -variation
      -prominent supraorbital torus
   D. Western Europe
      1. Western European
      2. Cro-Magnon
         -1868
         -rock
         -Aurignacian
         -30,000
   E. Asia
      1. China, 50,000
      2. *Homo erectus*, archaic *H. sapiens*
   F. Australia
      1. Sahul
      2. 55,000 y.a.
      3. 30,000 y.a.
      4. 14,000 and 9,000, archaic
   G. The New World
      1. Bering Land Bridge
      2. 12,000 y.a.

IV. Technology and Art in the Upper Paleolithic
   A. Europe
      1. 40,000
         -five, stone tool
      2. Several thousand, 30,000
         -flowering, vegetation
         -herbivorous
         -carnivorous
         -paradise
         -fish, fowl
      3. Sewn
      4. Colder
      5. Wetter
      6. Technology
      7. Specialized
      8. Solutrean
      9. Magdalenian
      10. Barbed harpoon
      11. Dental
      12. Prognathic
      13. Chin
      14. Art
      15. 25,000, Siberia, Africa, Australia
      16. Carving, engraving
      17. 27,000
      18. Southwestern France, northern Spain
      19. Grotte Chauvet

            -20,000
                -panther, hyena, owl
                -bears, humans
20. Human hands
21. Bas-relief
        -living sites
        -several animals
22. Horses, reindeer
23. Bison, horses
24. Groups
25. 20,000-18,000

B. Africa
    1. 28,000-19,000
    2. 38,000, beads, ostrich eggshells
    3. Bone, antler
    4. Ribs, splinters, mammals
    5. 180,000, 75,000

V. SUMMARY OF THE UPPER PALEOLITHIC CULTURE
    A. Slow
    B. Weapons, ornaments, tailored

ANSWERS & REFERENCES TO FILL-IN QUESTIONS

1. *Homo sapiens sapiens*, p. 468
2. Africa, other regions, p. 468
3. complete replacement, partial replacement, regional continuity model, pp. 468-471
4. Africa, replaced, p. 468
5. Archaic *H. sapiens*, modern *H. sapiens*, Africa, p. 470
6. African moderns, p. 470
7. organelles, mother, p. 470
8. trees, African lineage, p. 470
9. trees, no African roots, p. 470
10. skeptical, p. 471
11. Hamburg, p. 471
12. Africa, 100,000, p. 471
13. climatic, environmental, p. 471
14. archaic, hybrid, p. 471
15. hybridization, replacement, p. 471
16. evolutionary, anatomically modern humans, p. 471
17. Africa, p. 471
18. species, p. 471
19. polytypic, p. 471
20. Africa, p. 472
21. Klasies River Mouth, Border Cave, Omo Kibish 1,120,000-80,000, pp. 473-474
22. archaic/neandertal, p. 474
23. overlap, p. 474
24. 33,000, supraorbital tori, p. 474
25. Interested scholars happened to live there, it caught the curiosity and pride of the local population, p. 476
26. Western Europe, p. 476
27. eight, 30,000, p. 476
28. Aurignacian, p. 476
29. female, sexual dimorphism, p. 477
30. gene flow/breeding/mating, p. 477
31. Zhoukoudian, Ordos, Inner Mongolia, p. 478
32. Ordos, 50,000, p. 478
33. African, p. 479
34. 25,500, p. 479
35. 30,000, 55,000, p. 479
36. 25,000, 30,000, gracile, p. 479
37. receding, supraorbital tori, thick bones, p. 479
38. 12,000, p. 481
39. Bering Land Bridge, p. 481
40. stone tool, p. 481
41. hunters, p. 482
42. invented, tools, p. 482
43. teeth, chin, p. 483
44. art, p. 483
45. cave, engravings, ceramics, Venus, pp. 484-485
46. animals, dots, hands, p. 486
47. sculpting, living sites, p. 487
48. interpret, p. 487
49. adornment, p. 488

ANSWERS & REFERENCES TO MULTIPLE CHOICE QUESTIONS

1. A, p. 468
2. C, p. 468
3. C, pp. 468-471
4. B, p. 468
5. B, p. 471
6. C, p. 471
7. D, p. 472
8. B, p. 474
9. B, p. 474
10. A, p. 474

11. D, pp. 474-476
12. D, p. 476
13. A, p. 476
14. C, p. 477
15. A, p. 478
16. C, p. 478
17. B, p. 479
18. D, p. 479
19. B, p. 481
20. D, p. 482

21. C, p. 483
22. C, p. 484
23. A, pp. 484-485
24. A, pp. 481, 486
25. D, p. 487
26. B, p. 488
27. B, p. 487
28. A, p. 485
29. C, p. 479
30. C, p. 484